D1603643

Traces of Travel

Also by Gerald de Gaury

Rulers of Mecca
Arabia Phoenix
Arabian Journey
The Grand Captain, Gonzalo de Cordoba, The Spanish Viceroy in Italy
Three Kings in Baghdad
Faisal, King of Saudi Arabia
Travelling Gent, Life of Alexander Kinglake, 1809–1891

Editor
First edition in English of *Through Wahhabiland on Camelback* by
    Barclay Raunkiaer
Spirit of the East (with H.V.F. Winstone)★
The Road to Kabul (with H.V.F. Winstone)★
Introduction to *The Queen of Sheba* by H.St J. Philby★

★Published by Quartet Books

Traces of Travel

Brought Home from Abroad

Gerald de Gaury

Quartet Books
London Melbourne New York

First published by Quartet Books Limited 1983
A member of the Namara Group
27/29 Goodge Street, London W1P 1FD

British Library Cataloguing in Publication Data

De Gaury, G.
    Traces of travel.
    1. Voyages and travels—1951
    I. Title
    910.4   G465

ISBN 0-7043-2363-X

Typeset by MC Typeset, Rochester, Kent
Printed and bound in Great Britain
by Mackays of Chatham

Contents

Illustrations

Acknowledgements

To George Harrap and Co., Ltd, for extracts from my *Arabia Phoenix,* 1946.

To *Time and Tide,* December 1951, for use of 'The Quest of the Holy Grail' by me.

To Derek Verschoyle for use of 'The Sultan's Ball' by me, published in *Memorable Balls,* 1954, edited by James Laver.

For an extract from *Faisal, King of Saudi Arabia,* by me, issued by Arthur Barker, in 1966; and to the Middle East Centre, Cambridge University, for use of my 'Memories and Impressions of Ibn Saud', in *Arabian Studies,* Vol. II, pp. 19 *et seq.,* 1975, also by me.

To Hutchinson of London, for use of an extract from 'Three Kings in Baghdad' (Chapter 6 and Appendix II) in *A Visit to Republican Turkey,* published by them for me in 1961.

Forenote

Prosper Mérimée wrote in the Preface to his *Chronique de Charles IX* that he liked the anecdotes in a history above all else and particularly those that seemed to him to evoke the morals and characteristics of a given period: *'Je n'aime dans l'histoire que les anecdotes et parmi les anecdotes je préfère celles où j'imagine trouver une peinture des moeurs et des caractères à une époque donnée.'*

Since his day, an ever-increasing wealth of material faces the ever-growing number of writers of modern history. If the writers are more numerous, so are their chosen subjects, some garnished with special vocabularies and peppered with necessary footnotes. But the resulting form is often unsuited by nature to the inclusion of anecdotes. Where, however, as in the Middle East and in Arabia itself there have been profound or superficial changes, anecdotes from the past, even seemingly trivial ones, may be of interest.

Some that may qualify for the purpose of illustrating a period that has gone have been selected from diaries and notebooks I kept at the time. It is hoped that the reader will therefore forgive a certain degree of inevitable disjointedness for the sake of an interest in the whole.

G. de G.

Introduction: Kitchener

In the early years of the twentieth century, at the time of the new King Emperor, Edward VII, two military heroes were revered and famed for their courageous exploits.

Lord Roberts, V.C., 'Bobs', a hero of the Mutiny in India, of successful marches to Kabul and Kandahar, of the victorious Commandership-in-Chief in South Africa, was already in his seventies by the first decade of the new century. Before the end of the nineteenth century he had been appointed Commander-in-Chief of the Army in India, a post that the younger hero, Kitchener, held from 1902 to 1909.

Those of us who saw Kitchener, if rarely and fleetingly, might have doubted the accuracy of our recollections had it not been for a later biography of him by Magnus-Allcroft which confirmed them. There are sixteen references to his appearance and the same number of photographs. Only one of the references does not confirm that he was notably handsome. Among those recorded as having taken to him at once were the Emperor Franz-Joseph, when Kitchener, then a young officer, was attached to a British general attending Austrian army manoeuvres; Lord Desborough and his son Julian, who was a page at the coronation of Edward VII and was killed in the First World War; Queen Victoria, who noted that he was a striking, energetic-looking man, with a rather firm expression, but very pleasing to talk to; his troops in the Sudan, between 1896 and 1898, 'who revered him as a god'; Winston Churchill, who, on the way to Ondurman in September 1898, rode up to him with a message and found that his appearance 'made a vivid manifestation upon the senses'; and Sir Osbert Sitwell who describes him in *Great Morning*, in sensational language, having seen him at a ball given by the Household Cavalry at Knightsbridge Barracks in the last few weeks of the glittering London season of 1914:

> One saw only him for his partner sank into insignificance, since, whatever his faults or his merits, his genius was sufficient to concentrate attention upon him to the exclusion of all others in his neighbourhood, as if he were accompanied by an invisible limelight with an orange slide; for the colour of his face was tawny beyond sunburn, and pertained to the planet Mars. With an altogether exceptional squareness and solidity, he sat there as if he were a god, slightly gone to seed perhaps, but waiting confidently for his earthly dominion to disclose itself . . . he plainly belonged to some different order of creation from those around him . . . And you could, in the mind's eye, see his image set up as that of an English god, by natives in different parts of the Empire which he had helped to create and support, precisely as the Roman Emperors had been worshipped. Within a few months' time, when from every hoarding vast posters showed Lord Kitchener pointing into perspectives in space, so steadily perceived, if focused with uncertainty below the caption 'He wants you', I have often thought of that square figure glowering under the wreaths and festoons of smilax, from among the ferns, and palms and flowers . . .

The Cabinet knew the value to it of Kitchener's name. The Prime Minister had stopped his return to Egypt in August 1914 just in time. He was already on board the cross-Channel steamer and about to sail on his way to Egypt, when Asquith's urgent message arrived and Kitchener, to the relief of the nation, rather reluctantly found himself Secretary of State for War.

Men who saw Kitchener at that time – the trusted hero of his beloved country, he was raising a voluntary new army of seventy divisions – are not likely to forget him. Of titanic energy and autocratic resolve, though tinged with 'a touch of inarticulate Poetry', his word carried instant conviction, and 'individuals dwarfed in the menacing gloom of terrible events were eager to merge their personalities in his commanding one . . . He was the indispensable symbol of their will to Victory.'

In August 1914 he told his colleagues in the Cabinet, at first showing to him their bewilderment, that the war would last three years or more; and he must have known that officers and men he went to inspect in its early days stood no great chance of surviving unharmed until the end. Men of the new divisions had nevertheless been saying, as they continued training during the first winter of the war, that it would be over before they reached the front. Only when inspected by Kitchener and by the King did they become proudly sure they would be in time for the fighting.

Kitchener rode through the lines of troops, a splendid figure holding himself lance straight; still 'a perfect horseman', as he was named when young; on a horse suited to a man of his six foot two inches and proportionate breadth. So admirably did he appear one with his horse, both of them magnificent, that they called to mind a centaur of old.

Nowadays what writer would describe any contemporary general as god- or Caesar-like, or any young officer think of one as resembling a centaur? Or what lawyer-politician, seeking to denigrate such a hero a very few years after his death in 1916, write a malicious and disparaging book about him, as Lord Esher did; or note, as he did, that Kitchener's lower face and skin 'resembled that of a private soldier', one of the millions of them killed in the war perhaps, like Kitchener himself? Lord Esher's attack was a safe one: the war was over and Kitchener dead when he made it. Made when Kitchener was still alive, the reaction would have been very different.

So, in the early days of the war and just before leaving for the front, the thoughts of many young soldiers were drawn to their King and to Kitchener.

A Visit to the Ottoman Turks, 1915

Young men who hurried to join the colours either in or just before August 1914 answered with shy pride when questioned about the date of joining. It was true that, as months went by devoted only to training, the men who had rushed to join the army began to grumble: 'The war will be over, dammit, before we get to the front.'

When, however, at the end of May and the beginning of June 1915, first the King and then Lord Kitchener came to inspect troops of the 10th Division at Hackwood Park in Hampshire, it was guessed rightly that the time to go to war had come; and as sun-helmets and khaki drill uniform reached the regiments, it was thought that the destination might be Gallipoli.

On our way to entrain for an unnamed port, the soldiers' wives and sweethearts walked alongside them carrying kitbags or rifles. For a week it had been sultry weather and as we marched the pending storm broke, the thunder heavy and near. In the intervals between its crashes a band could be heard banging away at the head of the column. The lanes were dark with summer leaf and bordered with flowers. It was the very last time that most of our Hampshire men would see them.

Part of the divisional headquarters and many of the 10th Division were packed aboard a troop ship, the S.S. *Transylvania*. The crowding below decks was almost intolerable. The sea in the Bay of

Biscay was too rough to permit walking or parades on deck other than boat drill. Since there was a great deal of straw below decks for the animals and men to sleep on, smoking was allowed only on deck. A number of the horses died and had to be lugged to the gunwales and thrown overboard in spite of the storm. The men were nearly all seasick and miserable until we reached Gibraltar. There the finer weather, the sight of the famous Rock, leaping dolphins, the blue Mediterranean and other troopships with which to exchange cheers, heartened them again. Day by day the weather improved.

Nearing Malta, we wore khaki drill uniform for the first time and the donning of new dress, while at the same time receiving orders about preparing for battle, gave it a ritualistic significance. Hair on the head was to be cropped and that on the body shaved, in order to prevent lice. Before an assault, we were warned, the stomach and the bladder should be empty, for only thus could surgeons hope to save one wounded in the stomach. The officers had nearly all bought, from a chemist's shop in Bond Street, London, a little pocket book of medicines and drugs in leaf form, each section being perforated, like stamps, in order to make separate doses. We had had the forethought to buy some extra ones for our men. We were ordered from now on to wear identity discs. We eyed each other anew. I myself was eighteen years and two months old, having been given my commission in the army when seventeen years and five months old; we were mostly very young. The Navy had midshipmen in action who were even younger.

The sea, that had still been choppy in the western Mediterranean, grew less disturbed every day and the air warmer. Nearing Egypt the weather became sweltering. The troops stripped themselves to the waist. They came on deck for air and lay down in the shade, under the boats or wherever they could find it. The sea was without ripples, oily and sluggish, and the ship seemed to have difficulty in cutting it, hissing as it did so and seeming to move more slowly than before. The interminable cries from the parties that played the card game of House rang loudly on the still air. 'Housy, Housy – 'ere you are – top of the 'ouse.' The heat at noon was blistering. Since the nights were very hot, the officers began to sleep on deck. On the fourth day of heat, we saw the low Egyptian coastline swimming in a mirage ahead of us, and at night the lights of a town.

We were allowed on shore in turns. My own turn came in the

daytime and was short. Those who went in the evening came back with astonishing stories. To our amusement, a most respectable and elderly captain had been seen, sitting fascinated alongside a great fat negress; for several days afterwards he was teased about it. Since he was killed almost as soon as we landed in Turkey, the negress must have been the last woman with whom he talked. Others reported having seen a row of boys waiting, ready for anything, and been offered hashish cigarettes. It seems there were establishments of every grade, for every kind of pleasure. The constant passing of ships, the main form of transport between West and East, had long supplied Egyptians of the ports with numerous customers having every scale of income and kind of taste.

Next day the ship sailed northwards, so that Gallipoli was thought to be the destination. Final preparations were to be made on one of the Greek islands. There we lay in the open, having no tents, dosed ourselves against malaria and suffered much from flies. In a Greek village a potent wine was discovered, against which the men had to be warned, rather unsuccessfully. They drank it like beer and some quickly became drunk. Money running out, a visit was made by officers to the S.S. *Aragon,* to see the staff and ask for money for the troops. They passed a roped-off space, where members of the staff were lolling in deck-chairs sipping iced drinks, and were refused the money. In consequence we disliked the staff, and when the *Aragon* later went aground it was said to be on a reef of its own soda-water bottles.

The battalion reserves and transport section were separated from the remainder. They were to remain on the island. We had been told to leave our swords behind in England. Some officers felt ill-armed, having nothing but a six-chambered revolver apiece. Old regular officers said that with a sword you had a longer reach than with a bayonet and rifle and you could use a sword to signal a change of direction to the men behind you.

Maps were issued to the colonels of battalions and to a few others. There were not enough for all, and subalterns had none. It was in a hazy kind of way that we set out, if the extensive military preparations more usual today are compared with our arrangements then. On the other hand, we were supported by something rather more sustaining than the value of democracy as a reason for fighting. There remained within us a deep sense of obligation; 'theirs not to reason why' had for us a less ironical meaning than it received later.

6

The crossing to the peninsula was undertaken at night in a small steamer, every foot of which was taken up by the ranks of men waiting to land. One soldier was hit by a spent bullet while still aboard. Soon we could see the lights of candles and lanterns from dugouts in the cliff face and quick flashes from machine-guns, rifles and grenades constantly being fired on the summit. It was into Anzac cove that the ship was moving, on that night of 5 August 1915. Quietly we lowered ourselves into the ship's boats and were rowed to the end of a wooden quay. The rifle and machine-gun fire was continuous and near. As the boats clustered there, a staff-officer addressed us from above. 'Hampshires? I have orders for you from the General', and thereupon, before we disembarked, he gave us a kind of homily on war, embroidered with military directions and warnings. The gist of the orders given us was that we were to conceal ourselves by day most carefully, so that the attack to be made in a few days' time would remain a surprise.

An Australian guide led us away, up the cliff by a steep path. We stumbled on in the dark until we met other waiting guides. They showed us where they had prepared dugouts for us in the cliff face like their own. They warned us once more about being seen in daylight, gave us tips for our night life, the whereabouts of water, the ration dump and so on, and left us. Soon each shelter in the cliff was lit by a yellow candle. We were at last installed on Gallipoli, in Ottoman Turkey.

In the daylight the firing was less frequent. Flies worried us, until we made the dugouts dark by rigging a jacket or shirt across the dugout mouth, but this in turn made them so unbearably hot that we lay in the dark, sweating. The Australians wore shorts, boots and socks, a bandolier and a soft wideawake hat, and nothing else. We had trousers, shirts, underclothes, coats and puttees, and wore sun-helmets, and were uncomfortably overdressed for the heat of the eastern Mediterranean at midsummer.

Concentrated lime-juice and rum was issued in great earthenware jars at the ration dump, which by night became a sociable meeting-place. There would be a great deal of chatter and exchanges. On the second night, towards dawn, an orderly came from the captain commanding the company, passing the colonel's order to be ready soon for an attack. We were to move into position for it that coming night, marching off at about dusk. Accordingly we fell in as the sun went down, following Australian guides to hilltops on the left of their position. It was a gruelling climb, with many halts and whispered commands. From the Australian lines we went on without a guide, down a steep gully for what seemed many miles, until we came out near the shore, about dawn. It had been a tiring march and at one moment, when we crossed the Australian lines, the smell of dead bodies had been almost overpowering in its sickening sweetness and significance. We lay exhausted in the sand and slept. At that time we did not know that our whole column, under Brigadier Baldwin, had lost its way.

In the afternoon we twice fell in, ready to move, and twice were told to fall out again. Shortly before dusk we moved off in the direction of the hills. Entering a gully at nightfall, we were soon confused by its winding and branching pathways. Our line of march was further broken up by stretcher parties with wounded men passing us and by a succession of led mules coming down for ammunition and water. The climb became steeper, and soon we were very tired and thirsty, but by dawn we were lined up across the ridges; we saw to it that rifle-magazines were charged, fixed bayonets and lay down, waiting for the order to advance. It was the morning of 9 August, or so I thought.

The order to stand up and then to advance was passed across the hills, and we began our scramble upward through the bushes and across the rocks.

In a short time the line was no longer a line. As we neared a summit, towards Chunuk Bair, we could see beyond it and far below many ships close inshore, and away on our far left dozens of ships' boats rowing towards it. A great bay spread out into a haze. Here and there, through my field-glasses, I saw one or two very small parties of Turks. They fled before a great landing of British troops, but our men by the shore were not following them. Breaking out from Anzac, we were to support the attack from Suvla Bay capturing the heights on its right flank.

We struggled on. Men started being hit by snipers and machine-guns. After a time we came into a gully below the lee of some hills and rested. I had very little idea where we were going or what we were supposed to be doing, except climbing upwards over increasingly rough going. At times we were out of sight of other troops and mostly unsure of anything except the heat, our thirstiness and the constant sniping, from which casualties were becoming serious. We struggled on, with intervals for resting, until dark when we were so tired that we slept, in spite of bursting shrapnel and incessant crackling rifle and machine-gun fire. Near dawn, the firing mounted in a crescendo that woke us and kept us from sleeping any more.

There were shouts that the Turks were charging. Some of the scrub had caught fire and by the light we could see Turks above us leaping down from the nearby summits. My poor men were being hit one after the other. I got the survivors together and took them to a knoll, out of the gully. On the way we found Lieutenant Bell, with one arm blown off and his chest torn open, dying. By him knelt one of his men who looked up piteously. Far gone and unconscious as Bell was, I put two of my opium wafers in his mouth.

We continued to struggle on and upwards, sometimes clambering on all fours. Only six men were left with me. I felt a stinging pain in my right foot. Taking off the boot, I found blood where a bullet had gone in. William Sherren, my batman, bandaged it and then supported me. It was impossible for me to walk unaided. The men were already out of sight. Sherren and I made our way back towards the gully. The din of firing was increasing. Smoke from burning scrub was twisting over the hills and the sun was pale and low behind it. Flames were rising from some Turkish ammunition dump or post. Suddenly, as I stopped in my hopping to give Sherren a rest from steadying me, there burst from the smoke and scrub, a couple of yards above us, three Turkish soldiers, bayonets fixed. The nearest, plunging downwards and carried on by his impetus, swerved, scowling, as he came level with me. My revolver was ready. There was a second when a shot might have hit him in the back, and then it was too late; they disappeared with a rattle of falling stones and a curious smell. Afterwards I was not sure if I had hesitated to shoot a man in the back, ingloriously.

Slowly and with many stops, we made our way downwards, Sherren sometimes half-carrying me and sometimes, as a change, I would hop on one foot, my arm on his shoulder. After a time, exhausted by the heat and by past exertions, Sherren fainted. He was much older than I, had seemed quite old to me, being perhaps thirty. He would not, however, leave me and so slowly, all day until late afternoon, waterless and foodless, we made our way towards the sea. In the late afternoon, a gigantic sunburnt Australian stopped by us. As usual with them, he was stripped except for his shorts, boots, hat and a rifle and bandolier slung over his bare chest, which was the colour of chestnuts. He looked down at my bandaged foot. 'Want a lift?' he said, and added, 'Mount,' making me a gesture to climb upon his back. The last I saw of poor Sherren, he was sitting there in the gully, feet apart, head on a rock, an utterly exhausted man.

The Australian, who wore a canvas wristlet with a sergeant-major's crown, made light of his burden and chatted about the battle. He was going down with urgent demands for supplies of ammunition. When we came within sight of the sea he pointed it out to me. 'Here,' he said, 'I leave you. You can hop the rest. It isn't far.' My life had perhaps been saved by him, and I wanted to say something appropriate or give him something. He saved me any embarrassment. 'You won't want these any more,' he said, and stripped off my field-glasses and revolver. 'Good luck, sonny. You'll have it all right too.' He waved gaily. At a corner of the gully he turned and stood, a magnificent figure, and shouted to me, 'Tell them back home the Aussies can fight, and good luck to you.'

'I will, I will,' I replied, cupping my hand to carry the sound.

He gave a quick grin, turned swiftly away and went striding off out of sight, singing a verse with words of ribald kind at the top of his voice.

Between me and the sea, the gully was crowded with seriously wounded men, most of them Gurkhas. A doctor was at work upon them, using a packing case as his operating table. As I paused in my hopping opposite him, he was dealing with a Gurkha whose arm was so badly shattered that I thought he must lose it. The man squatted by the case with his arm laid across it and uttered no sound while the doctor worked. Other Gurkhas squatted or lay upon the ground in a queue, waiting their turn, some of them terribly hurt, but all of them bravely quiet.

When I reached the water's edge, a boat rowed by sailors and down to near the gunwales with its load of wounded soldiers had just left and was about fifteen yards away. Rather to my astonishment (seeing how full it was) and greatly to my joy, it turned back and two sailors leapt into the sea and lifted me aboard. It was already darkening and lights from the ships off the coast, far out, were beginning to show.

After a long row we came near the side of a small ship. Before we could come alongside the master shouted, 'All full here, we are sailing now.' It was the same at a larger and professionally marked hospital-ship: 'All full here.' We rowed further and further into the night until we came upon a caique at anchor and were transferred into it, the boat then and there being made into a hospital-ship, though without any facilities whatever for treating wounded men.

The British sailors ordered the master to sail at once for the islands or try any hospital-ship that would take us. The sea was choppy by now, and as soon as we sailed waves splashed over the deck and on to the wounded. A New Zealand officer and I, both less seriously wounded than most of the others aboard, conferred together. The more seriously wounded men were groaning piteously; some wounds become more painful after a few hours than they are immediately after being received. The boat was rocked more and more ferociously by the now dark sea. We approached the master and spoke to him urgently. Would he not try the ships we could see in the distance, overtaking us and moving slowly in the same direction? He agreed to hail the nearer of them as it came level with us. The captain of the ship, perhaps moved by the pathetic sight below him, agreed to take us, full as he was. With difficulty the wounded were transferred to a ship's boat.

While this was being done, a naval launch came up. In the saloon we found a number of less seriously wounded officers drinking tea and rum and discussing the battle. Bombardment of the heights by the Royal Navy while our own men were on them, and in consequence driven off them, was being angrily described.

At that moment the door of the saloon was opened and a dapper midshipman, about fifteen, stood there, saluting. 'Excuse me, gentlemen,' he piped. 'My admiral's compliments. He would like to know if any of our troops are still on Hill 971?'

There was silence. Then the officer who, a moment ago, had been most vehement said, 'No – there are none – now.'

The boy stood still for a moment, perhaps sensing that more could be said. Since no one said anything further, he saluted, thanked us and left.

Some of us were landed on Lemnos and there waited for transfer to another hospital-ship the following evening. The tents of the camp hospital were very hot in the daytime and we longed to be taken off. Gradually, from one officer and another and from the men, the story of the battle in which we had taken part could be pieced together into something hazily comprehensible. The battalion in which I had been serving lost every officer, either killed or wounded, and every company sergeant-major and quartermaster sergeant was hit. From midday on 10 August until nightfall, the men fought on without any officer. *The Times* published an article on 19 August 1915 by its correspondent, E. Ashmead Bartlett, on this part of the fighting:

GENERALS IN THE FIRING LINE
Generals and colonels fought with rifles and bayonets alongside their troops in the firing line. It was a fierce hand-to-hand struggle amongst the scrub, through broken ground, in which no man knew how his comrade was faring. Many commanding officers were killed, including General Baldwin, who had throughout these four days set a splendid example to his men.

Gradually the enemy was driven back, and the ground we had been obliged to abandon was regained. Throughout the day of the 10th the enemy continued his attacks, with gradually lessening power, but could not force our men from their hard-won positions. At nightfall the fighting gradually died down from the sheer exhaustion of both armies and the consequent impossibility of any further physical effort.

Thus closed for the time being, amidst these blood-stained hills, the most ferocious and sustained soldiers' battle since Inkerman. But Inkerman was over in a few hours, whereas Englishmen, Australians, New Zealanders, Gurkhas, Sikhs, and Maoris kept up this terrible combat with the Turks for four days and nights, amidst hills, *dongas,* and ravines, 900 feet above the sea, to which point all water, rations and ammunition had to be borne along paths which do not exist except on the map, and down which every man who fell wounded had to be borne in the almost tropical heat of August in the Mediterranean.

It was only a piecemeal account that was to be had of the men of my platoon. I never saw or heard of most of them again, though two of them, Curley from the Wiltshire border and Andrews from near Christchurch, I found at Catterick Camp in 1919 and had them transferred to my command. My company commander died of a stomach wound. All platoon commanders without exception had been killed or wounded. The colonel had been hit in the head. Murray Hicks was the only company commander to have survived, wounded. He alone, with five men, had reached the summit of the hills we attacked. There he fought, bayonet to bayonet, with the Turks and only gave up when a second heavy naval shell fell on his position.

On the way to England from the Aegean I spent two weeks in a temporary hospital in Malta, the Convent of the Blue Sisters. As far as I can remember there were no visitors. We had almost no books. Among those brought to me upon my asking for some was an Arabic grammar. It was thus I came to learn the Arabic alphabet, killing time in a makeshift hospital in Malta. (In 1981 the Blue Sisters were forced to leave Malta by the Maltese government.)

So it was not until the early autumn that I was brought again to the English coast, at Devonport, aboard another hospital-ship. She came in gently, on a smooth September sea, and the boys of a naval training ship manned their rigging and cheered us. We waved back to them, brushing our eyes as we lowered an arm so that our tears were not obvious to others.

The Australians and New Zealanders were in much excitement at the sight of the green English countryside; of its villages, houses nestling against a church, of an ancient figure cut upon a downside, the thick woods and small fields in valleys which the train passed on its way to London. When we reached Paddington Station at dusk, we found men of the St John's Ambulance ready to deal with us. The walking wounded, of which I, having crutches, was counted one, were directed towards large private cars waiting on the roadway inside the station. The wives of the cars' owners were there, as in wartime duty bound, but they wore their ordinary dress, and it was the chauffeurs and ambulance men who installed us in the cars. As far as I was concerned, the women were right. It was more encouraging to see women looking beautiful still than have them bustling efficiently about one in uniform. As we left the station the crowd that had been assembling at the barriers sent up cheers that sounded very loud under the station roof. The Australians and New Zealanders beside me were elated.

We were taken to the peacetime Military Hospital at Millbank and there tended by the scarlet-caped sisters of the Queen Alexandra's Military Nursing Service. They came and inspected us and took our names and addresses, then returned to give us a last cup of some warm drink and reduced the lights to a small night-light in the middle of the ward. As we bade one another good night, each of us gave the words a little more than their ordinary significance.

Not long afterwards a noise of guns woke us. The night nurses came hurrying into the ward, gliding over the polished floors which reflected the light of lanterns and torches in their hands. They were like figures in some modern ballet as they fluttered this way and that and bent over their patients. 'It is the enemy,' they said, 'an airship.' It was the first Zeppelin raid, on 7 September, on the capital. Searchlights, one or two, followed the Zeppelin. We had a magnificent view through the uncurtained windows and without stirring from our beds. An occasional crash followed, until gradually, like music that fades in a diminuendo, there came no more sound.

The ladies who met us at Paddington Station and many others who worked hard in hospitals and at useful war work were not the only ones who took up a part in furthering the nation's effort to win. While on sick leave in plain clothes in London I was able, by quickly turning aside, to avoid being given a white feather by a woman in Piccadilly. Another day, when wearing uniform, a tough-looking woman shouted at me, 'Ya – still playing at soldiers here in England – ought to be ashamed o' yerself.'

Afterwards, when officers who had been on Gallipoli met, they discussed its, to them, still mysterious nature. At the end of the war, in early November 1918, being on crutches following my fourth wound, three of them received in France, I met by chance an American officer in the Hampshire Regiment, who had lost an arm. We agreed to meet in a week's time for luncheon, on what, as it turned out, was Armistice Day, at the Carlton Hotel in Pall Mall. We found it in a state of pandemonium with a man called Winston Churchill standing on a table making a speech we could not hear. We did not then know how much he had been responsible for the initiation of the naval bombardment and the campaign of Gallipoli. It was only later when Sir Ian Hamilton's book, *Gallipoli Diary*★,

★A bibliography on the subject would have to include the following:
ASPINALL-OGLANDER, Brigadier General Cecil F. *History of the Great War based on Official Documents, Military Operations: Gallipoli*. 2 vols. 1929, 1932. Heinemann.
CROMER, 1st Earl of (Evelyn Baring). *Abbas Hilmi II, Khedive of Egypt*. 1915. Macmillan.
HAMILTON, General Sir Ian. *Gallipoli Diary*. 1920. E. Arnold & Co.
MAGNUS–ALLCROFT (Sir Philip Montefiore). *Kitchener: Portrait of an Imperialist*. 1958. John Murray.

was published, and the book on the Gallipoli operations in the 'History of the War' series, by Brigadier C.F. Aspinall-Oglander came out, followed much later by revealing books by Alan Moorehead and Magnus-Allcroft, on Kitchener, that it began to be clear how the history of the world might have been different if only that campaign had been better managed and won. Even when the initial Cabinet compromises had quite lost us the advantage of surprise, the final effort at Suvla might have been successful, had that landing been immediately exploited and plans made in advance for doing so.

With Turkey defeated in 1915, could Germany have long continued? If she had given in by 1916, the ghastly battles of the Somme would not have taken place and the appalling casualties in the Russian armies have been avoided. Russia might have occupied part of Turkey; but however it turned out, there can be little doubt that, from an earlier and victorious end of the war, there would have been a different and better world today.

When I looked down over the bay of Suvla and on our troops resting there, I did not know that I was looking at the losing of one of the decisive battles in the history of the world. Nor did I foresee that it was probably the last campaign to which in all about a hundred thousand men, on both sides, would go without any motorized vehicles or women.

MOOREHEAD, Alan M. *Gallipoli*. 1956. Hamish Hamilton.

WILKINSON, Norman. *The Dardanelles*. 1915. Longmans, Green. This admirable book contains sixty pages of text and thirty full-page plates in colour, reproduced from water-colour drawings made on the spot, and a number of black and white illustrations done on the scene in the summer of 1915, and was issued in the same year, in time, in my case, for a copy to be given to me as a Christmas present, which I still have. That the book was so excellently and quickly done – and in wartime – was truly remarkable.

For this and following section, 'France: a War Diary', see also

ATKINSON, C.T. *Regimental History – The Royal Hampshire Regiment*. Vol. Two: 1914–1918. R. Maclehose and Co., Ltd. University Press, Glasgow. 1952.

France: A War Diary

France – Belgium, 1916

11 July: Left England, on H.M.T. *Lydia,* with reinforcements to the 1st Hampshire Regiment and for other units almost destroyed on 1 July.

12 July: Reached Le Havre 1 o'clock a.m., steamed on up the Seine with a pilot to Rouen, which we reached at 12.30, and reported at 3rd Infantry Base Depot.

14 July: Left Rouen.

15 July: Reached Amiens and left same day.

16 July: Reached Berneiul, detraining at Montralet.

18 July: Left Berneiul for 11th Brigade Reinforcement Camp half way between Bus-le-Artois and Acheux.

19 July: Reported to 1st Bn at Mailley-Maillet, walking through Bertrancourt. Major R.D. Johnston in command, Flint Adjutant. Company Comdrs: A, (temporarily) Edwards; B, Cromie; C, Masterman; D, Sharp. A taken over by Guard, C by Smythe. Went into trenches same afternoon, saw Serre and Beaumont Hamel, where casualties had been much the heaviest at beginning of attack on 1 July.

The battalion of the Hampshire Regiment in which I had been in action on Gallipoli had lost in under one week every officer, from the Colonel downwards, either killed or wounded, and sustained extremely heavy other losses. On 1 July 1916 the 1st battalion had lost eleven officers killed and 310 men killed in a few hours. The 4th Division to which it belonged had been recorded as suffering a total of 6,000 casualties in the one battle. Surprise for the attack had been lost, owing, it was said, to the premature explosion of a heavy mine which led to the enemy coming out of nightly refuge in underground shelters to man their numerous machine-guns and so be ready for the assault. Among the casualties in the 1st battalion of the Hampshires were the very few remaining officers who had survived from the early days of the fighting in France, including Colonel the Honourable Laurence W. Palk, D.S.O., who had succeeded to the Colonelcy three months earlier, having come out in 1914 as a captain. The men still spoke of Palk's death with great sadness. He had been killed leading them in their attack and had always been admired by them for his character and bravery. Once, near Le Cateau during a night of resistance under fire, he had spent part of it reading aloud from Scott's *Marmion* to a group of his men. Another time, later, he had read out to young officers from Gibbon's *Decline and Fall*.

While much liked, even, it was said, 'revered' by the men, it was held that he was often unusually forthright. He told one young officer, the first time that he met him, 'There are three things I will never have said to me: "It always 'as been done, Sir"', "never 'as been done, Sir" and "I thought". It is your business to know and to act,' he had added. He was a thorn in the side of the Divisional headquarters and the senior staff-officers did not like him. In the regimental history he was to be described as 'a magnificent regimental officer, kindly yet firm'. With him had fallen, in addition to ten officers killed, fifteen wounded on the same day.

(*The Times* reported Colonel Palk as having died on 2 July 1916. Their obituary notice on 11 July said that he was the son of the second Lord Haldon, that he had entered the 8th Hussars as a trooper and in three years rose to sergeant and was then given a commission in the Hampshire Regiment, serving in South Africa. In the retreat from Mons he won the French *Légion d'Honneur,* later receiving the D.S.O. He was described as leading his men carrying only a walking stick. He was said to be a good horseman and a keen student of military history. Debrett states that the barony of Haldon became extinct in 1939.)

20 July 1916: Bde relieved. Marched to Hut Camp near Bus.
21 July: Marched to Beauval through Louvencourt.

22 July: Remained billeted in Beauval, No. 17 billet, rue de Neuve.

23 July: Marched to Doullens, arrived 4.30 a.m. Left by train for D'Esquelbec, reached at 1 o'clock. Marched from Esquelbec to Wormhoudt and billeted in Hotel de la Gare (Mess) and in saddler's shop (bed).

25 July: Left Wormhoudt 5.28 a.m. for Poperinghe by light railway and marched from there to Camp E, about 2½ m. east-north-east of Pop.

26 July: Reconnoitred trenches occupied by the Grenadier Guards and same night left for support position on east bank of Yser Canal.

27 July: Went into trenches for four days. Took over command of the snipers and work of Battalion Intelligence Officer.

31 July: Night march back to Château d'Elverdinghe. Relieved by 1st East Lancs.

1 August: Minden Day★. Roses worn and a rest day.

2 August: Defences of Elverdinghe reconnoitred by officers and sergeants, otherwise resting. Two companies, D and B, remained on Canal Base position during this rest.

5, 6, 7, 8 August: Trench tour. About 10.30 on last day the Germans heavily gassed the Rifle Brigade and the Somerset Light Infantry, who each lost six officers killed. D Coy Hampshires lost about 60. Total of our casualties under 100. One officer (Love, A Coy) slightly wounded and went down line. [I saw him again at Edwards, the bookshop in Marylebone High Street, in 1953.] Major Armitage, from the West Yorkshire Regiment I think, took over the command of the battalion. Presumably no officer of the right seniority could be found in the Hampshires. Even though Armitage was quite a good officer, a Hampshire Regiment officer should have come from one of its battalions to try, however hard it were, to fill Palk's place.

8 August: Rifle Brigade and the Somerset Light Infantry both lost equally heavily. About six officers killed and 25% men. Hants: 108 men casualties. One officer wounded. East Lancs: few casualties but Adjutant (Toswill) died from wounds received at Dawson's Corner on the Elverdinghe–Brielen road. I was marching back from the trenches at time of the show and had met C.O. and the Adjutant

---

★Minden Day: Commemorates 1729 victory of the British over the French at Minden in Germany, during the Seven Years War. The tradition was that the triumphant soldiers had plucked and put roses in their headdresses after the battle.

East Lancs just before they passed Dawson's Corner.

9 August: Sat on F.G.C.M. at Canal Bank position H.Qrs 1st Somerset and went strong point L.2 near Brielen same night. Went to our 1st Line Transport to sleep.

10 August: Still at Transport as ordered to proceed by a bus that did not arrive at Sniping School Range.

11 August: Still at Transport.

13 August: Went to Infry School, Mont des Cats, to test three new rifles on range (met Hall, 15th Bn), narrowly missed seeing the King who was visiting St Sizette (Divn H.Qrs).

Bn is in rest until 19 August.

After reconnoitring trenches, north-east of Ypres but south of old position, to be taken over from Duke of Wellington's Regt, we are told we are going elsewhere and rest is extended.

21 August: Moved to Ypres by train.

C and D Coys at Infantry Barracks. A and B, Zillebeke Bund. H.Qrs at Ramparts.

22 August: We relieved the Canadians (R.C.H.). Left Ramparts for Dormy House (our H. Qrs). Relieved by 1st Bn East Lancs, night of 27/28th. Much sickness in this tour. Lockhart, Mann, Sparrow, Combes sick. Smythe, Prynne, both buried by shell, the former wounded as well, both evacuated, also McEvey (wounded).

29 August: At the Zillebeke Bund.

1/2 September: Moved into trenches again, Sanctuary Wood Sector. This tour the enemy shelled with trench mortars, not very severely but more or less continuously. The right company sector particularly received a great many trench mortar shells and had several casualties. Otherwise quiet tour.

BRITISH OFFICIAL.
From Sir Douglas Haig.
General Headquarters,
Sunday, 27 August, 12.54 p.m.
The enemy shelled Roclincourt la Couture and our trenches east of Zillebeke during the day, and there was also much trench mortar activity on both sides near Hohenzollern. Yesterday our counter-batteries successfully engaged many of the enemy's gun positions, some of which were destroyed and others damaged.

(*26 August 1916:* In the shelling mentioned, Smythe and Prynne were wounded. Nearly all the casualties were in the right company, C. The Royal Irish Fusiliers 10th Inf. Bde on our right suffered heavily and also the West Yorks Pioneers.

This shelling and the wet have made our trenches particularly bad just where St Peters St comes into the front line.)

5 September: Left for Camp F (Montreal) – relieved by East Lancs.

Left Camp F (Montreal) for Bollezele from Cheese Market Station, Poperinghe, by light railway through Watou, Herzeele, Wormhoudt, Esquelbecq, Zeggerscappel.

10 September: Left Bollezele next morning early for Cappelle by road through Zeggerscappel, Bissezeele, Crochte, Steene and Gd. Mille-Brigge. Billeted at Cappelle.

Marched next day – 12 September – to Dunkirk, embarked in the docks and disembarked on far side of the harbour. Left for Cappelle again same evening.

Next day marched to the Sands, Dunkirk, and returned same evening.

Same programme third day, returning earlier. (Three hours spent in Dunkirk, 13 September)★.

15 September: Left Cappelle and marched back to Merchinghem.

16 September: Addressed by General Hunter-Weston, on leaving his Corps to go to the Somme.

17 September: Left Merchinghem for Esquelbec by road.

Entrained at Esquelbec for Amiens via St Omer – Calais† –

★We were not told at the time what this exercise at Dunkirk harbour and sands was for, but the *Regimental History,* page 175, gives the explanation: 'The battalion was in camp at Vlamertinghe and then near Dunkirk, where it was practised in embarking. This aimed at making it appear that we intended landing on the Belgian coast, and it seemed that coupled with naval activities in the Thames and elsewhere the threat did arouse German apprehension and lead to their devoting men and materials to strengthening the coast defences.'

Incidentally, the *History* mentions just before this, on page 174, the lake in the château grounds at Elverdinghe providing good bathing and then the gas attack 'on 1st Hampshire front, the discharge lasting ten minutes' (phosgene, on 8 August). 'The Hampshires had nearly 70 casualties, 14 killed or died of gas or missing, as many wounded and nearly 40 gassed, 2nd Lieut. Love being wounded.' He was able to return soon, his wound being slight.

†Passing south of Calais by Guines, and near Ardres, the area where 500 years earlier British soldiers escorting Henry VIII were camped, during the meeting on the Field of the Cloth of Gold.

Boulogne – Etaples – Abbeville, etc.

Marched from Amiens to Cardonnette near Allonville, north-east of Amiens.

Remained billeted in Cardonnette 18th, 19th, 20th and 21st.

On the 20th, Brig. Gen. Sealy visited the Mess for a few minutes.

On 22 and 23 September remained in Cardonnette.

Moved on 25 September to Corbie-sur-Somme, practised fighting a rearguard action on the way.

Newnham and two other officers from England joined the Bn at Corbie Station.

Excellent news of the fighting comes in pretty continuously now.

During the night of 25/26 September German aeroplanes bombarded the district – only one bomb fell in Corbie – killing a Somerset man (in the same brigade) at 12.30 a.m. This was at the very end of the raid, which had started at 9.30 p.m.

Bn and Brigade training in Corbie during the week. 30 September/1 October we put time back an hour on the ending of Summer Time.

Continue training for the attack at Le Transloy. Leave Corbie 7 October for Sandpit Camp near Meaulte. Leave S. Camp for the Citadel Camp, 8th.

Leave Citadel Camp, 9th, for Talus Wood Valley near Carnoy.

Bivouacked on a ridge to the right of this valley 9/10 October.

On this afternoon – 10th – I went over some of our captured ground with the colonel and other officers of my Bn. There are shell-holes everywhere – one never could have believed it without seeing – the desolation and the way the old trenches are torn to bits. Villages have completely disappeared – only red ground, from powdered bricks that once were houses, shows where they stood. We went as far as the top of the big ridge behind Lesboeufs – through the trees of which we saw Le Transloy, the village we are to attack. At present it is not very badly knocked about, though the church tower is down and some of the bigger houses. The 2nd Bn of the Hampshire Regiment is again near us, in the Guillemont district – we last saw them at Ypres. The whole of their Division, the 29th, which was at Gallipoli, is said to be here on the Somme. Further orders for the assault of Le Transloy have been issued to Coy Commdrs today. The 10th and 12th Brigade are assaulting the 'Brown Line' today, the 12th, and we have moved into a new tent camp at the south-western edge of Bernafay Wood, relieving the Monmouthshires.

15 October: Still in this camp which we have occupied since the 12th. Church Parade today. I walked into Montauban, 200 yards west of camp, inspected German cement dugouts, in southern side of Support Position and sketched the Madonna. That the shell at the foot of the pedestal of the Madonna had not burst was considered by some to be a miracle. Like the story of the Angel of Mons, it was widely known. All houses are flat in this village. Hudson left today for Comdg Offrs Course in Aldershot.

[He survived until the 1980s, living in retirement in Winchester, having been Colonel of the Regiment. In a last letter to me in September 1979, he said, 'How pleasant it is to hear from you after so long a time. One gets a bit mixed with some memories but one clear one is of your very smart tin hat which could easily tell us where you were when you were walking round the trenches and another was the superior pig-sty which was your headquarters and where you were cared for by an excellent butler-like batman.

'(I hope your wounds are not too troublesome? I shall always remember the gallant efforts of the two devoted men who gave such devoted service to their Company Commander.)'

Hudson's remark about being visible going round the trenches was in part no doubt because the front of the trenches, that is the enemy side, was higher than the rear. Unless one was very tall or stood on the firestep, the head would not be exposed to the enemy although visible to the rear. One who was seen going round the trenches whenever his brigade happened to be next to ours was Brigadier Carton de Wiart, V.C., who did not walk in the trenches, but always went outside them. By the end of the Great War he was reputed to have received thirteen wounds, some of them in other wars. Like Nelson he wore a black eye-patch over one eye and a shiny hook owing to a lost forearm. How it was that enemy snipers did not kill him was a mystery. Perhaps even the Germans refrained from shooting at such a stunningly brave man.]

The following officers have joined the Bn lately:

Lieut. Pearce, 2/Lt Jones [Gassed 1 Sept. 1918.]

2/Lt Hawkes, 2/Lt Fall.

Fall has gone to hospital today. Guard is now 2 i/c.

17 October: Moved to Guillemont in the evening. Trench kits only taken by officers. Seaforths came into our camp. We relieved the

East Lancs in the bivouac.

18 October: E. Lancs attacked Dewdrop and Rainy Trench at 3.40 (zero) a.m. onwards. R.B.s [Rifle Brigade] also in the assaulting line, Somersets in support. Hampshires in reserve. Stood to 3.30 a.m., but Bn not called on. A very wet night.

19 October: The East Lancs lost two whole companies and gained no trenches, chiefly owing to their being hurried into the line to attack without proper preparations. The Rifle Brigade lost 200 to 300 other ranks. East Lancs lost nine offrs. We are to go into support relieved by R.B.s. Very wet weather.

20 October: Bn went into support position at Hog's Back. First-line reinforcements left the Bn for the Transport Lines near Carnoy. Some casualties from shelling. Left Hog's Back for the line 22 October. Bn ordered to attack from the line they hold – the right subsector of the British Line – in conjunction with the French Army, and to take Buritza Trench. Zero-hour fixed at 11.30 a.m.

23 October: The zero-hour was put back to 2.30 p.m. owing to thick mist, and because the artillery had not completed registration, for which was required a clearer light. The mist cleared at 12.30 p.m. Three prisoners of the 15th Regiment (Bavarians) were captured during the night and brought down. They said they had only just entered the line and had recently been at Verdun. Bn 'went over' at 2.30 p.m. At 2.30 and at intervals onwards, lights, mostly white, were sent up from the German Line. Our own artillery was intense, but not *very* intense.

I was at Bn Headquarters during the afternoon. No information arrived until about 5.45 p.m., when a message came from Icke to say the right had been 'hung up' but that the left was entering Buritza. Dallas Moor, V.C., (liaison officer to the French) reported that they were held up. At 6.15 I went up to the line to send back reports to the C.O., since no other messages had been received owing probably to the barrage fire. Line, who was brought down severely wounded, reported nearly all officer casualties severe ones. I reached the front line about 7.10 p.m. and found all officers of B and C *hors de combat.* Icke left only in A. German, Foster and Charles in D.

The remaining men of the Bn were just crawling back from no man's land, when I arrived, as the machine-gun fire had become too heavy to dig in. Work of getting in the wounded and reorganizing the Bn was at once started. Girling was brought in from in front at

10 o'clock and died at 11.30 p.m., when I was with him. Small party of Rifle Bde and the Dublin Fusiliers having entered Frosty Trench, we communicated with them by small fire trench: *Frosty. Hampshires. French Army.*

OFFICER CASUALTIES

A Coy:	Harrison	killed
	Gullick	wounded (arm)
B Coy:	Cromie (Capt.)	killed
	Wood	missing
	Line	severely wounded (side)
C Coy:	Capt. Le Marchant	killed
	Masterman	wounded
	Hodgkins	wounded (stomach – thigh)
	Lapthorne	slightly wounded (neck and cheek)
D Coy:	Girling	killed (died of wounds at 11.30 p.m.)

1 Sergeant-Major (B Coy) wounded.

Currie (B Coy) was wounded when reconnoitring the line the day before, being hit while taking photographs of bursting shells.

Sergeant-Major New (A Coy) and Sergeant Hentest, two very good N.C.O.s, were shot by snipers while standing on the parapet when it was just getting light next morning (24th). D Coy found to have suffered most casualties in men, and A and B most in N.C.O.s.

We were relieved on the night of 26/27 October by 2nd Royal Welch Fusiliers. I took over temporary command of B, it having no officer and no sergeant-major, Sergeant Pugh being senior rank left. Foster had taken over C for the time being.

Marched back to bivouac near Guillemont (Trones Wood). Large fires and hot food were ready, but very wet night. Roads impassable and open country very slippery and muddy. It was the beginning of the end of the worst two days' soldiering I have yet experienced. The mud in and outside the trenches had covered us literally from head to foot – all rifles were unworkable. Food supply was scanty owing to the dump being sniped continually the day after the show – and little could be done the night before. What few dugouts existed were absurdly small – mere niches in the trench wall.

From Trones Wood the Bn marched to a camp (tents near Carnoy) on the 26th. Left Carnoy on the 27th for Méaulte. I took over C Coy. Left Méaulte Monday, 30 October for Mericourt Station where the Bn entrained for Arraines near Abbeville. Detraining at Arraines, the Bn marched to Merelessart (8 kilometres). I went to Hallencourt from here, 3 km off.

Left Merelessart on 2 November for Le Transloy where training recommenced. Half the Bn and H.Qs in Ramburelles. C and D Coys in Le Transloy.

Draft of 15 men arrived for C Coy on the 7th. Moor came to dinner and slept, 7th Coy training until 22nd.

Bn training continued after 22nd (I left the Bn on 22nd for Flixicourt – 4th Army Course).

Division said to be moving (1 December).

Division left billets, 7 December.

Extracts from Diary of a Brother Officer, Mr Love

January 1917: A discussion on presentiments after dinner. I remember when old Stokes was my platoon Sgt (No. 4 A Coy) in August last, he used to say, amongst his usual grumbles, that he had been wounded once, but the next one would finish him. It did, on 23 October, though Icke says he was pretty cheerful. I cannot swear that Girling had any presentiment, or whether it was only the usual doubt of what may happen. He wrote out his father's address in my diary. My idea is that he felt what was going to happen. Icke says Sammy Harrison never expected to come back. After supper the night before he was gloomy, and gave his mother's address to Icke. Cromie had been out here long enough (and come through) and yet he knew what would happen (killed 23 October). Does one have a presentiment which does not come true? Is it common to everyone going into action? I have none, but on the contrary am convinced I shall come through.

(Love's remarks in his diary about presentiments jump with my own feelings at the time. The average 'life' of a subaltern during the worst period of the battles of the Somme was about a month. Within that time he would become a casualty. Sickness, wounding or death was all that he could expect. A Company Commander could expect about six months' 'life' and a Battalion Commander about a year. I had an impression that not only did some officers and men know their fate when the time drew near, but in certain cases knew what it was to be. Some subalterns had hardly joined before one felt they would not last long, and about others one sensed that they would stay longer.

Like Love, I did not anticipate death. I was, however, wounded four times, once in Gallipoli and three times in France.)

18 January 1917: . . . De Gaury and Foster back from leave, and Mann back with the Coy.

15 February: De Gaury came in with the news that another plane had been brought down by shell-fire.

23 February: De Gaury is quite wonderful. An hour after coming in he was completely changed and looked fresh and spotless.

Sunday, 30 September 1917: . . . Officers with the Regiment were: . . . C Coy: Lt. de Gaury, M.C., 2/Lt. Stannard, 2/Lt. Scrivens, Lt. Collett.

In a following year, going on leave from the trenches on the Somme with a brother officer in the Hampshires, Dallas Moor, who had won a V.C., in Gallipoli★, we had travelled down to Boulogne in a comfortless railway wagon, of the kind labelled 'horses and men'. Told by which boat the next midday we should leave France, we were left to find room for the night in a hotel, all of which were full. Going from one to another and quite late we at last tried a small one, explaining our need to the dozing proprietress. Looking us up and down she said that there was nothing save one bed in a corridor, which we could have if that would do. After the trenches and the railway truck we did not hesitate to accept. Hardly had we tucked ourselves in than the owner came back with a large mug of hot toddy, saying that she had been making some for herself and we might have this mug between us if we liked. If we were leaving early we should tell her so that she could call us and we did not miss our boat. We thanked her warmly. As she turned to leave, she said gently, 'I lost my son early in the war. Good night.'

Next day she charged us almost nothing for 'a bed without a room' as she described it.

★He died in the influenza epidemic in 1919.

Coming into London very late at night, we took refuge in the Piccadilly Hotel. Finishing breakfast next morning in the large, almost empty dining-room, we lit our cigarettes; when we did so, a waiter came across the room with a message from a man sitting alone far away, telling us to put out our cigarettes at once. The waiter told us he was the owner of the hotel. We did as he asked, packed our small bags and left the hotel, as anyway we would have done, at once.

Thus passed the first two nights of our short leave, from the trenches in France.

Wounds

The second wound, in France (I received the first in Gallipoli) led to a report to battalion headquarters of my death. It came from a shell-burst against the remains of a brewery wall of brick. Being very near it, bits of brick hit me and their impact knocked me over; I was concussed into temporary unconsciousness, while blood poured heavily out of an ear and a shoulder, making a most untidy sight. A passing orderly returning to battalion headquarters understandably reported my death.

Recovering in a few minutes and helped on my way with a drink, I was in time to stop the report of a killing, though a visit to an advanced dressing station was thought imperative. Injections and a night of hospitalization followed.

A third wound introduced a piece of shrapnel deep into my upper left leg, where it has remained without the slightest inconvenience for the last sixty-five years. (The last time I saw it was by X-ray at the request of the Air Ministry staff, London, in 1934, on vacating an appointment as G.S.O.II Intelligence, Iraq Command.) After an operation to retrieve the metal in my leg I asked if I might have it as a souvenir, but the wise young surgeon in the field hospital concerned told me it had been thought better to leave it where it was, a very right decision for which many thanks are owed to the young surgeon.

The fourth and last wound was more serious. Running forward to the German, Quean–Drocourt Line of trenches in the attack on 2 September 1918, I was shot down by machine-gun fire, some six bullets being later found in my right leg. Having lost much blood and given drugs, I was not conscious at the time of being taken across the Channel and to the place where in the end I was taken, a very large temporary hospital at Wandsworth. Memory, however, did not exclude recollection of the way stretcher-bearers and runners had tried to help me where I had lain, wounded, until our line later advanced again. Three men lost their lives in the same gap in the wire.

My mother came to see me at Wandsworth each afternoon, and on about the third occasion, when I had told her I believed that they intended to amputate my right leg below the knee, to my astonishment, she left me, almost at once.

Late the same evening, in the dusk, two men with a stretcher came into the ward, going from bed to bed. Asking my name, they said at once that transfer to another hospital had been ordered from the War Office. They had a written order. Picking up my few belongings, they carried me off. On our way down the long main corridor we came upon the Sister in charge of the ward.

'Just what are you doing with that patient of mine?' she demanded.

They told her.

'It is highly irregular. I shall report it,' she said.

I was taken to Londonderry House in Park Lane and given a bedroom to myself, where I was at once asked what I would prefer for dinner and was recommended the wine to accompany my choice. Bullets were removed from my leg the next day. New well-being was thus begun, though crutches were still needed.

A day or two after lunching at the Carlton Hotel in Pall Mall with Morse, an American officer in the Hampshire Regiment who had lost an arm in the war, circumnavigating our way to the hotel in a taxi with difficulty because there was already chaos in the streets as it was Armistice Day, I was given a ticket for an afternoon concert at the Albert Hall for wounded officers and men, many in blue. Queen Mary attended it. The programme was, I believe, slightly amended; from being a somewhat routine affair for giving pleasure to the wounded, it became a celebration of victory in the most horrible war in the history of the world.

When it came to an end with 'Land of Hope and Glory' and the National Anthem, with the entire audience turning to the Queen, I cannot think there was a single dry eye among those many, many thousands of wounded soldiers.

In mid-November, by which time I had been moved down into the drawing-room of Londonderry House, we were asked by a member of the hospital staff where we wanted to go. Lady Londonderry, now that the war was over, understandably wanted her house for a party at Christmas. The Sister in charge said that I should be walking again, without crutches. She tried to make me walk and used the word 'cowardly' when I said that I would try but could not manage it, as I knew would be the case.

It was arranged that I should go to Lady Dudley's hospital, a house at Chichester Terrace, Kemp Town, Brighton. I had only been there a few hours when an elderly doctor, highly recommended by a great-aunt of mine in London, saw me and, examining my wounded leg, made me feel it near the ankle.

'Tell what you think that is,' he said, lifting his hand for me to feel in the same place.

'Like a bullet,' I thought.

'Yes. I could remove it easily, but we had better tell your doctor, whom I know.'

The next day the bullet was taken out, and soon I began to walk again; I went to Lymington (the Whitakers' place) in Hampshire, for convalescence. Time was needed for the leg to recover.

By the Marne in 1920
The river is full and flowing fast.

Among the anecdotes told by General Sir Louis Spears of the days when he was on liaison duty with the French was one concerning Joffre's custom of stopping to chat with soldiers he might come upon. He did so when he found some of them bathing and idling by the river Marne. 'And do you know the name of this river?' he asked one, who hesitated before replying, 'Well, at home we would call it the Loire.' Joffre nodded understandingly.

One summer's day after the war, while resting sleepily in long grass near the river's bank, a boy came wandering through nearby thickets.

He began to whistle 'Malbroucq s'en va t'en guerre'.

The Somme

The Somme was thought of by British soldiers in the 1914–18 war as an area, a wide area where had been, or were still, spells of heavy fighting.

Comparatively few men had seen the river Somme and it was not thought of firstly as a river.

A Colonial Colonel, 1924

In January 1924 I sailed to join the First Regiment of Arab Levies at Baghdad. It was stationed on the west bank of the Tigris, between the desert and the date gardens, and was a unit of the forces under the Colonial Office, Iraq then still being a mandated territory.

The Minister for the Colonies was the Duke of Devonshire, and even my instructions to embark, issued from Downing Street on 27 December 1923, were in his name.

> Downing Street,
> 27 December 1923

Sir,

With reference to your request to be allowed to proceed overland to Marseilles to join the Peninsular and Oriental Steam Navigation Company's S.S. *Plassy* which is due to leave that port on 4 January 1924, I am directed by the Duke of Devonshire to inform you that there is no objection to such a proceeding, on the understanding that you will be required to make your own arrangements for your journey to Marseilles, and, in the event of your failing to embark at that port on 4 January, no claim in respect of detention allowance or other expenses incurred can be entertained.

2. As you are proceeding overland to Marseilles your appointment to the Levies will take effect from the day preceding the date of your embarkation at Marseilles.

3. In receipt of information from the Shipping Company that you have actually embarked at Marseilles, arrangements will be made to credit your account with Messrs Lloyds Bank Ltd (Cox & Company's branch) with the difference in cost of a passage from London and from Marseilles, less Government rebate.

I am, Sir, Your obedient servant,
(signed) Gerard L.M. Clauson
    for Asst Under Secretary of State
LIEUTENANT G. de GAURY, M.C.

'I am directed by the Duke of Devonshire to inform you . . .' appeared frequently in the letters we received. There still lingered an old-world orderliness and grace about our correspondence and much that we did. We usually had 'the honour to request' even forty-eight hours' leave of absence.

Nevertheless, although it had taken me some six weeks to reach Baghdad travelling via Bombay by ship (then the quickest route, other than the supposedly hazardous new way across the desert by car of the Nairn Company from Damascus), we felt in closer touch with and of more concern to those at home than do most junior servants of a Ministry who are abroad today. As interpreted to us by his staff, the Minister for the Colonies might seem conservative and pernickety, but at least – if one could trust the letters which punctiliously replied to ours – he was following our careers with almost grandmotherly solicitude. The British abroad had closer ties among one another than now. They were nearly all administering or soldiering, and the majority of them had had the same kind of upbringing. Home leave to the United Kingdom was infrequent. The local inhabitants seldom spoke English and lived quite different lives, their wives and daughters, if they were Muslims, being strictly in purdah so that is was difficult for the British to mix freely with the local families on an everyday social footing. Circumstances thus threw the British very much together.

In consequence, it was with rather more anxiety that would be the case today that I met my companions-to-be, the Commanding Officer of the Arab Levies and his four British officers.

Long experience of how to live in the outposts of Africa had taught the Colonel a way of getting on with his officers. He kept himself almost entirely to himself and we seldom saw him except at his orderly room or in the Mess at mealtimes. He was not a man one forgets easily, being six feet four inches tall and proportionately broad. He had dark brown, wavy hair and a longish, wispy moustache. The amount he ate was astonishing, though perhaps imperative for the support of a body so large. He would eat side-dishes, between courses, as others crumble and nibble bread. His favourite side-dish was a ham from England which would be placed at his left hand and remained there throughout the meal. For the game course which always followed the meat, he preferred a turkey; and to follow the turkey there would be a very large welsh rarebit. Exceptionally hot curries were favoured by him, especially when accompanied by chutney, bombay duck and various spices. A new supply of these accessories from India was always greeted by him as good news and spoken of with relish. The meal was washed down with shandy-gaff, a concoction of ginger-beer, a jug of which, wrapped in damp linen, would be kept cooling in the breeze outside the Mess.

The Colonel did not speak much to us at mealtimes beyond some inquiries at the beginning about our health, the arrival of mails and the results of our games of polo. Thereafter he would hardly speak, except to give orders to the Arab waiters who, barefooted, were kept nipping about him. Sometimes he would be obliged to send reprimands to the boys outside who pulled the punkah cords through openings in the mud walls of the room. Every now and then, drowsing in the midday heat, they needed slapping into renewed attention and being threatened with the Colonel's anger. With the self-confidence of Arab youth, they would squeak some reply to his reminder through the hole in which the cord ran. 'May God cool you, Colonel Sahib,' or they would answer with some cheekier phrase.

I seldom entered the Colonel's bungalow; when I did for the first time, after knowing him for about a year, I was astonished by the number of large, silver-framed photographs of exceptionally beautiful women, nearly all of them in court dresses and sur-mounted by ostrich feathers. There must have been at least a dozen. The only photograph of a man was that of another giant, his brother, who governed Somaliland.

In the orderly room the Colonel was a particularly imposing figure. Contrary to the custom in other regiments, with his khaki uniform, he wore a cap with gold braid and coloured band, one that correctly belonged only to blue, undress uniform. His belt and boots had been boned and boned until they looked more like patent leather than the genuine leather of which they were made. He held himself bolt upright and seldom spoke except to announce the punishment or dismissal of the offender. Under the regulations then in force, he could and quite often did award a caning.

After a few days of attachment to one of the older company commanders, I was given command of the right company of the Levies, which had no man under six feet tall. The regiment had been recruited from the province of Amara, on the lower Tigris, where there were great inland lakes and marshes; perhaps it was the way of life upon them that had made the men longer-legged and bigger than other Arabs. They had first been levied four or five years earlier, as guards and escorts to British political officers. When the British district officers were reduced in numbers, their guards had naturally been reduced too; but the men from Amara, having proved better-disciplined than others, had been kept on as a reserve and so in time were formed into an organized battalion.

At first they had been given a khaki-coloured dress based on their own native clothes. Gradually, as they fell under more regular military administration, they were supplied with and accepted more traditional military clothing, though barelegged and bare-foot. Thus, instead of an ankle-length shirt, they were issued with a khaki coat of the kind called a *kurta*, worn by the Indian cavalry and descending to a few inches above the knees, and khaki shorts. Since the shorts were shorter than the drill coat and the men had not yet abandoned the waist-long hair-plaits of which they were proud, the effect was odd. That the men had taken to the wearing of shorts was, however, considered a pleasing advance in the direction of military conformity, and as such earned praise from the staff at the faraway headquarters at Mosul, in northern Iraq.

A few days before I joined it, the battalion had been transferred from Nasariya on the Euphrates. The marsh-men were happy to be in the capital and proud to be on public guard duties there. For some of them the attractions of the city proved rather too much. There would be cases of lateness for parade or even absence with which, as a company commander, I had to deal. If they were serious offences, or repeated, in the customary way I took them to the Commanding Officer's orderly room. Thus, soon after taking over my company, I heard the Colonel award one of my men twenty strokes with a cane and was astounded to hear the soldier thank him, apparently with genuine feeling. I learnt that they preferred a punishment that was soon over to a loss of pay, with its effect on their families, or to imprisonment, which they held to be both shameful and almost unbearably irksome.

The arrangements made for caning were doubtless much the same throughout the forces under the Colonial Office, wherever it was then still in force. There was no great hurry made over it. My Arab sergeant-major, Chichani by name, would put down the parade of the company with all its camp-followers for the following day or even the day after if it were more convenient. I noticed that I was not consulted very closely by him.

The company would be drawn up in three sides of a square facing a triangular scaffold. The camp-followers, Indian clerks, some Persians of the contractor's staff and the boys who laundered and polished equipment for the men, stood at the corners. Beside the triangle was the offender, dressed only in a pair of shorts. The orderly corporal was ready with a couple of canes.

Chichani would ask permission to begin, and he and the corporal then tied the man to the scaffold by the wrists, one to either side. The corporal loosened his shorts so that they fell to his ankles. The sergeant-major took up his stand near the man, feet apart; taking a cane, he would stretch his arm several times, aligning the cane to see that the distance was correct. When he said, 'All ready, Sir?' it was time for me to begin counting strokes. At first, the soldier held his head back, turning it over his shoulder in order to see when the stroke was coming. It was a matter of pride not to show signs of pain but, try as they might, they did so. The buttocks writhed, the back would be suddenly arched and the neck tautened, as each blow fell. The man would then no longer look over his shoulder, but stand braced to receive his punishment.

With the last cut, he was released and, shuffling round, would lean forward to try to kiss my hand, as a sign of submission and an absence of vengefulness. He would attempt the same thing with Chichani, who with the modesty becoming to his lesser rank would withdraw his hand in time, waving it towards me, like a prima donna indicating the conductor.

For a year or two these canings were regularly awarded and carried out. The procedure was always the same and I never heard more than a quickly suppressed whimper from the offender. When it was abolished by the Colonial Office in accordance with some new general regulation, the troops said that they regretted it. They always had numerous dependants who suffered from the deductions in pay that went with other punishments and no one had yet told them that it was shameful to take physical punishment or to exhibit fortitude under it.

In the process of putting the battalion on a more regular footing, the Colonel and I, the only two regular officers, would be consulted by the Adjutant, a former footballer of distinction who had somehow found himself at the end of the war in charge of the marsh-Arab levies, and by the other British officers.

Among the matters we debated was the case of the mullah, a dignified and turbaned priest who had come with the battalion from the south, usually distinguished by a saffron robe and long-pointed sky-blue leather slippers, a hennaed beard, a prayer on his lips and prayer beads in his hands. There was no place on the new establishment for a chaplain, but it was felt right that we should have one. In the end it was decided to leave it to the men to subscribe voluntarily at the pay-table towards his upkeep. Life in the capital, however, was more expensive for them than it had been in the marshes, and so the mullah's emoluments fell. At about the same time the camp became haunted. There are a number of supernatural beings in marsh life, and one of them must have moved with the battalion. In the dead of night bricks would come crashing into the reed huts of the married quarters. A sentry would fall over something that felt to him like a wire, but that could not afterwards be found. Ghoulish yells would disturb the hour before dawn.

The mullah was asked to exorcize the camp and was paid for it, achieving complete success . . . but only for a time. The trouble would soon begin again and the efficacy of the mullah's prayers seemed to last for shorter and shorter periods.

The British regimental sergeant-major of the battalion who, like most of his kind, was a practical man undertook, with the help of two stalwart Arab orderlies, to investigate these happenings. For a time he had nothing to report. At last, with great satisfaction, he was able to tell us that he had solved the mystery convincingly, and he brought his evidence to the orderly room. It was the mullah, in nothing whatever save his turban, but greased all over. He had been found by the R.S.M. at midnight, slipping through a narrow conduit that led into the married lines. We decided to do without a mullah in future, and no one complained.

We were always on parade soon after dawn; we had no air-conditioning machine and seldom obtained enough ice; we slept on the roof and were much disturbed by the howling of jackals and by the bites of mosquitoes and other insects, in spite of using citronella oil. We had hardly any social invitations except from officials, no theatres to visit except Arab ones, where boys danced as girls, no films or radio, and only a few new books sent out by slow ship-borne mail from England.

The three-roomed separate huts in which each of us lived had immensely thick mud walls that kept them cool. We each had a punkah boy who tugged away at his cord during the hot afternoons from his place on the verandah. When we went to our quarters through the blaze of heat after the midday meal, orderlies would drench down the camel-thorn screens across the windows with water, turning the hot blast to a cool one as it passed through the dripping thorn, making a refreshing, sweet smell of damp vegetation in that otherwise intensely dry air. A bath of wind-cooled water from the porous clay amphorae outside was always ready. We woke from siesta in time for an evening game of polo on the sun-baked 'field' behind the camp. After it, we would ride back on our sweating ponies to the Mess and there sit on the roof while the sun went down, trying to quench an unquenchable thirst, until it was time to change into thin white mess-kit. So our days passed, healthily if unintellectually. On a subaltern's pay and foreign allowance we led a life with no anxieties.

Sherqat, 1926

During the British mandatory governing of Iraq, a small military detachment was stationed at the then railhead at Sherqat on the Tigris, close to where the main river is joined by a tributary, the Lesser Zab.

The huts of the detachment, which I commanded for a time, were on the higher, western bank of the river and between them and the sweep of the main river below where numerous mounds marked the site of an ancient Assyrian capital, Asshur. One of my very few visitors was the young Shaikh Abood of the Jibour tribe, whose forebears had helped British excavators on nearby Assyrian sites almost a hundred years earlier, as was confirmed in the book on Nineveh by Austen Henry Layard, whose astonishing work brought him new success and changes of career.

Hereabouts in Iraq the country begins to change a little; it is more rolling than in the southern part of the land. There are remains of ancient sites other than the Assyrian. To the west of Sherqat is the Parthian al Hatra and, still further west, Tudmor or Palmyra with its extensive ruins.

As Gertrude Bell wrote in her foreword to *Amurath to Amurath*, to Lord Cromer, 'the banks of the Euphrates echo with ghostly alarums, the Mesopotamian deserts are full of the rumours of phantom armies, you will not blame me if I passed among them *"trattando l'ombre come cose salda"* '.

My friend Abood, in case of some unforeseen military emergency, could, I supposed, raise a couple of hundred camel-mounted soldiers with carbines or rifles and some spears – not firearms, for which they would expect to have their ammunition supplemented. My men were all well-trained marsh Arabs of the Albu Muhammad, now accustomed to marksmanship with the Lewis machine-gun. Diminutive though our force would be, its morale and arms were such that we could, I reflected, have given quite a good account of ourselves in the face of one of those phantom hordes of the past which had come conquering through this land.

Sayid Jaafar al Ataifi, 1926

Sayid Jaafar al Ataifi, a descendant of the Prophet Muhammad, was venerable and rich, an owner of large properties in Kadhimain, near Baghdad.

Distinguished European visitors were taken to see him; the senior officers of the services called upon him and he would even invite them, if they agreed to take the precaution of arriving discreetly the night before, to view the annual Muharram passion play from a window overlooking the mosque. When it was only a matter of a courtesy call, he would receive at his garden outside the city. Messages were exchanged with him beforehand, so that he would be ready at the large wooden gates of his orchard, itself hidden by a fifteen-foot wall of sunbaked mud and straw.

However frequently he had visitors, he never refused to meet them and his picturesque appearance and old-world behaviour provided the exotic note which visitors expected in Baghdad – one which it hardly yielded them otherwise. So Sayid Jaafar had become a kind of 'showpiece', and probably knew and rather enjoyed the position.

Like most men of his standing, he still wore a turban and a robe, a dress nowadays almost entirely confined to religious dignitaries. Then, except for a few of the new ruling class, it was an almost obligatory sign of respectability, similar to the bowler hat and umbrella of the City of London, and no less reassuring in fact.

Strange secret passions or ghastly rectitude may, of course, belong to wearers of either kind of hat. The Sayid's turban was a billiard-cloth green; his long dress was usually of light-grey face-cloth, embroidered in black braid at collar, cuffs and fastenings; his foot-wear was generally canary-yellow or sealing-wax-red leather slippers with long curling points, and he carried a string of amber beads with a silver tassel. His brows were prominent and large and his nose was equally distinguished. His beard and moustache were hennaed bright red, or dyed bootblack black. They might, discon-certingly, be either, according to his whim.

He would hold each of our hands a long time in turn. 'How very gratifying.' 'How welcome and fortunate.' 'Welcome again.' 'How do you do?' 'How goes your health?' 'Again, how is your health?' As many times we had to reply. The multitude of ejaculations and the succession of inane inquiries would continue as we advanced with him into his garden and until we were seated on long wooden benches covered with Persian rugs, set out on a shady path between the gently gurgling water-channels.

'And how,' he would say, this time with a show of greater earnestness, 'does Sir John? . . . and Sir William? . . . how are they?' They were the names, we knew only by hearsay, of military commanders long since gone to England or India. No one, includ-ing the Sayid, I fear, really cared a straw. His questions were no more than the safe exchanges of the polite society of a bygone, oriental world.

Formal relations having at last been satisfactorily established, the Sayid ordered his waiting servants to bring the tea. For it, we were taken, at the funereal pace which his dignity demanded, still further into the depths of the garden, where the shade was so profound, from close-set palms, orange trees and pomegranates and the humidity so relatively heavy from the slow-moving water in the channels, that it was as dank as a cave. As we moved along at ceremonial pace, in time with the water, it seemed to be the dusty, corrugated palm trunks that were moving, not us. Ahead, giant frogs hopping ponderously on the dark, mud paths lowered them-selves into the channels, and edged their way obscenely out again when we had passed. The leaves of the fruit trees were grey with the dirt of dust-storms; it was the murkiest garden imaginable. Only here and there and far overhead gleamed shafts of sunlight, where the fronds of palm trees criss-crossed like prison bars and the doves cooed and fluttered lazily in and out of a zephyr we could not feel below.

There were never more than eight of us . . . and the table was never laid for fewer than twenty-five. Dignity demanded that it should be so. His reputation for generosity and hospitality would suffer, were he ready for less than twenty-five guests at one time. 'Is that all we are?' He would peer about him, as if some of the party might be lost. We sat in a huddle at one end of the long empty table while servants poured out tea for twenty-five from immense, heavily decorated silver teapots into tiny waisted tea-glasses standing on miniature china saucers. We nibbled the cakes and crumbled the hard sweets. He would press us to eat more; but even twenty-five guests could have made little inroad into that great quantity of food, laid out so that plate touched plate, over the length and breadth of the table, concealing its fawn, muslin and gold-embroidered cloth.

I remember one visitor, Sir Hubert Young, acting High Commissioner, leaning forward when the Sayid was not looking and gently stroking an icing-covered cake. 'Just as I thought – my initials are still there from our last visit,' he said to a guest from Europe, Lady (Edwina) Mountbatten. Lady (Nada of) Milford Haven, sitting beside her, giggled and turned to ask the Sayid about his harem and about his daughters. But the parting presents, wooden boxes of Persian sweetmeats, were already being brought to us, a signal for departure from his century and world to ours.

Mar Behnam, 1928

It was an inspiriting, warm and cloudless morning when we rode out on our way to an annual festival on 19 March, at the monastery of Mar Behnam, fifteen miles from Mosul in northern Iraq. The monastery stands beside the village of Khidhr Elyas in rich corn-lands between the Tigris and its tributary, the Greater Zab, and dates from the fourth century A.D. Close behind the monastery with its tomb of Saint Behnam is a great grassy mound covering a Sassanian or earlier ruin. The festival in the spring is known today as that of Saint Joseph, father of the Virgin Mary, the monastery following the Syrian Catholic rite. The church, however, contains some lively representations of Saint George slaying the dragon; one of them, the biggest, is a stone wall-carving six feet by four, and about seven feet from the stone floor, immediately to the left of the chancel. As we entered the church some girls, dressed in their bright new festival clothes, were laughingly throwing up kerchiefs at it, in order that they might catch on a large nail in the rump of Saint George's horse. There they would leave them, so the Archbishop of Mosul, Monsignor Georgius, told us, while they made a wish – 'usually for a handsome young husband or bouncing children'. Young seminarists kneeling at the chancel rail turned to look at the girls and then smilingly glanced at one another before sinking their heads in prayer again.

The Archbishop showed us all the monuments, described in

scholarly records, before leading us out to the baptistry and down underground to see the tomb of Mar Behnam. For all his seventy years, he led us with agility, lighting the way into the depths with a small taper.

Beside the tomb, in a dark recess forming one side of the octagonal walls, were manacles and an iron circlet for the throat, in which men and boys were fastened who had some special wish for penance or were to be cured of an illness, in particular of madness. They remained in the shackles for a whole night, in the dark on the cold stone flags beside the saint's resting-place.

In another corner, facing the tomb and the manacles, is a cell-like entrance to a blocked passage in the rock, its interior inky black, its doorway a few feet from the ground, with holes where bars might have been placed across it, an eerie place of now unknown usage.

As we came out into the sunlight at the top of the stairway leading from the tunnel to the tomb, we encountered Yezidis from Jebel Sinjar, followers of a strange cult; the Archbishop told us with pride that not only did the Yezidis come here but even Muslim Kurds and Arab bedouin. He explained that 19 March is the anniversary of the death of Saint Joseph, not of his birth. An interesting gloss, for it was in fact the death of winter and of her representative, the dragon, that they were unwittingly celebrating, as well as reverence for the less cogent human.

Khidhr Elyas (Khidhr means green in Arabic), the nearby village, is closely connected with Saint George, 'Green George' of England and of the European countryside. He is, or was until recently, to be found throughout northern and middle Europe, the Middle East, and even in India. Always his festival, as successor of Adonis, is in the spring. Sir James Frazer in *The Golden Bough* says that in White Russia a song represents Saint George as opening with his golden keys (the sunbeams) soil which has been frozen all the winter. The Wallacians and the Bulgarians looked on Saint George's Day as holy, the Huzuls in the Carpathians and Rutherians and Estonians had age-old ceremonies on his day. In England he was so revered that Edward III founded an order of knighthood in his name, and by an order of the great national council at Oxford in 1222 his day was ordered to be held on 23 April every year, as it still is.

According to Frazer, there is evidence to connect Saint George or Adonis and the earlier Tammuz with the spirit of trees and vegetation. His shrines are found in various parts of Syria and are particularly resorted to by childless women. According to one story there, the fight of Saint George with the dragon, who held captive the daughter of the Phoenicians, took place under a cliff on the shore near Beirut, in the Lebanon. He is variously described by the Muslims as a rich Palestinian merchant of the third century, a general martyred in a revolt at Mosul, or even as a contemporary of the Apostles. In his *Lives of the Fathers*, Dr Butler gives the year of his martyrdom as 303, and his cult certainly existed before A.D. 495, in which year there is a Papal Bull referring to his 'Acts', which are condemned. It was not, however, until 1972 that Pope Paul VI desanctified him.

In Iraq, 'Khidhr' or 'al Khadir' is found in many places other than Mar Behnam: at Baghdad itself, on the Tigris, on the Euphrates, and at the outlet of the two rivers. There is a shrine on Abadan Island and another on Falaikha Island at the head of the Persian Gulf. In Persia, too, Khidhr was much revered. Imad at Kirmani, who died in A.D. 1374, wrote: 'What cares he for the road, the pain, the trouble and the sickness who has Khidhr for his friend and Christ for his companion?' Three hundred years later, Sa'ib of Isfahan wrote: 'What profit is there from a perfect guide to those whom fate hath left empty-handed? For even Khidhr brought back Alexander athirst from the water of life.' For Khidhr could make himself immortal but not confer the gift. In Kurdistan, as in Persia, the spring festival of Naurous coincides with that of Khidhr and, some say, they celebrate then the defeat of an old tyrant prince, whose effigy is burnt by a lowly youth named Kawa.

A whole branch of the Khidhr tradition rests on his relation to Alexander. He is said to have been a commander of the advance-guard of the army, in its search for the source of life. In another account, he is a cousin of Alexander and given a more mundane role. In yet others, he accompanied not Alexander but Elyas. In some versions he lived on an island at the meeting-place of the seas and was the patron of navigators. Here and there, off the Arabian coasts, he used to be invoked by mariners in distress. In the Indian Ocean, under the name Khodja Khidr, he becomes a water-god and is represented astride a fish. There are associated stories of a human being who married a water-maiden. As al Khidr, Pir Bader or Raja Kidar, he is known in many places in India, in Bengal and Bihar, with a shrine on Bhakr Island in the Indus opposite Sukkur in Sind. In the eighteenth century he was adopted as the emblem of a ruler of Lucknow, when there was a revival of his cult there. In brief, Khidhr was originally the symbol of a fertility cult which came to be associated with the prophet Elyas or Elijah, with Alexander and finally with Saint George.

Leaving the village of Khidhr Elyas at Mar Behnam, we made our way along a track through the young corn to Qaragosh, Keremleis and Bartalla, three Christian villages. It was hereabouts that Alexander began the action of Gaugamela which ended in his victory over the Persian Empire, called the battle of Arbela; his army must have advanced over the ground by which we had come towards the crossing of the Zab.

We found the inhabitants of one village gathered in their old stone church of Saint Shimon, a lady martyred with her seven children in the time of King Antiachus. The women were on the right of the nave, the men on the left; the small girls stood close-packed together in a bunch, as if for safety, although there was plenty of room in the large cool church. The boys, seemingly all choirboys, were clustered at the rails, being directed in their singing, or rather yelling, by a closely head-shaven man of devout but unprepossessing appearance. The women would all have been subjects fit for Rembrandt: turbaned, shaggy-haired, with long hanging sleeve-ends and baggy *sharwal* trousers. They prayed rather like Muslims, going down on their knees in frequent genuflexions on little prayer-mats, though crossing themselves with sudden fervour whenever, repeatedly, the Lord's name was spoken. It was clearly a more serious affair here where there was no Khidhr Elyas tradition, as at Mar Behnam, and later the priest told us that the day was one of fasting and of three full services.

As we rejoined the main track outside the village, there came into view another monastery associated with Khidhr, high up on the hillside, that of Mar Matti which overlooks the plain, green from young crops.

Did some Greeks stay hereabout, after the great battle, to guard the route for mails? Perhaps their wounded were with them? Did they celebrate here, in the following spring, the defeat of the winter?

Twenty hours later, in Baghdad, on a Thursday evening, I saw little flat pieces of wood, with lighted candles on them, floating down the Tigris, and was told that they had been set out on their journey just above the mosque of Khidhr Elyas on the west bank at the north end of the city. They were propitiary offerings in hope of a heartfelt want: a wife, a husband, children, health, life itself.

The waters of the Tigris were rising. Soon the melting snows in the far north would be adding to its size and force.

So Adonis, and Saint George, under one alias or another, still lives on.

A Present for King Abdulla

Being comparatively often in the Palace at Baghdad, I made friends with Abdulla al Misfir, or al Madhaifi, the Guest Master as he was later called, an Hejazi who dealt with bedouin visitors. He would talk to me about Arabia and Mecca and excite my fondness for the esoteric. His knowledge of distant tribes and parts of Arabia forbidden to Europeans was equalled by his knowledge of Arab customs, of such things as perfumes and essences for various uses, of medicines and salves unknown to the Europeans, of bygone manners and ways medieval, of courtly habits that smacked of Africa and Byzantium and trading in slaves, black and white.

Since, as he had heard, I was leaving for Jordan and Egypt, one day he asked me in courtly terms whether I would be good enough to take with me in the R.A.F. aircraft a trifling present intended for the Emir (as he then was) Abdulla in Amman. If I thought of it, I must have supposed that the present would turn out to be a bottle or two of rose-water or essence of sandalwood or some such thing. I found that in fact it was four large packages done up in carefully sewn calico, containing camel-hair cloaks of a kind, as his letter now explained, that had been made in Iraq and were unobtainable in Jordan.

A slightly irritated R.A.F. pilot agreed that their weight was not too great in his load. All day we lumbered across the desert and sat down at last – it was a Vickers Victoria, as far as I remember – on the small and awkward landing-ground at Amman late in the evening, intending, as the pilot told me, to leave for Egypt, at precisely ten o'clock the following morning.

Early next day, I went to the Palace with my bundles. The Caucasian guard inspected me and let me in, a letter from Abdulla al Misfir my passport. At that hour the Palace, though open, was nearly deserted. A young negro page flitted away and was never again seen by me, but he had shown me an open door into a drawing-room and there I waited until at last a suave young Trans-jordanian in European clothes appeared.

My packages were in the doorway and, in Arabic, I explained my desire to deliver them and to see the Emir.

'His Highness will not be long coming,' he assured me. 'But tell me,' he said, leading forward confidentially, 'how goes Iraq?' His next questions were subtly leading ones. They showed a knowledge of politics in Iraq, doubtless acquired from his role on the Palace staff, whatever that might be.

Cautious as I was, he picked out from my replies something on which to base further questions. It was done supremely well.

The Arabs, I reflected, are natural diplomats and, given a position in a palace, know how to cull from a visitor in the politest way his news from afar.

But time was going on. Without, I hoped, his noticing, I cast a look at my wrist watch. His extreme politeness was catching. I did not wish to offend the young diplomat by so rude a gesture as looking at a watch while talking to him.

But perhaps he saw, for he reassured me: 'His Highness will really not be long now,' and continued conversing on topics piquant for their introduction of live comments by the King on matters of high policy.

But by now it was time to leave. 'I must go,' I said firmly.

He looked at me as one in pain. 'I can now assure you, and once more, that His Highness is coming, at this very minute. He is most regular in his habits. Exactly half an hour ago, as usual, I trimmed his beard and touched it up a little, you know, and from the moment when I finished him, His Highness takes precisely half an hour before appearing. I do therefore assure you . . .' But at that moment the double doors at the end of the drawing-room were thrown open by two Caucasian guards who, advancing towards us, announced, 'His Highness,' with which the Emir's barber and I rose and bowed. As I talked I found myself admiring the Emir's complexion, its pink freshness, and the cut of his beard and its colour.

I had, however, to cut short our talk as far as I dared; and I arrived at the landing ground only just in time. The propellers were already turning and the pilot was anxious to be off. 'More of your high politics, I suppose,' he said, tolerantly enough.

I saw the King from time to time, in Baghdad and elsewhere, and some years later, while I was writing a book on the history of the rulers of Mecca, of the family of the Hashimites to which King Abdulla belonged, I visited him in Amman. He received me to discuss the book and material for it, and invited me to lunch with him. While we were discoursing about the history of Mecca, he spoke of a strange stick or wand which had recently been brought to him from Medina. It had been closed up in the wall of the great mosque there and found during repairs. A friend of the Hashimites had secured it and brought it to him. With it was found a short document; and both the wand and the letter, the King said, he would show me after our meal.

The King still wore Arab dress, with the small turban worn by the Hashimite princes in Mecca, with gold-embroidered centre and the outside of fine and spotless lawn. His ankle-length gown was embroidered with flowers. His cloak was light in weight and almost transparent. Like all his family, he was always very well dressed, in good taste and extremely clean. He was very strongly perfumed.

The luncheon party was made up of his personal suite, one of his Ministers and myself. I sat opposite him in the middle of a long table. The conversation was rather limited. Arabs do not speak much among themselves at meals, or did not do so until Western manners began to be adopted. They relied for sociability very largely on quotations and the capping of quotations from poetry, a trial for the knowledge and patience of foreigners, however well-known the language may be to them. Our conversation was of the old-fashioned kind.

After luncheon, the King invited me to go up to his newly decorated pavilion on the hillside above the Palace. He would come there, he said, and join me for coffee. I went off with the Chamberlain and found that it was a pleasant, white-plastered little building in the old oriental style, but the interior decoration had garish touches. The brilliant emerald-coloured cushions had bunches of artificial pink roses fixed to them, so that one feared to lean back and thereby crush them.

In consequence we stood about instead, idly conversing, until a fusillade of shots interrupted us. I looked askance at the Chamberlain. 'It is only His Majesty, I think,' he said. But what he meant, I did not understand. Was he taking an assassination very calmly?

Then a soldier arrived, walking at unhurried courtly pace. 'It is the King trying out one of the new automatics supplied to his bodyguards, on the sparrows. He shoots as always very well – and has killed several of them,' he said.

The King, possibly elated by his postprandial bag, was smiling and happy when he arrived. At once he began to speak of the book and of material for it; and after a time, remembering his promise to show me the find from Medina of which he had already spoken, he called a guardsman and told him to fetch his particular confidant, a reader of the Koran. There was a long pause, then the King sent another soldier after the first on the same errand. At last an unusually handsome, bearded bedouin arrived, clearly in a very ill-temper, having I daresay been roused from a siesta in the warm afternoon or from some other private diversion. He stood in the doorway while the King gave him instructions for finding the wand and letter, then loped away in silent sulkiness, without the customary words of obedience.

After a time Abdulla sent another messenger to hurry up the delivery of the stick. We continued our conversation until, the midday heat becoming overpowering, I asked leave to say farewell. Still another messenger was sent to hasten the bringing of the stick, but since it did not come and there were no more messengers left in sight, the King expressed the belief that we should not receive it. He said it sadly, then, becoming brighter, told me to come to the Palace in the morning, 'I shall have it by then. I can get it myself,' he said, like one who has had a clever and unexpected thought.

The next day I went to the Palace, taking with me the local Government Archaeologist, Gerald King, and his photographic equipment. The wand was of grey-white wood, with tiny ridges along it and a crook carved like foliage. There were some very small holes on the crook that might have held some metal covering or rings. The letter with it had every appearance of being genuinely of its very early date, but the statements in it and the titles employed did not fit with the facts known from the surviving chronicles of Mecca. We wondered if it was the stick known as the Prophet's Wand but it remained a mystery.

The ex-Khedive of Egypt, Abbas Hilmi II

One day in the early 1930s, while G.S.O. II Intelligence, at Air Headquarters Iraq and living in the city of Baghdad, I received a message from the Palace that King Faisal wished me to come to see his guest, the ex-Khedive of Egypt.

In case it is thought that the Palace was an ancient survival from the days of the Abbasid Caliphs, perhaps their green-domed palace, it should be explained that when Faisal I had arrived in Iraq, following the 1921 Conference in Egypt promoted by Winston Churchill and attended by Gertrude Bell and T.E. Lawrence, among others, no suitable building had been found for the new monarch. In consequence, he had taken into use a number of huts put up by the Germans for themselves or for their allies, the Turks, on a sweep of the Tigris, north of the city. No one was sure what had been their military purpose, but the huts had been connected by covered ways. Until winter rain had washed it away, the huts and nearby date palms were still murky with dust from spring and summer dust-storms. It was hard to imagine that this assembly of huts was the palace of a king, the romantic figure of the Arab revolt.

I was told in the Chamberlain's hut that the Chamberlain was with the King, but that the ex-Khedive was waiting for me. It was the elderly deputy Chamberlain who dealt with tribal visitors and persons from Mecca and the Hejaz, from the former princedom of Hail in north Arabia and the Shaikhdoms and Emirates of the south, one Abdulla al Mudhaifi, who received me and who bowed me onwards to where the former Khedive awaited me.

As we walked slowly through the midday heat, he whispered to me that they had just received a present, from the King of the Yemen, of many bags of the best coffee from the slopes of the Yemen mountains. 'Did you not like it when some was sent to you last year? I remember that you did so and have given instructions for a bag to be placed in your car.' This was Yemeni coffee and the best of it, long exported from Mocha, had become well-known by the name of that seaport on the Red Sea.

It was therefore with such places in mind that I was shown in to meet the ex-Khedive of Egypt, schooled in Vienna, descendant of Muhammad Ali Pasha the Albanian, from Kavala, son of a merchant living then on the Mediterranean coast, who had been first of his line, being a successful soldier, to rule in Egypt. The Khedives of Egypt, though in fact almost autonomous, were regarded by the Turkish Ottoman Sultans as their subjects. Lord Cromer, the British Agent in Egypt, said in his book about him, that Abbas Hilmi's main wish in life was apparently to enrich himself by every possible means in his power, and the presence of British officers and officials in the Egyptian service was an obstacle in his course. Fortunately Cromer had taken a strong line in support of Kitchener when he was Sirdar of the Egyptian Army, and the young Khedive had introduced Maher Pasha, a favourite of his, as Deputy Minister of War, during the temporary absence of Lord Cromer on leave in England. Lord Rosebery, the Secretary for Foreign Affairs, supported Kitchener and Cromer, so Abbas Hilmi was obliged to write a letter that was published in the *Gazette*, saying that he was entirely satisfied with his army under Kitchener, thus contradicting what he had been saying for many weeks and his attempts to destroy the morale of the army; he was also unable to keep the anti-British Maher Pasha any longer.

Cromer's book about Abbas Hilmi was published in 1915; the character and attitude of Abbas Hilmi was in consequence fairly widely known. Earlier, Kitchener had become worried about the position in Turkey. He had written to Lady Salisbury in 1910: 'We are out of it altogether, as our present Ambassador does nothing and the German is allowed to do as he likes.' Kitchener had long been convinced that, as Ambassador at Constantinople and given a free hand, he could retrieve the situation. For success, however, he would have needed to be provided with funds in order to outbid the Germans in purchasing the support of Turkish leaders; and Grey, the Secretary for Foreign Affairs, was much too high-minded to make sufficient funds available. Moreover, Grey was strongly opposed on trade-union grounds to the idea of appointing ambassadors from outside the Diplomatic Service. Kitchener therefore contented himself by characteristically securing a private understanding in Constantinople that Turkish approval would be forthcoming in the event of his being offered Gorst's post in Cairo as British Agent. That approval, known as an 'exequatur', was necessary because Egypt was still technically a part of the Turkish Empire.

Had Grey been other than he was, and had he appointed Kitchener to Turkey and directed Gorst's successor in Egypt into close harmony with Kitchener, giving Kitchener the money he needed, Turkey might have stayed out of the war and Germany have postponed or put off declaration of war. It can be understood how the return of the Khedive from Turkey to Egypt in 1914 had rightly been prevented, a change in rulership made without any trouble in Egypt.

Abbas Hilmi spent most of the war in Turkey, Austria and Switzerland. Among those in touch with him was Bolo Pasha, an Armenian financier who had at one time been a dentist practising in Egypt. Bolo was reported to have been in touch with W.R. Hearst, the American press magnate, and Rosenburg, a Germanophile financier based in Austria. Paul Bolo was arrested in France and tried by military court-martial for complicity and commerce with the enemy. Among those who gave evidence was one Saddiq Pasha, described as *l'homme de confiance* of Abbas Hilmi, whose evidence veered to the side of the prosecutor. Bolo admitted paying visits to Abbas Hilmi, saying that it was about a debt owed to him; but Saddiq said that it was about sums for buying the French press. He planned to buy *Le Temps, Le Figaro, L'Homme Enchaîné, L'Information* and some provincial papers. During Bolo's trial early in 1918, a number of other orientals were arrested, including one Farkouh, a Turkish arms salesman from Smyrna with a luxurious villa in Evian from where he went backwards and forwards to see Turkish agents in Switzerland . . . or so it was alleged. Another arrest was that of Joseph Caillaux, former *Président du Conseil* of France, whose wife shot the editor of *Le Figaro*, M. Calmette, in his office but was eventually released, unlike her husband who was convicted of complicity with the enemy and imprisoned. Bolo was also convicted and shot at Vincennes on 17 April 1918. Abbas Hilmi certainly saw Bolo during the war. How deeply he connived with others is probably revealed in the archives of the trial of Bolo, presumably preserved still with records at Vincennes and by now available to students.

Abbas Hilmi, like most of his family, was small and squat, as was noticeable when he rose to greet me in Baghdad, a dozen years after the trial of Bolo. He was courteous both in manners and language to me; he spoke flatteringly of my abilities, of which he said he had heard. One of his main interests now, he told me, was in banking and investment. He hoped that he could persuade me to see his friend and assistant, Watson Pasha. He had heard that I was to go on leave soon. Watson knew what his own moves were likely to be, in his yacht visiting Mediterranean ports. Perhaps he could keep in touch with me.

Jimmy Watson did get in touch with me the next day and inquired when I expected to be in London; he invited me to lunch with him at the Naval and Military Club in Piccadilly. He said that he was retiring soon from being A.D.C. to the ex-Khedive and knew that the latter was interested in finding an English officer as his relief. He encouraged me to take up the opportunity.

I never took any further steps in the direction they proposed or heard from King Faisal or his Chamberlain what might have been in Abbas Hilmi's mind, why he had picked upon me. And Watson, on being drawn indirectly on it, avoided it or did not know what the answer was.

A Midnight Dinner, 1930

British political officers during the Great War, and perhaps before it, had toyed with the idea that the Shaikhdom of Mohammera on the left bank of the joint waters of the Tigris and Euphrates might be added, with Basra, to the States of the Persian Gulf, thus rounding off the British-Indian sphere of influence thereabouts. Towards the end of the war, the Shaikh of Mohammera's 'Arabian Nights' entertainment of British officers became well known. He did not seem averse to ruling under British influence. However, the formation of Iraq, apart from any other considerations, ruled out his survival as a ruler independent of Persia. The time came when the new Shah invited the Shaikh to visit him in Teheran, a fearful but inescapable visit from which he never returned. He left twenty-two sons and many female dependants. Dealing with their claims, the estates being in three countries, was one of the main occupations of the Sayid, his man-of-law in Basra. He was to visit me at intervals in later years, to discuss aspects of their claims, bringing one or two of the sons with him.

When I called upon him in Basra he let me browse in his library in which were splendidly illuminated oriental books, as well as some rather rare books by European travellers in the East. The house was situated across the river from where the Shaikh of Mohammera had lived.

On being asked to an evening party in the early summer by him, I accepted but, for some reason, it was put off and it was midsummer before it was renewed. Even for Basra in summer, it was a period of record heat: a policeman on traffic duty, a duty then new, had collapsed and died in the street; a dozen workmen loading an iron barge had all died from heat stroke. A message from the Sayid begged me not to come until three hours after sunset.

Even at that late hour, one's clothes were soaked as soon as put on. A small fan made from palm matting was carried though ineffective. The city was almost empty of passers-by as I drove through it slowly in an *arabiya*, a small two-horsed Victoria carriage. The driver excused the slow pace. 'The horses are exhausted. Their coats are wet. I can't ask them to do more.'

The few lights in the streets were dimmed by the haze of heat, and sounds were given a curious resonance by the thickness of the humid air. In the date gardens, crossing rills near the river, it seemed a trifle – if only a trifle – less stiflingly hot.

As the Sayid's house, half concealed by date palms, oleanders and orange trees, was reached at last, I freed myself from the sticky seat of the carriage. I saw glimmering in the garden the light from candles in many small coloured-glass containers. They only partly lit up a path onwards through a corridor of pomegranate bushes and apricot trees. A footman in (then rarely seen) old Persian dress, a long close-fitting blue coat and a black felt conical hat, led me to a pavilion, by which were jasmine and tuberoses, their scent heavy in the stagnant air. Beside a table laid for eight or ten at the side of the pavilion were couches with blossoms strewn on their seats. A row of porous amphorae, poised on wooden stools and used for cooling water, were ready. Beside them two youths were endeavouring to cool glasses in silver filigree stands by waving fans over them.

The Sayid appeared from one of the alleys, leading his guests. First was the Governor of Basra (or *Mutasarrif*), a bulky dark man, and his deputy, small, pale and bespectacled. With them was a Senator of Persian descent and name from Baghdad and two German canoeists, aged about eighteen, wearing only shorts and singlets. They had come, it was explained, all the way by canoe from Germany, except when canoeing was impossible and they had been obliged to take a train. As a means of livelihood they sold signed photographs of themselves posing alongside the canoe. Out of politeness to the Senator, it seemed right to ask for a photograph, rather like taking a ticket for a lottery or some side-show in order to please one's hostess at a charity ball in Europe. The German boys trotted off to get one from where they had left them in the house. Lastly there was the mate of a British tramp steamer then anchored in the Shatt-al-Arab who had just arrived with several blocks of ice, the Sayid having a business connection with the shipping line. The mate said the ice was sent as a present by his master on the ship.

The main course was a Persian pillau, chicken with rice on which were raw eggs and a sprinkling of chopped red wood, followed by water-melons, manna from Hamadan and grapes which tasted of roses and, according to the Sayid, were the result of grafting a rose tree on to a vine; he denied that it was achieved by dipping the grapes in rose water. Sitting on the couches after dining, we were brought water pipes or *narguilehs*, then date araq or sherbet, whichever was preferred. The latter, made from the stamen of the male date palm, is thought to be an aphrodisiac, and the conversation turned on that subject for a time. The Governor said that sharks' fins were profitably exported from the Persian Gulf to China, which was true; the Senator dismissed the efficacy of powdered pearls; the Deputy Governor quoted no less absurd recipes from a book published in Cairo. Only the canoeists had nothing to contribute, and giggled bashfully. The bold Welsh mate, perhaps tactlessly, said that he had no use for such things; the Sayid opined that variety was the best remedy. The minstrels who had been strumming in the background struck up once more for a short song; then, fatigued by the weather and the night being nearly over, leave could be taken. The drive through the palm gardens while dawn approached was enjoyable, the first moment in twenty hours to be a little cool.

Many years later, visiting a friend in Belgravia, I am introduced by him to a man who had given him a lift and arrived with him at the house just as I too arrived. 'You know each other already,' my host tells me. It was one of the twenty-two sons of the Shaikh of Mohammera who had visited me with the lawyer and whom I had not seen since 1930. He was now a diplomat working in London, I gathered. Before he sped away in his car, he mentioned his lawyer in the past . . . but no more than that, not the midsummer night long ago in Basra that his name conjured up for me.

The Lure of the Desert

When Faisal, a son of the last Grand Sherif of Mecca, took up the kingship of Baghdad, Gertrude Bell showed him respect and devotion publicly in a way that persons not embroiled in local politics found to verge upon the absurd.

Sometimes in those days and later, when T.E. Lawrence was becoming well-known, it would be asked in England what exactly was it that attracted certain Britons to the desert, to the Arab world. The questioners sought some characteristic they all had in common.

The difference between the desert travellers, in personalities, in build and in their approach to, in most cases, self-set tasks, was so marked that it seemed unlikely anything could be found in common. And they were not all British, for a few foreigners had also been lured to the desert lands. A comparison between Gertrude Bell and Sir Richard Burton, for example, shows how hard it was to find anything in common. Sir Richard was dark, dark as an Italian or an Arab, with full lips and pugnacious jaw; a magnificently built man. Gertrude was slight and very fair, with a pointed face and a long (too long), thin, intelligent nose.

Burton was tempestuous, an extravagantly industrious *bashi-bazouk* travelling in all the continents, master of some thirty languages, author of very many works and papers, some of them erotic; upsetting officialdom wherever he went, not always exact in his facts and often wild in his criticism. His life was one long gesture against social conventions.

Gertrude, on the other hand, was precise and scholarly; she was carefully dressed in clothes sent out from Europe; she travelled – apart from some remarkable mountaineering in Switzerland during her youth – mainly in the Middle East, and was in friendly touch by letter with the most distinguished officials and politicians of her day in England.

Gertrude Bell had gone up to Lady Margaret Hall at Oxford and obtained a first in history, the first woman ever to do so. Burton also went up to Oxford, but failed even to graduate, though it was at Oxford that he first began to study Arabic. Instead, he induced his father to buy him a commission in the Indian Army – the 18th Regiment of Bombay Native Infantry. In India, with the haste of a fish returned to sea, he at once plunged into a study of the peoples of the country. He qualified in several tongues: Marathi, Sindhi, Punjabi, Persian; he studied also Pushtu, Sanskrit and more Arabic. He acquired native teachers with whom he lived for weeks the life of a native. He practised the religious ceremonies and exercises of Islam. He was at home; but he never obtained what he longed for, the chance to go into military action. Seven years later he left India, a sick and disappointed man.

It was during his leave that he planned to traverse Arabia from sea to sea and, when permission for this was refused, he prepared for a startling journey – to penetrate Mecca, the forbidden city of Arabia, disguised as a pilgrim. It would be almost certain death if he were discovered. He carried off this extraordinary feat, which entailed a complete change of manners and behaviour, sustaining the change night and day for months with entire success. He travelled, disguised, first as a Persian, then a Dervish, then a Pathan educated at Rangoon. He called himself Al-Haj Abdullah. Afterwards he returned to India, and his *Personal Narrative of a Pilgrimage to El-Medinah and Meccah*, published in 1855, was seen through the press in England by a friend.

But he was a natural wanderer, Elizabethan in spirit. The year after his Mecca exploit found him attempting to penetrate another forbidden city in disguise – Harar, in Abyssinia. Next he tried exploring the mountains of Somaliland. Then came a year in the Crimean campaign; then he attempted to reach the sources of the Nile with the explorer, Speke. After several years in West Africa and several more in South America, he next appeared in Syria; Iceland, then Trieste, then India. In 1877 he was seeking gold in

Midian in Arabia; in 1881 it was gold on the Gold Coast. He was a constant thorn in the flesh of the Foreign Office, and it was his wife who, never leaving the Office alone, obtained for him a succession of consular posts, in one of which – Trieste – he died in 1890.

By comparison – but only by comparison with Burton's restless globe-trotting – Gertrude Bell's life was a quiet one. Her travels abroad began by visits to a relative who was, first, British Minister at Bucharest, then at Teheran. While in Teheran, she industriously learnt Persian and later translated the works of several Persian poets. In 1899 she settled in Jerusalem to learn Arabic, and travelled to Baalbek and Petra – then an adventurous journey, particularly for a woman alone – and began her archaeological studies of Eastern monuments. In 1905 she was in Turkey and Syria; in 1910 in Iraq, where she rediscovered Ukhaidir, a hunting palace in mid–desert. She next made an attempt to journey to the heart of Arabia, but only succeeded in reaching Hail in northern Arabia, where she was kept virtually a prisoner, returning, a disappointed woman, to Baghdad in 1914.

In the autumn of 1915 she was invited to join the Arab Bureau, then forming in Cairo. She was an invaluable and industrious compiler of information for the armies fighting in Arab lands, and was sent to join Sir Percy Cox, the Civil Commissioner in Iraq, as his Oriental Secretary, a post she held until just before her death, while Honorary Director in the Department of Antiquities in Baghdad, in 1926. She was described as 'a connecting link between the British and Arab races without which there would have been dislocation both of public business and private amenities'.

One could scarcely imagine two people more distinct in temperament and achievement than Burton and Miss Bell. What was there, then, in the Arabian lands and peoples, which attracted each of them with so strong a compulsion? In Kinglake's *Eothen* there is a sentence which may define the attraction of Arabia for Gertrude Bell: 'I can hardly tell why it should be, but there is a longing for the East felt by proud people when goaded by sorrow.' In that sentence, I suspect, lies Gertrude Bell's secret. A passage from one of her books reads:

Life seized upon us and inspired us with a mad sense of revelry. The humming wind and the teeming earth shouted 'Life', 'Life', as we rode, 'Life'! the bountiful and magnificent! Age was far from us – death far; we had left him enthroned in his barren mountains, with ghostly cities and out-worn faiths to bear him company. For us the wide plain and the limitless world, for us the beauty and the freshness of the morning, for us youth and the joy of living!

And the final lines of the book are these: 'Morning breaks fresh and cool through the soft mists to light mysterious lands and wonderful.'

'We' is Gertrude Bell and Henry Cadogan of the British Legation in Teheran. The year was 1892. She was young and in love with him, but her parents had hesitated, his fortune being small, and, a few months later, while she was in Europe, he had died of cholera. She never married.

I cannot help feeling that her love for the East was at least partly caused by the love for Cadogan which she had experienced there, and that in all her expeditions and explorations one can discover an attempt to recapture it, after his death, in 'mysterious lands and wonderful', some of which he had known.

The impact of the oriental lands on Burton was quite different. He became, to all intents and purposes, a native of the East; he identified himself with its peoples, its atmosphere, far more intimately than did Miss Bell. Was his dark colouring, perhaps even his name, an inheritance from some gypsy ancestor? He, a natural wanderer, was not so much an alien, a European visiting the East, as one just finding a natural home. During his childhood his parents dragged him all round the continent: the nomad instinct was in his blood as the record of his life, apart from his Arabian experiences, declares. In one of his books, he describes what he felt in the East:

A strange, inexplicable melancholy which accompanies all travellers in *tropical* countries. Nature is beautiful in all that meets the eye; but she is a siren whose pleasures pall, and one sighs for the rare simplicities of the desert. I never felt this sadness in Egypt and Arabia; I was never without it in India and Zanzibar . . .

That is it, 'the rare simplicity of the desert'. In another of his later works, which describes his search for gold in Midian, in north-west Arabia, he wrote:

At last once more it is my fate to escape the prison life of civilised Europe, and to refresh body and mind by studying nature in her noblest and most admirable form – the nude. Again I am to enjoy a glimpse of the glorious desert, to inhale the sweet, pure breath of translucent skies that show the red stars burning upon the very edge and verge of the horizon, and to strengthen myself by a short visit to the wild man and his home . . .

Burton and Gertrude Bell were fundamentally different in character; and in their reaction to the Arabian spell there was a deep difference. Burton was an instinctive nomad, at home in a nomadic civilization; his own lines sum him up:

Do what thy manhood bids thee do, from none but self expect applause
He noblest dies and noblest lives who makes and keeps his self-made laws.

To Gertrude Bell, that phrase of Kinglake's applies . . . the 'longing for the East felt by proud people when goaded by sorrow'. But in each case, the lure for them was very strong; for each of them, Arabia was suffused by a romantic glow.

Today, naphtha fields, light industries, air-conditioned apart-ment houses, television, film theatres and fleets of motor-cars are gradually but inevitably replacing the 'stage properties' which decorated the traditional Arabia . . . the herds of camels, slow marching; the desert dawn; the grace and dignity of being, whether it be in brocade or in rags; philosophy under the stars; ruins of cities from which forgotten empires ruled a trembling world; the archaic manners of a different age, that scene which soothed the mind, and, as Kinglake noticed, effaced sad memories.

Poor gawky Hester Stanhope, for example, hostess for Pitt and one of the most complimented girls in Europe, became unwanted after her uncle's death and, travelling abroad, at last found in the Arab world, until the end of her days there, some tranquillity; perhaps too much – 'tranquillity carried beyond the point of virtue', as Gertrude Bell once wrote. Though Hester Stanhope ended her days in the Lebanon, she did travel earlier in the Syrian desert, went to Palmyra and wrote of it enthusiastically.

The desert has one quality which has not been mentioned by its

European travellers of the past: its *security*, as it can be called; and that in spite of it having brought death to some of them. It is a form of security that is the very opposite of that experienced in cities in the industrialized Western world, or in mountainous lands, tropical forests or any jungles. In these latter parts of the world, though it may not be consciously thought of, safety is lacking because danger can spring out upon you; whereas the desert's horizon is very far off and no murderous enemy can be hidden and concealed until the last moment, be able to leap out, catching you unprepared. Here a deep and primitive instinct is touched.

About the time that Gertrude Bell was setting out for Hail in northern Arabia, just before the Great War, a very young Dane, Barclay Raunkiaer, was leaving Kuwait by camel caravan for Riyadh. He was so impressed by what he saw there, in spite of his frightening misadventures on the way, that he hoped to return, and would have done so if the illness brought on him during his journey had not led to his death in Denmark. He ended his short book:

> Our little vessel glides eastward to a low accompaniment of creaking tackle, over leaden shallows whence the backfins of attendant sharks emerge like black triangles to sink again lazily into the deep. Blood-red the sun goes down on the desert coast of Arabia and gathering darkness veils a land where there is hardly a thing living or dead that is not hostile and abhorrent to a stranger. But, nevertheless, that same land casts an irresistible spell over whosoever has come unscathed from its better acquaintance, just, perhaps, because it is there that the oldest society on earth stands revealed ever and again in the light of day.

The very last of the Arabian desert travellers, Wilfred Thesiger, who described his journey in *Arabian Sands,* published in 1959 after his dangerous crossing of the Empty Quarter by camel, ends his book by saying of his bedu companions:

> I realized that the Bedu with whom I had lived and travelled, and in whose company I had found contentment, were doomed. Some people maintain that they will be better off when they have exchanged the hardship and poverty for the security of a materialistic world. This I do not believe. I shall always remember how often I was humbled by those illiterate herdsmen

who possessed, in so much greater measure than I, generosity and courage, endurance, patience and light-hearted gallantry. Among no other people have I ever felt the same sense of personal inferiority . . .

Yet I knew that for them the danger lay, not in the hardship of their lives, but in the boredom and frustration they would feel when they renounced it. The tragedy was that the choice would not be theirs; economic forces beyond their control would eventually drive them into the towns to hang about street-corners as unskilled labour.

So whatever it was that drew persons of intelligence once and again to Arabia for times short or long, small or little, none can ever again experience quite what they did. The lands where telephones don't ring, where manners are the manners of a slower-moving past, are ever narrowing. In central Arabia now jeeps have replaced jinns, and geologists have meticulously explored that mysterious jinn capital, the mountains of Kaf. The oriental dawn breaks behind a herd of oil derricks while Arabs in dungarees begin a machine-controlled day. Their manners are changing with their life; the gentler civilization of a former, fairer world, the civilization which was still there for Richard Burton, Gertrude Bell, Barclay Raunkiaer, Wilfred Thesiger and others to explore, is gone.

Funeral of a King, 1933

The officer on night duty at the Royal Air Force camp fourteen miles away from the city rang after midnight: would I tell the British Chargé d'Affaires that King Faisal had died suddenly in Switzerland and that his body was being brought by ship to the Levant and onwards by R.A.F. aircraft.* (Faisal was a son of the Grand Sherif of Mecca; he became King of Iraq in 1921, having played his part in the 1914–18 war by making a diversion with Arab tribesmen on the right flank of Allenby's advance into Syria.)

Long before the hour of arrival, the streets were lined by the inhabitants of Baghdad, many of them sobbing. The women, covered by black veils and cloaks, lined the balconies and roof edges, where they rocked and moaned and made that peculiar and repetitive noise of ululation reserved for emotional events.

When the aircraft arrived at the city airport and taxied towards the waiting soldiers and notables, the crowd behind began to wail in earnest; their cries were echoed and carried on through the city in one great and continuous sound of emotion. Meanwhile, the front part of the aircraft having been removed by airmen of the crew, the coffin was eased out of it by them on to the shoulders of eight senior Iraq officers. It had not been foreseen that the British Consular authority and Swiss undertakers would be at pains to provide a

*The present author wrote an obituary notice of Faisal for the *Iraq Times*.

coffin fit for a king, one of the heaviest kind with solid fittings. Moreover the pall-bearers were coffin-bearers and of coffin-bearers as such there were none. The portly Generals began to sag and the young British airmen ran forward to lend a shoulder only just in time to bring the coffin safely to its gun-carriage.

As the procession made its way slowly through the city to the mausoleum seven miles away, many men from the grief-ridden populace in the streets joined the cortège, for such was held to be a pious thing to do at any funeral. So great was the pressure of them after the first mile or so along the main street that senior officials and foreign representatives lost their positions, were jostled and forced out of the procession. Some of them took to their beds afterwards, and two of them were several days recovering.

In the towns of Iraq it was considered a worthy thing to take part in a funeral. When a coffin passed, carried by hand and shoulders through the lanes, bystanders would lend a shoulder to the coffin for part of its way, even if the dead person was unknown to them. As they did so, they would mutter suitable formal phrases about death and the departed.

It is said by some people that the Middle Easterners are materialistic and unsentimental, but opinions vary about the meaning of such words as sentimental. If the meaning given in the Oxford Dictionary is taken as acceptable, the Arabs are certainly sentimental: 'a tendency to be swayed by feeling rather than reason' and 'nursing of the emotions' is how it explains the word. The Arabs are often swayed by feeling rather than reason and they certainly nurse their emotions. They themselves, I think, would admit that they nurse emotions and even proudly do so.

In cities of the north, like Baghdad, when a death comes the women relatives and attendants sometimes appear quite unhinged in the extravagance of their behaviour. They vie with one another in tearing clothes and hair, beating themselves and wailing. If one is exhausted before the others, her sister mourners may take her up and throw her down to continue. By this standard, the men are only partly deranged. They come prepared for the scene with handkerchiefs and may appear incapable of giving the simplest orders to retainers. All must be in disorder like the minds of the mourners. When the whole people of a city are mourners, the scene for Europeans is truly eccentric.

Baghdad Craftiness

12.11.33.
Faraj was an elderly Solubbi, a capable guide in the Syrian desert. The Solubba are the smiths of the bedouin, sellers and repairers of arms and pots and pans. They are people of unknown origin, reputedly descended from Crusaders or their mercenaries. Some of their customs vary from those of other bedouin whom they visit and follow about in the desert in pursuit of their trade. Faraj had never been in Baghdad before he came to see me.

The bell on my door kept ringing; after the door was opened to him and while he waited by it and the servant came to see me about him, the bell rang again. Asked why he kept ringing after the door was opened he said, 'I like trying it. Leave me be at it. I haven't done this before.'

When he left he fumbled with the lock and door handle, and stayed waiting by the door for it to be opened for him; he said, 'It is crafty,' as he was let out.

My First Visit to Ibn Saud

I left Jedda by the Medina Gate at 9 p.m. on Friday 28 June 1934, in a heat temperature of 95°F with humidity at 86°.

The guards at the Gate shouted, 'Stop. Where do you go?'

The leader of my bedouin escort, sitting beside me, answered a trifle scornfully, 'We are for Riyadh,' and to the driver, 'Drive on.' The guards fell back, repeating, 'To Riyadh,' as if we were 'the Royal Mail' or something deserving immediate respect.

The Chargé d'Affaires, a Secretary of the Legation, the Vice-Consul and the Pro-Consul (afterwards murdered by an Arab in Jedda) and his wife came with me as far as Umm as Salam to sit awhile on the coffee-house benches there, before saying goodbye. Three miles was as far as they could go without requesting special permission to go further into the Holy Land from Jedda. A journey to Riyadh was so unusual that it merited a send-off. No one from the British Legation had ever been invited there, lest other diplomats clamoured for a visit. The King's message for me said that I was welcome provided 'he wears Arab dress and travels with an escort furnished by us'.

We follow the track along the Wadi bottom into the depths of greenery in the Wadi Fatima and camp there at 9 p.m. Starting very early the next day, we come to the stone-lined well of Jaarah, whence Ibn Saud sends out for his water when in Mecca. The Arabs are connoisseurs of water, as pernickety about it and appreciative as college dons are, or were, reputed to be about their burgundy.

Flocks are being watered and a row of grave children, aping their elders in formal salutations, seat themselves about me, making polite inquiries. One, the youngest, aged about six, asks for a shirt, which is all they wear. His, as he said, is ragged. I apologize for having none small enough for him. He gives a rueful, understanding little smile.

We travel on past Zaima, where there is a fort and a plentiful spring, with *humr* trees, bananas, maize and millet. Some of the hills near it are the colour of burnished copper.

In mid-morning we reach Sail, a hamlet of stone-built houses. It was at Sail that, some fifty years ago, Charles Doughty was threatened with death, assaulted and robbed before being taken off to the Sherif at Taif, as he tells in *Arabia Deserta*. For us, a sheep's blood gushed out of its throat as we came up. Fifty minutes later I am bidden eat from the choicer morsels of the same animal. I sleep in a hut while the escort snore gently in the shade outside. The people of Sail take me for a Damascene, the most foreign kind of foreigner they can imagine me to be. Salih bids me keep this up: 'In Najd we must not let you be known.' At 12.50 p.m., somewhat late, the fat Meccawi coffee-house keeper, a self-appointed Guardian of the Faith, stalking confidently with stick in hand, cries, 'To prayers – to prayers.' It is the time for the noon prayers. I am left alone, but espied by the Meccawi on his second round. He makes his stick whistle and repeats his call, this time with puritanical venom. Abdulla, my driver, comes back just in time to make excuses for me; I am ill, he says, and the King's accountant – 'a financial wizard', he adds, with a touch of brilliance. The Meccawi's expression changes at once.

Rid of the Meccawi, Abdulla stays with me. He says that he has been in three armies: the Ottoman Turkish, the Hashimites' and the Saudi. The Turkish was the best. 'You fought and they paid monthly, or almost so. The Hashimites you could leave if they did not pay you. Ibn Saud you cannot escape and he does not pay except when in a panic. In the Yemen war we used to sell sacks and sacks of rice to the people of Hodaida at four riyals and Ibn Saud had paid twenty-five riyals the sack.'

I slept in Ibn Saud's new fort at Muwaiya.

The next day the track becomes worse and worse onwards from Dafina, where many of the Ataibah bedouin were watering, and so continues through groves of *sidr* trees to Afif; and at last to Qaaiya about 3 p.m., by which time everyone is so tired from the bumpings that we make camp.

Salih, head of the escort, says to me in his bedouin way, 'I don't like the ride by steam, I want riding on a riding camel.' He uses *vapoura* for motive power other than the human or animal and, to him, natural ones. When some tax-gatherers come up, Salih tells them with a wave in my direction, 'These are officials of the Finance Department for whom the King has sent.' He explained to me afterwards that the King had ordered that my nationality and religion were to be concealed.

A bedouin caller asked if he should kill a sheep or bring it alive.

We said, 'No, neither,' and he sent camel milk. We had just come through country near Muwaiya, where there is much meat; sheep and gazelles were plentiful thereabouts and I had bought two gazelles and had their haunches cooked for the bedouin. In the end our visitor asks us for tobacco, sugar, coffee and tea, explaining that he has had guests for four days, presumably the tax-gatherers, and all his supplies are gone.

Near Murad we had trouble over the guides. Driver Abdulla found his car deep in sand and the guide said that he was to go on, which was clearly impossible. Abdulla, a Somali, is hot-tempered. Salih is concerned to keep up his position. The argument rapidly degenerates into a wild exchange of abuse. The whole party, except Abdu the truck-driver, a Sudani, join in. I write some of the more unusual curses down in my notebook by light from the headlamps.

They were gathered together about thirty yards from me and I pretended ignorance for a time, but could not remain long subjected to this row, which was getting nearer to bloodshed by the moment. My position as a mere passenger had to be abandoned. I stalked forward and, with full force of lungs, as on a parade ground, I expelled the name, 'Salih.' There was an immediate silence in which I said very quietly, 'Enough – your wrangling bores me.'

Fortunately, at that moment some bedouin arrived from their nearby camp. In the customary interminable exchange of salutations and inquiries about health and news, their tempers cooled. The bedouin helped to free the vehicle from the sand and by morning the quarrel was forgotten.

Next day we see in the distance the Jebel Tuwaiq, the backbone, as it were, of Najd; and have a first sight, away to the north, of giant sand-dunes, shining as gold in the early sunlight. By some wells at Awaina or Ain al Mumammar, Salih tells me that the settlement of the Muammar was abandoned over a hundred years ago because it was overcome by ants. In point of fact it was captured and destroyed by the Al Saud. Perhaps as a sop to Muammar pride, they were afterwards said to be as numerous as ants, and so the story is turned today.

The bedouin speak of Ibn Saud either as such or as *'ash-Sheukh'*, the plural of Shaikh. When I once used *'al Melik'*, or King, they said, *'Melik aish – manhu jabhu melik?'* (King of what – who made him a King?).

In the now appalling heat – it is 2 July – I drink frequently of water and the camel milk which bedouins offer us. The heat and glare dry the lips and redden the eyes. I use fat for the former and *kohl*, or powdered antimony, for the eyelids, as do the bedouin and all our party.

Ten miles from Riyadh we stop for me to change into fresh clothes, so that I may enter the place in better order after five nights of dusty travelling. This halt to change is customary.

Salih went ahead to see the King and report our arrival.

On reaching the walls, I dismounted and sat in a tent outside them; some other travellers, rather to my astonishment so near the heart of Wahhabism, were there discussing the price of cigarettes. Within a few minutes Shaikh Yusif Yassin, the King's private secretary, a man from Tripoli in the Levant, arrived to take me to his house near the Eastern Gate. We went by a narrow lane, winding between small windowless houses on either side, reaching his wooden gate in a few minutes. It is a nest or hive of humans, this village capital, where the inhabitants hide themselves in box-like houses, burrows as it were, reminding me of the cubby-holes children make with a blanket over a table on wet afternoons in England, perhaps from the same primitive instinct and pleasure.

Yusif excused himself, to go to court once more, leaving one of his servants to look after us and give us time to bathe and change. Yusif is plump and white-skinned with a carefully trimmed and black-dyed beard, and so is very different in appearance from the lithe, darkly bronzed and little-hirsute Arabians about him. After dinner he would take me, he said, to the King.

Our baggage was brought on a camel into the small courtyard and quickly distributed. The bath, if any, in these houses is only a closet with a tank for water which can be heated in winter by burning brushwood below it. A servant stripped to a loin-cloth pours water over one as required, and offers a towel. Neat and clean once more, we sat in Yusif's coffee-hall waiting for him. As soon as he returned he said dinner was ready; but before it, without a word of warning, he goes into a corner of the small room, turns his back on us in the direction of Mecca, and goes down on his knees, forehead to the ground, backside in the air and on through the habitual risings, turnings and genuflexions for prayers in a way that he manages to make aggressive – or so it seems to me.

At dinner, he talked airily about the aircraft service they would be having as soon as the pilots being trained in Italy returned. As to the aircraft, he said that it was not quite decided yet from where they would buy them. The learners had crashed two Italian aircraft, complete with officers. Luckily it had been in the contract that they were covered for all damage incidental to training by the lump-sum payment made for the training. Yusif laughed gaily about it and seemed to feel that they had brought off a victory over the Italians. He spoke about the American Oil Company, its intentions and the areas likely to be selected for testing. He said that the concession went by default to the Americans. The A.P.O.C. (British) company refused the contract they could have made earlier on far more favourable terms, which is true – if he meant many years ago.

It is only a short time since cars have reached Riyadh. People still ask one how long the journey took one and are astonished if you do Jedda–Riyadh in under six nights. Three and a half days is the record so far.

We dined rather uncomfortably because Yusif had produced a table, chairs and some knives and forks, which clearly dismayed his servants. I wish it could be definitely one thing or the other: on the floor with fingers, or in a fully ordered European style. The food was only passable, the Riyadh grapes not so good as those eaten at Murad on our way to Riyadh, the sweetest I have ever tasted.

Dr Hussain, the Director of Health for Riyadh, came in for dessert. He is a Turk, I think.

Before we left for the Palace, Yusif sat on the floor, his ears close to his radio to get the latest news. This done, he shuffled on his sandals and scuttled out of the door and along the lanes in front of me. His lantern-bearer preceded us, saying in a commanding tone whenever the very few passers-by were near enough to hear, 'Way-

Way-for the Shaikh Yusif.' His repute as Ibn Saud's secretary was enough to ensure me protection. No harm could come to one among the fanatics as his guest, but the cold dislike behind his perfunctory courteousness only injured one's pride, ridding one of ability to expand in such company.

The absence of traffic in the quiet sandy lanes, already dark save for our lantern light, the windowless walls broken only by a few wooden closed doors, and the mouths of narrow lanes all much alike, made a maze in which a stranger would be quickly lost and at night find none of whom to ask his way.

The only open space is before the fort-like Palace, the home of Ibn Saud. 'Home', I reflect, is hardly the word. The English word 'home' is not easily translatable and certainly not into Arabic, in which the nearest word means tent, house, women of the family, a verse, conduit, etc. The old Palace in Riyadh was the winter military headquarters of Ibn Saud, first and foremost somewhere he could leave his numerous womenfolk and children while campaigning. It is even more mazelike than the streets, for another dimension is added. Rambling stairs, glimpses downwards into great courtyards, one after the other, confuse the visitor. The nearer we came to the roof, the more numerous were the bodyguards —men squatting in the passages, rifles held between their knees.

The old warren was where Ibn Saud's grandfather, Faisal, received Sir Lewis Pelly, Resident in the Persian Gulf in the mid-nineteenth century. Pelly's reception had been so uncertain, because of the fanaticism of the people, that he burnt his papers and cut short his stay. When he told Faisal that he felt he should leave, he was clearly relieved.

As we came out on to the roof, Yusif kicked off his sandals in the archway and I followed suit. Guards rose to their feet and we passed, and across the lantern–lit flat I saw Ibn Saud himself rising to his six feet four inches. Even among the slender, tall, specially picked bedouin guards he was of tremendous height and bulk, a mountain of a man.

He stretched out his hand and drew me to sit down by his right hand. The lanterns were of poles at two of the corners of the Persian carpet on which we sat, and they threw a low yellowish golden light which made our camel-hair cloaks and faded scarlet head-kerchiefs warmer in colour than in daytime. The King smiled as he inquired in the usual way about my journey and the road, and it was one of the most conquering smiles I had known. These Arab rulers, some of them, have overwhelming charm – and Ibn Saud's begins to work on me.

This first audience was not very long; but the following morning he received me early, before the heat of day began, and spoke at once of matters in his mind, of trouble on the Iraqi frontier where raid after counter-raid had been following until no one knew who was most to blame or who had gained or lost the most in sheep and camels. . . No one, that is, except Ibn Saud, who was very sure that the Iraqi tribesmen were most to blame and that the Iraqi junior officials near the frontier were inexperienced in desert control, which does seem most likely.

'We are habituated to desert matters,' he said, and emphasized it with anecdote after anecdote. Sometimes he spoke of battles rather than raids, his part in them, his wounds. 'It is the morning cold and cold baths that bring out the rheumatic stiffness in them, don't you agree?' he remarked tactfully, somehow having come to know that I had been wounded several times in war.

His smiles were bold, his language strong, his phrasing classical, with bedouin sayings interlaced. Once he was well started, his talk became a flood which nothing stayed until the call to midday prayers rang out.

Usually at these talks, twice daily, he spoke about tribal matters, their politics and history, or the history of his own family and of the rival desert-oasis dynasties, of Hail and al Hasa, or about the Hashimite lands to the north of his, of Jordan and Iraq, by which he complained he was 'surrounded'. He would harp upon 'the lost treaty', made by Sir Lewis Pelly with his grandfather. The archives had been examined and it could not be found. It had been lost since the time of his father's exile. Given then to a woman of the family for greater safety, it had in the end been mislaid.

'Where is your copy?' he asked. Sir Lewis Pelly never mentioned it, as far as is known, when he returned to the Persian Gulf. Had he destroyed it when he left Riyadh, or rather notes on some talks on the subject which Faisal had fancied were binding? Nothing has come to light, but Ibn Saud was convinced that there was some 'treaty' with the British, advantageous to the Saudi dynasty.

His strength, it seemed to me, lay in his intelligence web. All comers were examined by his chamberlains and bedouins and by himself if they had anything of consequence to say. He had recently installed Marconi sending and receiving sets in his provincial head-quarters, then an astonishing novelty in Arabia; they were of exceptional value for the maintaining of security in his vast kingdom.

Mountainous meals of mutton and rice, presents of arms and clothes and sometimes of gold sovereigns would induce a talkative mood in Arabian visitors to Ibn Saud's court. His charm and understanding did the rest. More and more visitors came from across the frontiers and from far afield, as flies to honey; so much so that he had to fix visiting seasons and keep other months free for his travels and administrative business. The administration was fairly simple, not much more than the approximate assessment of the income from the poll-tax and customs dues and the revenue from the pilgrimage and setting of them against expenditure. Expenditure had equally few headings, only his Privy Purse and the amount required by provincial governors, over and above that collected by them when their expenses had been deducted. A third and new expense comes under 'Foreign Affairs'. Everything is under one of these three main headings and is dealt with by his 'Minister of Finance', who in a land without any banks himself guards the cash, mostly in English and Turkish gold pieces, in person with guards for the purpose. Incidentally, Queen (Victoria) sovereigns are worth slightly more than Kings', but no one knows why. The silver coins most in use are the Maria Theresa (of Austria) dollars and Indian rupees.

'We Arabs,' said the Treasurer of Internal Affairs to me, 'prefer the millions.' He meant, in preference to hundreds or thousands of pounds.

Ibn Saud is a practical joker when the mood takes him. I was a victim. Dining, seated on the floor as usual, before a great dish of chickens in a huge mound of rice made tasty with herbs, he pulled out a chicken by its projecting legs and handed it to me with a gracious gesture. Taking it by its other end and finding it burning hot, I dropped it quickly, as the King foresaw. It was an old trick and everyone smiled at my discomfort. Before I had recovered my equanimity, I heard him ask me, 'After dinner, you would like to visit my *haram*?' I thought that I had misheard and gave a little smile and nod, hoping that, whatever it was he had said, that would do for answer. The King sometimes used old bedouin sayings and proverbs that nonplussed even educated Arabs from the north. To visit another man's harem is of course unthinkable, except to very close relatives with permission or to the eunuchs, where there still are such, or to accepted attendants.

After dinner, however, as we walked away, after washing, to return to his reception room, he reminded me that I was to visit the harem and called his private chamberlain to take me there. Ibn Saud waved me away with a smile and the Chamberlain, drawing a key from his gown, unlocked the great double door and bowed to me to precede him.

We were on the balcony of a great oblong courtyard. Far down the balcony two young black girls in purple silk looked round a corner, giggling, and were shooed away out of sight by my companion. As we advanced I saw that the side rooms, one after the other, were empty of women. Each room had satin-covered bedding and silk pillows neatly folded and little brassbound boxes and trinkets arranged in order in alcoves.

I felt somewhat like an orderly officer inspecting barrack-rooms. Below in the courtyard were piled heaps of brushwood for fires and in the rooms at the side of it were cauldrons and cook-pots of every size, mostly large, blackened by smoke outside, clean and white inside.

When we emerged and rejoined the King, he asked the Chamberlain how our visit had gone. 'All well. Just as I said, there is not a soul left, for all have gone to the wedding.' It was thus that I became, or so I presume, the only Christian ever to have been in Ibn Saud's harem.

Next day, Salih pointed out to me Philby's house, its door in a side lane we were passing. He added that he has two girls, one for bedding and one as a servant. The former he described as 'thamin mowater' (eight motors or cylinders), i.e. good in bed. Philby did not take Mrs Philby to Riyadh.

Almost everyone smokes in Riyadh, though all of them pretend not to do so. No one does so in public since it is strictly forbidden. One of his sons smokes, though Ibn Saud does not know it. Whisky and women can be and are bought in the Wahhabi capital.

In summer, the King comes in from the Badia summer-palace outside Riyadh at about 2.30 at night Arabic time, i.e. after sunset; he works, either signing letters which, each one done, he drops to the floor before him, whence or on the way down they are retrieved by his secretary; or in receiving visitors and listening to summaries of the news from the provinces and from the radio. To listen to music is forbidden. At midnight, or six o'clock Arabic, he reads or has read to him the Koran and the names of the Martyrs, and then sleeps until dawn. Dawn prayers being over, he sleeps again for a time and then works once more until the noon prayers. In the early afternoon he goes to the summer-palace in the tree-lined Wadi Hanifa.

Before going to him after dusk, Yusif and I sit on the floor by the radio to hear, as well as may be, the news. Cairo comes over indistinctly. The news gathered, he rushes off before he forgets what he has heard, to see the King. A few minutes later his servant, a swordsman and a lantern-bearer come for me.

When European politics are discussed they are sometimes all at sea. I found that the phrase 'balance of power' was not understood. Yusif, who had been caught out in something he did not know, started catching my eye. The King refused to let me go when I suggested leaving and called for more coffee, '*Qahwa,*' which is repeated from man to man, the sound dying out far away. It is only *gishr* or husk coffee, very pale in colour. There is doubt about the permissibility of bean-made coffee, since it could be an intoxicant and thus forbidden. We got on the subject of Abyssinia and the war there. The King thought that the material the Italians could produce would bring them out the winners. These Arabs see in it the approach of another great war. So the conversation ranges widely and on the whole interestingly.

It is not easy to sleep on the open roof-tops in Riyadh. The wooden water-wheels make a sound like untaught players toying with a stringed instrument. The mosquitoes and *muedhdhin* calling to prayers are disturbing.

After taking leave of the King, Yusif brought me the King's present of camel-hair cloak with gold wire embroidery on its collar and a headdress, plus a gold dagger. My party bound for Kuwait with me comprises Salih the headman armed with a rifle, two guides with rifles, two drivers having revolvers, one assistant-driver unarmed, one relative of Ibn Sabah, the Shaikh of Kuwait, carrying a large automatic pistol, my servant with revolver, two soldiers with rifles and revolvers and myself with pistol and sword. A baker of bread, aged about fifteen, joins us; he has only a dagger, which of course all the others have. We are well enough armed for the journey to Kuwait.

We leave two hours before nightfall. The ascent of the Armah plateau cliff is difficult. The Chevrolet, which has no handbrake, started plunging backwards towards the cliff side. It looked like death until a boulder stopped us at the very edge. It caught under the sump, the only boulder of its size in sight on the track. It is cold at night on the Summan open desert, even now in summer. I begin to feel very tired and rather ill. Nevertheless I manage to keep up my observations and route books. Hereabouts there are, of course, no water-wheels, mosquitoes or professional *muedhdhin*, but dung-beetles make more noise than might be supposed in the hard, otherwise silent desert.

I was thankful to reach Kuwait three days later and distribute parting presents of new kerchiefs and three riyals all round to each of the party, except to the cook and second driver and baker boy, who get two. I had given three of the party two riyals each for pocket money in Riyadh. All except my servant are in the pay of the King, so they are well satisfied. Rice and other food (except for extra meat bought by me from bedouin twice and some supplies for us bought in Jedda) were supplied by the Saudi Government, together with the transport and petrol, so the crossing of Arabia from sea to sea did not cost me much. My only European or Western predecessors to cross from sea to sea are, I believe: Sadlier in 1819; Shakespear just before the First World War; Philby during it; Hamilton of the American Oil Company just before me, though I am not quite sure whether he returned from Riyadh by the way he had come or not.

It turns out that I should not have been allowed to leave Jedda on such a journey. I was ill before I left, having seen the Indian doctor there about a sickness which he wrongly diagnosed; they now say in Kuwait at the American Mission that I should have remained very quiet for three weeks at least. Except for the relapse, however, it does not seem to have done me any harm.

I tried the water at all the wells en route and took samples of it, which in some cases horrified the Royal Air Force doctors in Iraq. They looked at me in astonishment when I told them that I had tried all of them. One can become inured to such tests of oneself by practice. Americans of the oil company, who take most exceptional care and use tinned food, are apt to go down seriously ill when they have to take the local food and water.

Portrait of a Shaikh:
His Metamorphosis, 1935 to 1955

'Every Arab, however poor, has an Aladdin within
him all ready to blossom forth; at the first touch of
fate – behold him a King.'   André Gide, *If It Die*

When I first met him in 1935, he was twenty-eight years old, a
younger brother of an uncle of the then ruling Shaikh of a small
principality on the Persian Gulf shore of Arabia. We did not then
call him a Shaikh. The people of the state lived by pearl-diving, by
carrying cargoes, mostly dates, in their wooden sailing ships and
importing goods, many of which were smuggled into neighbouring countries at great profit. He himself was not at all wealthy. He
lived in the town, the only one in the state, in one of the small
windowless coral-and-clay houses, though with brass-studded and
well-carved wooden doors, which were all that most of them then
used. But it is chiefly in the desert, sitting alone on a rug in his small
black goat-hair bedouin tent that he was memorable to me. When I
used to visit him then, on one of his spring camping expeditions, I
never thought, and I am sure he did not think, that in some fifteen
years he would be travelling *en prince* abroad in the Western world
and that we should even go to see the Pope together.

By then fate had touched him. His elder brother had succeeded as
ruler of the State of Kuwait and the State was found to be rich in oil.

He was head of three of its newly formed and hastily expanding government departments.

His meeting with the Pope, Pius XII, in 1950 was fortuitous. The Shaikh had asked to see me in London and then pressingly invited me to accompany him to Naples where he was to embark for Egypt. On the first of two days in Rome he rang me, surprisingly early after a late arrival the night before, to ask me what I planned for him. Saying that there was an adage 'When in Rome do as the Romans do', I proposed that we might act as pilgrims do in Mecca on arrival there and go at once to the shrine, in this case the church of St Peter. I would be ready for him in an hour.

Going slowly round the church, it was noticeable that numerous parties, of nuns, of boy scouts and others, were entering it. On halting in front of the Pietà by Michelangelo, a small monsignore who had been hovering near us came up to ask me who the visitor in Arab dress might be. Having told him, he at once asked us to come with him to a position where we could see and be seen by the Pope who was due to enter in forty minutes. As he guided us up the nave, the great crowd of visitors was being shepherded behind barriers or into high-up galleries. It was the last public audience of the Marian Year. We were placed by the throne under the baldachin of Bernini, where some twenty others were already seated and waiting.

The Shaikh was impressed by the Pope's entry. He was dressed entirely in white and sitting on his *sedia gestatoria,* escorted by the Swiss and Noble Guards, accompanied by shouted *Vivas,* the waving of handkerchiefs and throwing of blossoms. After the speech by the Pope in five languages, he made a tour of the few persons by the baldachin, talking to each of them in turn. Placing myself on the side of Shaikh from which the Pope was coming I was able to present him by name and country, adding, '. . . where oil has recently been found', thus giving His Holiness a clue, of which he took advantage in speaking to him. Before the Shaikh reached his home from Egypt, his brother had received a medal from the Pope through the nearest Papal Delegate.

When in the Persian Gulf two years later, invited by the Shaikh to stay in his new house by the sea, I find that my dusky, handsome and energetic friend is taking home files at night. He does not go through them after dinner but between the dawn prayers and the time when he leaves for one of his three different offices in one of his half-dozen American motor-cars. The precise moment of his morning departure is uncertain because there is his cook to be given orders and numbers of petitioners to be seen. The supplicants stand waiting for him near the main doors of his new house, and are nearly all bedouin. Wild, bright-eyed creatures, they clutch in unaccustomed, horny hands a piece of paper on which some literate friend or professional letter-writer has inscribed the gist of their request or complaint. At this hour the Shaikh is in a happy mood, and while he scribbles an instruction on the corner of their papers he usually asks some provoking question. The answer is given forthrightly in a high-pitched voice; that of bedouin whose throats are constricted from shouting at one another in the open desert. In the case of one of them, the complaint was about a bride; and the Shaikh's pertinent question draws a reply so unabashed that the bystanders, the Persian cook, myself and some armed retainers all smile at its simplicity. Women petitioners, when there are any, stay away at a decent distance, cloaked and unidentifiable. A servant is sent to collect their papers. Today there is only one. She replies through her veils, in a patient, muffled voice. Given her letter back with a note upon it that will further her cause, she murmurs a prayer for the Shaikh's long life and disappears round a corner so quickly that it seems almost as if she had never been there, as if she had been a conjuror's trick.

The last petitioner is even more outspoken than the others and raises an open guffaw. The Shaikh steps into his Cadillac. Two of his riflemen squeeze in beside the driver and another squats before him in the tonneau. Everyone is smiling, the petitioners most of all. The large American car slides away to a chorus of 'God bless you,' 'The Lord protect you,' 'May He lengthen your years.' The ragged clansmen from the desert go scuttling after the car, towards the city, barefoot, but each happy now in the possession of valuable 'chips' to play in the casino of the new bureaucracy, the office doors open to them by order of the Shaikh.

I am in no hurry to go to town myself and, having a large car with a driver at my disposal all day, can go when I like. I return to the four-roomed, air-conditioned flat for guests, fitted with hot and cold running water, that looks out on the gently lapping Persian Gulf. The house is furnished by a well-known English furniture store and, apart from the Persian carpets, the only *objet* is a superb ivory chess-board with its men, from India. By error, there are no less than a dozen air-conditioners in the main sitting-room, one under each window. The inner door of the flat for guests opens on to a court some forty yards square. It is only one of three courts in the public or guest quarters of the Palace, a one-storey building in modern Arab functional style, that is, without a single arabesque or archway.

The main dining-room is habitually set for eighty covers but can take over a hundred. On most nights there are fewer than thirty men at dinner, which seems an intimately small number in the great length of the hall. On the verandah outside are seven modern bathroom basins, where the guests, who eat with their fingers, wash after the meal. After these smaller everyday dinners, some of the cronies drift away and then, reduced to a mere dozen or so, slip down from the European armchairs in the drawing-room, to sit cross-legged on the floor. The Shaikh calls for his briar pipe. 'Don't you smoke a briar?' he asks me in some surprise – and calls for cards too. The game is 'six', a kind of bridge for six persons. It usually takes about forty minutes to reach the score of a hundred that terminates a rubber. Between rubbers the coffeeman is called and goes his round with little handleless cups. Like everyone else except me, he wears a long, white shirt of Chinese silk that clings to the form in the damp atmosphere of the Gulf. Late at night, some of them take off their headdresses and sprawl on the floor. The conversation is brisk and the jokes sometimes broad. No one has drunk anything but water, coffee or whey all the evening. When the Shaikh leaves he turns in the doorway and begins gently, in a careful way, to sing to me 'Good night, Aileen'. It was a fashionable song three years ago when he was travelling for the first time in Europe and America. I was with him for part of his travels and it is a reminder by him of our days together then. He continues the song as he goes, turning round every now and then to smile at me. He so likes Arab singing that he arranged his return journey from abroad to coincide with a concert given by the famous Umm Kalthoun in Egypt; and he plans to hear her again.

Breakfast in his house, with its eggs, honey, unleavened bread, cheese and tea, is the meal nearest to the European arrangement of one. Since the main dish at dinner is always mutton and rice, the jovial Persian cook's morning orders run to little more than being told the numbers of guests expected. . . one night it was a hundred and fifteen. Three earth-moving machines were put to work all day clearing a way through a small sand-dune that had covered the main track in his house the night before; the wind rising again might make it impassable. The Arab guests arrived mostly to time, the Europeans late, having missed the cleared track. The latter came in, dismayed by the sudden coldness in the room, and the women by knowing that their make-up was spoilt by sand in the hot wind outside. They were all grey with dust which drifted about the room as they spanked themselves to be rid of it. The Arab guests had been sitting in order of their seniority by age in chairs arranged along the walls, obedient to Arab custom, until the Europeans arrived and then stood up in disorder, like guests at a cocktail party without cocktails, until dinner was served.

The main dish, the mutton and rice, is very well cooked, the pudding a cornflour mould and pink jelly. It is followed by the usual strong Arab coffee served in the little handleless cups that are handed back at once to the waiting servant.

The Shaikh says of his cook, 'He is a good man,' and adds, 'He slept in my room when the family was away last month.' They dislike being alone and, like medieval European gentry, see to it that a trustworthy man is nearby at night. Privacy, except with the women, is almost unknown and seldom sought.

Ali, the Shaikh's little son aged about six, is dusky, like his father, with large roving eyes and appealing manners. He and his younger brother and sisters are in part charge of a governess from the United States who was found for the Shaikh by American missionaries. On Sunday evenings she is lent a car to go to a service at the small Mission-house; otherwise she hardly leaves her charges. It is even said that the conditions of her engagement forbid her to do so; thus it is rare for other Europeans to see her. I had only heard of her, although her rooms were a few yards away from mine, when there was a tea-party for two visiting American Congressmen. She brought her charge to be seen, at my suggestion, and stayed, sitting next to me. 'I go about with the Shaikh's wife to other households and I know how lucky I am to be in this one,' she says. She is full of praise for it.

The Lebanese doctor, on my other side, has much the same story. 'Few there are in this State who do not swaddle their children until they are old enough to walk.' How do they walk after being swaddled so long, I wonder. He goes on to tell me that 'wives in this part of Arabia often become pregnant while still suckling, which is bad for their infant and reduces the quality of milk for the next child. Among animals the female is not disposed to go with the male during the time of suckling. The human female, being less natural, most wretchedly does so quite often.' I glance at the governess, whom I am relieved to find is looking away, observing the antics of the boy across the room. I am not sure that the doctor was right about animals. Tribal Arabs possessing a good mare have her served nine days after she has delivered.

A fellow guest in the Palace is a resident of Hama on the desert side of Syria. He seldom converses, but often calls for a *narguileh*, or hubble-bubble water pipe. He shows no sign of leaving and has seemingly settled down for a long stay. Another, who has recently arrived, is brighter, hailing from Baalbek and having been educated in the Lebanon. He is in business with a Yugoslav maker of pre-fabricated houses, but tells me that he is dropping him for a German-Swiss who will partner him in the more profitable import business now abounding.

One night I came back late, that is to say about ten o'clock (or the equivalent of about midnight, since we all get up at dawn). The *muedhdhin*'s call to prayers then wakes us, whether we like it or not. It is a genuine call, in that it is given by a human being and not a gramophone record working on a tannoy, as is nowadays generally the case in Syria and the Lebanon. At night, in the distance, this new Palace looks like some Western seaside amusement park or pier, being illuminated outside by several hundred coloured electric-light bulbs. Although it is late when I return, the lights are still on inside the Palace, the double doors open. The guests are awake and the Shaikh with them. Cloaks and headdresses have been discarded with the water pipe now abandoned by the silent man from Hama. The Shaikh is in a happy mood although, as he tells me, he has been twice beaten at 'six'. The room is smoky from tobacco and he rubs his eyes.

'Would you like some drops?' asks the guest from Baalbek, and flashes out of the room to return in a moment with several jujubes in paper twists. We roar with laughter and the Shaikh and I both say in the intervals of our laughter, 'We thought you meant eye drops.' This homeliness and simplicity of humour is becoming rarer. Others of his family have already bought expensive villas in the Levant and properties in Egypt, where they sport mistresses who run through fortunes and are contemptuous of homeliness.

Once, however, the Shaikh was in a different mood. It was my first night as his guest and there were no others then staying with him. After dinner he reviewed for me this history of the last two years. It was the history of the development of the city, of the mistakes made. He is utterly convinced that it could have been done otherwise and better and that the method was unduly advantageous to the foreign contracting firms. Some of them, he insisted, had made money from the payment of commission on orders, in spite of quantity surveyors and a 'cost-plus' accounting system, and through 'juggling' with their local partners. The very next morning the Ruler's private secretary opened his conversation with me by saying that 'contracting is a dirty business – I am getting out of it'; but he has not done so.

One of his chief complaints the Shaikh did not mention. A European was appointed to direct development, not a member of the ruling family. Only five merchants were making much money from the development and others not so; thus, many merchants and the ruling family were put out. In his fervent explanation to me the Shaikh sometimes repeated himself and once or twice, asking a rhetorical question, did so even more often. His face worked. He brushed off a bead of perspiration from time to time. At last he flung himself back in his chair, like an exhausted actor. 'Well, that is how I see it. You tell me if I am wrong.' He had wanted to talk himself out and be listened to.

The ruling family, I reflect, expect a hand in all patronage. The development of their city is the greatest opportunity for exercising patronage ever known to them, and there had been failure to allow for the inevitable reaction against a Western controller who did not have one of them at his side. The new ruling Shaikh was harried until he agreed to change the arrangements and remove the foreigner from control. He had been replaced by my host, his brother, now head of the Development Board, head of Public Works and of the Municipality and a member of the Ruler's Council.

The population of the city is doubled in a short time and some say that, with the oil-field labour, there are more 'foreigners' now than there are locally born residents of the State. On Fridays, the Muslim holiday, in the great square where a few years back the camels of waiting caravans were couched and sheep were brought by hundreds to stand for sale, where once the merits of slaves were canvassed, there are now parked a hundred or so American cars that

King George V arriving at Hackwood, 28 May 1915

Lord Kitchener inspecting the Hampshires at Hackwood, 1 June 1915

The author being carried out of action by an Australian sergeant-major at Anzac, 10 August 1915. Drawn by the author soon afterwards

Drawing by the author of the entrance to his dugout, Iser Canal bank, No. 6 bridge, France, August 1916

The mill in ruins, the west end of Zillebeke Lake, drawn by the author, 1 September 1916

The towers of Corbie Abbey, France, drawn by the author, 7 October 1916

The Madonna of Montauban with the 'miraculously unexploded shell', drawn by the author, October 1916

Arras Cathedral, drawn by the author, 1916

Sentries of the 1st Hampshire Regiment in the front line, with periscope. Drawn by the author, 1916

'Praga Waga', as Edward, Prince of Wales was called, with staff-officers near the front line on the Somme. Drawn by the author in a notebook kept in his pocket during the Battle of the Somme, 1917

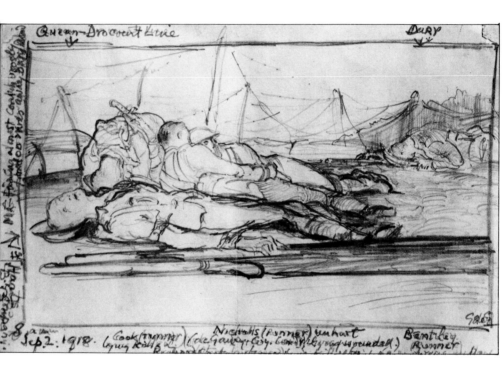

The fallen — three killed and one wounded beside
the author — in an attack on the Quean-Drocourt
support line, France, 2 September 1918. Drawn by
the author shortly afterwards while in hospital
recovering from a wound in his right leg caused by
machine-gun bullets

A photograph of the author taken by Langfield, London, 1919

With Shaikh Abood of the Jibour at Sherqat in Iraq, 1926

Prince (later King) Abdulla of Jordan

An excursion to the ruins, Samarra, Iraq. Left to right (sitting): three members of the R.A.F. crew, the author, Richard Halliburton (American writer and traveller), the Emir Hussain (King Faisal I's brother-in-law), the Emir (later King) Ghazi, in uniform, members of the Nowwab family. Foreground: an R.A.F. pilot

King Ibn Saud with two of his sons, photographed by the author

Bringing the Grand Cross of the
Bath from George V to Ibn Saud.
Water-colour by the author, 1935

Portrait of the author by
Anthony Devas

Abdililah, Regent of Iraq, with the author and
Ismet Inönü, President of Turkey, on a state visit to
Turkey, 1945

Shaikh Fahad of Kuwait, brother
the Ruler, with the author, visitin
Pope Pius XII, 1950

The Christ by Benvenuto Cellini, 1562, in the Escurial near Madrid

The Coming of Age parade of King Faisal II of Iraq, 1953

Victor Cunard, Freya Stark and Sir Harry Luke,
drawn by the author, taking tea in the drawing-
room of Villa Freia, Asolo, 1957

The Prime Minister, al Hassan, later Commander
of the Northern Forces of the Yemen, with his
secretary Ahmad Sharif ad Din, in his cave near
Burqa during the civil war in Yemen. Drawn by
the author, 1964

Soldier in North East
Yemen, drawn by the
author, 1964

bring shopping foreigners from the labour camps and from new, gardenless, garden-city suburbs. Camera-hung, with green eye-shades or white peak caps, in blue jeans and coloured shirts, in striped singlets and shorts, they roam and slouch and eye and buy – Americans, Lebanese, Palestinians, Iraqis, Indians and British.

On Fridays my host's offices are all closed. On weekdays his hours are so arranged that he misses none of the five prayer times. There is no fuss or fanaticism about his attentiveness to the rules and religion. He just keeps carefully to them. In orderly fashion and in accordance with religious precept, he divides his nights, equally and regularly, between his two wives, one of whom he keeps in town and one out.

Ever since his visit to America and England in 1950 he has discussed from time to time his next visit abroad, to be in 1954 – 'God willing', he always adds. He had been only a week in England and two and a half days of that short time were taken up by a long train journey – in bitter cold weather – to the north of England, where the Oil Company which had sponsored his tour was insistent that he should launch an oil tanker. 'Next time,' he said, 'I want to see everything – old and new.' He was ready to be away for some three months. He wants to see both 'the great houses and families' and 'many things historical', as well as modern installations. History he reads quite often; having asked me for a book on the Crusades, I sent him Steven Runciman's two volumes, which he described as 'deep and broad', though I doubt if he found time to read them to the end. He is the only one, of his generation, in his family who reads English, learnt by him while at the American University in Beirut for a short time.

He is delighted by the news that there is now an agreement for the supply of water from the north. He has planted six Jerusalem thorns in holes left for them in the brick courtyard of his Palace and, regarding them, quotes Bacon, without knowing it: 'A Palace without a garden is poor handicraft.'

One day the conversation turns to schools in England. 'Is Harrow or Eton better?' I am asked. It is the matter of his son's education. The Shaikh listens. I have the feeling that he has told my Lebanese questioner to raise the matter. I suppress a sigh as I embark on this difficult subject; though I reflect that such is the charm of the boy that he could hardly be other than popular. . . However, in the end he was sent to a school in Chicago.

The next day, the news from Taif where the King, Ibn Saud, was lying ill was again a subject at dinner. The little Lebanese said that he had news. The King's French doctor had returned immediately to Paris after visiting him. The news came from Beirut where the doctor's aircraft refuelled and a Lebanese journalist interviewed him. When he was asked about the King's health, the doctor replied that the King was in very good health '. . . only he has to have oxygen continuously'.

This account was received with the serious attention the news deserved. The Ruler of Kuwait said that he would not go to India as he had planned, if the state of the King's health was serious. He would have to go to the Saudi capital if the King died. Every day they speak of the King's illness.

Sometimes the Shaikh proposes that we travel together to the city, the car lent to me following us. The car he uses is one of the largest and longest American ones. It has numerous gadgets and special fittings. There is a small step between the 'master seats' and the quite wide space, with removable swivel seats, that separates them from the driving cab. In fact the car has a kind of mezzanine floor. Whenever the Shaikh wishes to say something confidentially – and many things seem to be confidential – he touches a button conveniently by his hand, at which there is a faint whirring and a glass slides up and cuts us off from other passengers. As soon as he has finished, down goes the glass. Then perhaps he has an after-thought. Whirr goes the glass. Down it goes once more, only to whirr again a few moments later.

The Shaikh's days are divided with as much regularity as may be between the several offices under his control. He is the busiest of his family. At the Public Works Department the corridor is quite full of waiting applicants when we arrive. Half a dozen blue-gowned orderlies make a way for us through them. He deals rapidly with his papers while committees file in to see him or foreigners come for interviews. On certain mornings he goes first to the Ruler's Advisory Council, the 'Signoria' as it were. Here there is a quieter scene. The elders of the city come forward to greet and salute him gravely and speak weightily – of trivialities as likely as not. Or he goes to the Health Directorate, where there may be questions to discuss about foreign personnel or the amount to allot for the annual supply of drugs and so on. On another day it is the Municipality that claims his first attention. New fire-engines, water-towers or streets, and all the matters that arise when a city is growing day by day, may there detain him. So his week passes, and every week brings another two million or more in sterling from oil royalties to his brother, the Ruler's, account.

One day I am alone with the man from Hama. Suddenly he is loquacious and confidential. He has a fine idea. The fine idea goes something like this. Very many firms, as he has come to learn while sitting around in the Shaik's office, are tendering for the Port contract. There are Yugoslav companies for example in for it. The whole thing is a lottery. He could make an arrangement with one of them, as their Arab agent. Then, if they won, a British company could do the actual work. Do I know a British firm who would like such an advantageous arrangement? I say that I do not know such a British firm. He is not put out and says that perhaps later on I shall hear of one and let him know. Anyway, the mystery of his long stay is cleared up. He is waiting around like others for the opportunity to make money.

A long and insecure past in the deserts has taught Arabians to be adaptable and quick in assessing new situations and unknown people. The Shaikh is less bemused by new schemes put forward by his foreign visitors than might be supposed. If he likes or trusts them, he says so afterwards. So he did after his talks with a British engineer. 'A sincere, straight-looking man,' he called him, and seemed loath to let him go, keeping him for dinner, sending messages for him and lending him a car. The engineer thought that the matter discussed could be arranged 'in an hour' when the Middle East director of his firm arrived, so agreeable was the Shaikh to him.

Fifteen years or more ago, when I first knew the Shaikh, it was the custom for the members of the ruling family to camp during the spring in one of their grazing preserves. Camel milk is then plentiful, light green grass and blue irises colour the ordinarily bare plain, and certain of the bushes are sweet smelling. At that time it was habitual to ride from one camp to another, visiting. The Shaikh being then merely the younger brother of one of the uncles of the Ruler, his camp was a small one, but he was more intelligent, quicker-witted and better-educated than most of his family. In the summer he used to go to an island some twelve miles off the coast, and there too I used to visit him, perhaps taking guests: British naval officers from a ship that called, or adventurous English ladies. Sometimes now, he and I recall those days, 'When we used oil-lamps because oil had not been found – before we were so popular,' he adds, smiling.

The perspicacity and inquisitiveness of such men as these merge to make them highly sensitive in certain directions. When recently I had to argue a case at length to him and finished, he trustingly asked no questions, only smiled and said, 'I would like to help you – may this do so,' and gave me at once the letter I needed from him. This is the patronage of an Arab chieftain at work, the prerogative of a Shaikh of standing. By cultivating obligation they cultivate a harvest of support, the instinctive aim of the politician.

In the summer of 1954 the Shaikh invited me to stay a weekend with him at his camp on the seashore, some thirty miles south of the city. This was no longer the single black goat-hair tent of fifteen years ago, but a large hut and several marquee tents. The guests included some musicians. A short love-song preceded our first meal, eaten on the *stoep*, seated on the ground and with the fingers. The fellow guests, cronies of the Shaikh, were introduced one by one. There was an elderly man, small, with a wisp of a beard and a distinguished air who, like his father before him, had imported horses from central Arabia, selling them in India for racing and for light cavalry regiments; an elderly pearling captain, honorary master of the Shaikh's yacht and his adviser on seafaring matters; a doctor from Palestine; and a handsome young Tunisian merchant, cosmopolitan, wearing Mediterranean-style beach clothes, including orange-coloured shorts, under a Tunisian toga. In the background the orchestra rose and bowed in turn, the *canoun,* the *oud* and the *dunbouq,* as they are called after their instruments.

During dinner the servants were all males, as is usual. It is absurd how unfounded are the stories in the faraway town about life at the camp. This is on the seashore, away from frequented paths – on a no man's land between two domains where no bedouin come and no travellers pass, because there is no hamlet or water-hole nearby. So tales had grown up of a palace built at vast expense, of a swimming pool, of troupes of dancing girls and boys, of halls of marble, of materials from Persia and India, silken carpets and mattresses of down, of unlimited pleasures of every kind. Instead there was nothing but a prefabricated air-conditioned small bungalow fitted with radio-telephone, and camp-furnishings and a few white tents. Instead of dancing girls there were only these male servants, fully clothed from head to foot.

After dinner there was more music and singing and quotations from the classical Arab poets. 'You have fired my energy and imagination; you have revived my lost hopes.' The Shaikh smacked my forearm, grinning with satisfaction. 'It is for you I remembered that line,' he said, clasping my hand in his.

It was just then that a girl of some eighteen summers went flitting across the end of the *stoep*. As she came and went about some task, I looked again. Her dark hair was long and straight, reaching her shoulders. Her complexion was ashen, through having lived a twilight life, I supposed. The eyes were large and dark. Her figure was good, though there was a hint in its curves of rotundity to come. My glance and question were as uninquisitive as I could make them. 'What make?' I said, with a slight toss of the head in her direction. 'Lebnaniya,' (of the Lebanon), replied the Shaikh, lightly dismissive, as one might say 'Persian' or 'Siamese' of a cat. She alone represented the troupe of girls of which rumour had spoken. Her name was Alice and her dress was proper.

'At what hour,' at last asked the Shaikh, 'would you like to be called?' We had talked far into the night. It was past midnight. I hesitated, as one usually does, wondering what would be convenient and customary. 'At half past four?' he suggested and, seeing my astonishment, explained that he proposed a fishing and swimming expedition to islands some two hours off the coast. We ought to start, he said, in his yacht, about five o'clock. His secretary conducted me to one of the marquees for guests pitched outside a six-foot-high rabbit-wiring fence that at a distance of fifty yards enclosed his wooden bungalow. He pointed out, a little way down the shore, 'a shower and lavatory'. A short pier led to a kind of sentry box over the water; in its floor was a very large circular hole and in the roof there was the rose of a shower fed from a tank above. The two facilities were, rather surprisingly, combined in one. It was the full-moon night, or rather the last of three nights, all of them called by the Arabs full-moon. The sand was already cold and the moonlight and stars bright enough to read by. The moon-path on the sea glittered so strongly that it was uncomfortable to look at. Soon not a sound was heard. Under the shadow of the marquee and in that splendid silence, sleep came without waiting.

The sea next morning was a trifle less smooth than the day before. The faster we went in the two-seater speed-boat, the Shaikh and I, the harder we bumped on the wavelets and the more he seemed to like it. A long detour round a sand-bar brought us to the yacht. On the way he pointed out an islet above water at low tide. 'Called Wolf Island,' he shouted. 'Once a man escaping from a wolf ran down from shore to islet,' he bawled, repeating the parts I had not heard above the noise of the engine and rushing water. 'He swam away, and the wolf stayed on the islet and was cut off and drowned when the tide rose. That is why it is called Wolf Islet.'

The remainder of the party arrived in a home-altered barge. It had been quite a trim and commodious yacht once. Its lifebuoys still bore the letters R.T.Y.C., but its standard of upkeep had gone. The Shaikh had borrowed it from a local company, his own new yacht not being ready. In the cabins the mirrors were cracked, paintwork was much neglected, the engines were not working in rhythm. Sailors would have noticed much amiss. A second yacht accompanied us in reserve, in case we broke down. Both borrowed boats were manned by the Shaikh's men. We sat on the afterdeck, cross-legged on Persian rugs and Dunlop rubber cushions. The retired horse-coper adjusted his spectacles and turned the pages of an old English paper, *John Bull,* slowly, from front to back and back to front again. The others shot at tern and cormorants with rifles, without success. In an hour and a half we passed a tiny sandbank called Umm al Maradim – Mother Pounding – and in two hours came to Garru Island. Thousands of birds rose as we fired at them. The northern end held cormorants and the southern side tern. However often we disturbed them, they always returned to the same parts of the island – leaving a no man's land of twenty yards between. In this otherwise empty ground there stood about three of either species – in the middle, and near together. Since the main parties were closely packed and their front ranks more or less straight, the oddity of this behaviour was noticeable. The younger cormorants were grouped together, behind the main mass of cormorants on the shore of the island.

The sea was very green and very clear, as it can be off the coast of Greece and unlike the thick, greyish-green water usual by the Arabian mainland. Brilliantly coloured fish lazed past. One of the brightest, with blue stripes and a yellow tail, is called Bint al Nakhoudha, the Master's Daughter. Turtles came up to stare at us and, sinking, would do 'falling leaf' turns which we could follow in that clear water. When the Arabs shot at them they would only submerge at first about a foot under the surface and stay there for a minute, as if thinking over the unexpected occurrence. Curious and mystified, they came up again and again.

The Shaikh went fishing from his speed-boat with a large spoon, and soon caught a tunny and some twenty-five other large fish. I bathed from the island with the Tunisian. The birds wheeled about us and came in to land nearby. 'It snows cormorants,' he said. The elderly members of the party bathed from the yacht. They wore nothing except a cotton *lungi*. Standing on the gunwale, they held their spectacles in one hand and their nose with the other, and jumped feet first. They went straight down to a great depth, where one could see them; coming up, they looked like large moray or giant newts, owing to the refraction of the water. 'It is five fathoms,' said the retired horse-coper. Both he and the pearling captain were spare men with wispy beards and fine large eyes – the old-fashioned Arab, a disappearing caste or a caste at least disappearing in the more northerly Arab lands where blood is mixed and where westernization has set in and altered man's way of life and thus his appearance and manners. The diminutive, fine-boned men of south and mid-Arabia still remain much as the men of the mother tribes of most of them, the Qahtan – or Joktan of the Book of Genesis – and the larger Ishmaelite Anaza have looked throughout the ages.

Luncheon on the deck included that delicious drink, ice-cold *leban* (whey), and marmalade sandwiches made rather too thick. There was fruit, too, now habitually flown from the Lebanon, fish-cakes and newly caught and grilled fish and unleavened bread. Afterwards the party fell asleep on the deck, Shaikh and all, here and there like battle casualties. Refreshed, we woke on nearing land once more. Soon everyone, with numerous boxes and weapons, was piled into the home-made barge. It was dangerously overloaded, to within an inch or two of its gunwale, but no one seemed to mind. On the contrary, all laughed when it shipped water and nearly sank. . . all, that is, except the engine-man, who baled sourly.

The barge drew too much water to be able to land us dry-foot. We pulled up trousers or long shirts and waded ashore. Alice, the Lebanese, was waiting for the Shaikh in the bungalow. We sat outside on the *stoep*, and drank draughts of almond sherbet.

After a time we heard the Shaikh busy on his wireless-telephone. Orders and messages and invitations to brother shaikhs. The echoing, harsh replies from the other end came over clearly. 'Yes, my uncle,' 'God prolong your years,' 'Oh, long o'years.' Such phrases have no more significance than 'O.K., Boss,' 'Thank you,' or 'Nevertheless, sir,' but they sound strangely over such an unbiblical instrument as the wireless. We went off to rest awhile, then use the *douche* and make ready to depart. The Arab valets had packed for us our simple luggage and stood around hopefully. The musicians were tuning up and the next guests arriving when we went to sit with the Shaikh for a few minutes before leaving.

We plodded up the sand-dune once more to regain the car parked half a mile away on the hard desert. The Shaikh's secretary promised marvellous food and the coldest drinks, on the way to the city, with his American friends on a ship moored in a creek as headquarters of an oil company.

The daylight was going as we arrived at the creek. The electric current was being turned on in the ship. Boy stewards in white uniforms came forward to welcome us and shake hands. They conducted us with polite waving of their arms to the big saloon where the staff were dining in twos and threes at separate tables, as on a passenger ship. None of the secretary's friends was there. They had all gone on leave to the United States. Those dining were mostly Texan, husky, enormous men with shoulders like prize-fighters, in singlets and jeans. There was an Englishman or two, and one elderly American with white hair and gold-rimmed spectacles. A middle-aged American was complaining while a boy steward stood by him, quite undisturbed and smilingly soothing him. The American was a little tipsy, and I thought might be an 'ugly customer' if not rightly handled. The Arab boy's attitude was somewhere between that of an animal-tamer and an experienced and slightly amused housewife. These young stewards draw about 250 rupees a month, and double it by tips from the Americans. Five hundred rupees is roughly £40, a good wage for a boy of fourteen or so whose living expenses and uniform are provided free.

A Lebanese we knew came forward to look after us. He took us round the ship and down to the big sitting-saloon where we were given beer in cans with two holes, one for drinking and the other to admit air. We sat on straight, hard, rexine-covered seats of which there were only a few. In the middle of the room was a long table stacked with rolls of cloth for sale. Behind, in a wide serving hatch, were shelves lined with such things as toothpaste, cans of American shaving soap, electric razors. In another corner was a small table covered with silverwork inlaid with designs in antimony, work done by Sabeans from Amara in Iraq, one of whom, resembling John the Baptist in early paintings, pale, round-bearded and robed, was standing by his wares. The Texan shoppers handled the small objects in their huge hands. The Sabean pretended to check the cost, which doubtless he knew well enough, in a small account and stock book. Neither prospective purchasers nor salesman wished to show much desire to settle. Against the wall on the other side sat two drillers side by side, one clearly tipsy; a cardboard tray steadied by the other was balanced on the knees of the drunker of the two and contained half a dozen beer-cans on their sides, empty. From time to time, and slowly, they adjusted the position of the cans, while exchanging slowly spoken confidences. At last they rose and with careful gait, glassy-eyed, made their way out.

We were taken to see the radio-operator's cabin. He was an Indian. It was possible to talk direct with the United States of America, but he was engaged, speaking to an incoming oil tanker. As we went on down the corridor I noticed that some joker had put up a notice over a lavatory door. LADIES, it said. There was not a Western woman within many miles.

On the great long foredeck of the ship, we made out in the dark some slow-moving figures. About four in all, they were slouching round the deck, each separately, hands in pockets, shoulders hunched, like lonely prisoners or patients in some hospital compound who had no immediate hope of release.

On the upper deck there was crooning; a film was beginning. Some of the huskier men were up there, attending to the projector and joking. The figures on the foredeck seemed to be the less robust kind.

As we drove back to the city, under the moon, I dozed. There is drilling in the sea not far away on this coast, and Captain Cousteau has been exploring hereabouts. 'As one turtle to another, don't you think the time has come to move? What are these strange humming craft? These new fish? Let us take the Master's Daughter with us, dear brother turtle, and go away.'

I woke as we entered a gate of the city ablaze with coloured electric lights, to rejoin a stream of cars, the total number in the place having now reached eight thousand, where the Shaikh and I had know it to have less than forty in all.

At another, later visit, turmoil constantly increasing in the town itself, the Shaikh gave me an appointment in his house, or Palace as it became known in English, on the sea. There we would be tranquil, though we could not expect to be quite undisturbed. Servants and engineers came in to ask for instructions, to report or attend to their work. 'Engineers' have become a part of daily life. There are air-conditioning plants, private power-stations, electric wiring and gadgets, cars and boats that require attention. Everyone of standing has an 'engineer', if not several, apart from numerous servants and coffee-servers. At most big houses there is a gardener too, though there are only a few dusty sunflowers, thorn trees and zinnias to look after. Various forms of acacia fill up corners of the yards called gardens.

The Shaikh had made one appointment with me for seven in the evening. There was no sign of any bustle which might herald his arrival. We sat for forty minutes in his much over-air-cooled guests' sitting-room. It was clear that he would not be coming. The telephone was an extension and when it rang I listened in. He was talking from the Municipality office to a servant and making arrangements about leaving by launch for his bungalow on the sea further south. I went and joined the servant and arranged to speak when he had finished. He was still engaged by work at the Municipality, was polite, but not in the least apologetic. As time means little to them, they cannot understand that it matters to anyone else.

Just as we were leaving, the official who should have attended our meeting at seven arrived in a great hurry. He had had other things to do. We talked to him for about two hours. He made appointments for the following day with the Shaikh, not believing that he would be going away. As we left, an elderly crony clutching his luggage – to wit, two packets of cigarettes – arrived. He said that he was meeting the Shaikh with a view to going south with him that night. Our tentative appointments were, therefore, once more altered. The Shaikh would not return for two days at least. We left, and later heard that he had arrived about ten o'clock, asked for us, and left by launch almost at once. If, trusting to such experience, one were to turn up next time an hour or so late, the Shaikh would be dead punctual and have been impatiently waiting for us. An appointment is an expression of good intent, and not necessarily to be kept. King Ibn Saud, when invited by the British representative in this city, turned up very late and left immediately after dinner.

Nevertheless, these Arabians never miss the times of prayers. When once I gently chided the Shaikh for a delay in putting through a matter he had already agreed upon, he replied that everything takes a long time in this new world. 'Even a dinner takes two hours to cook. Come and dine with me this evening.'

He and some others had taken to using, when talking Arabic, the English expression 'business is business'. This cliché has become something of an idiom hereabouts, meaning roughly, 'I do not know what to say, and anyway I do not say anything.' Its use by them approximates the European civil-service meaning or lack of meaning in such expressions as 'the matter is under consideration'.

In the past, unpunctuality was accepted and allowed for. When camel caravans left this place only a few years back, the same held good for all over the East at one time, the hour forecast for setting out was an approximate one, as everyone understood. When at last the caravan was marshalled and began to move, it was only for a short day's march. A halt was then made for twenty-four hours or more, to allow for sending back for anything or anyone forgotten, for laggards and private persons to catch up.

So when all the new hurly-burly of westernizing came in, with its exacting new disciplines, it was not everyone who was able to adjust their ways as to the manner born or, if they seemed to be doing so, could keep it up without sometimes backsliding. To change one's racial way of life when a grown man and even in what might seem to a Western observer trivial matters is after a time nerve-racking. Two Englishmen who did so, in reverse, in Arabia, Sir Richard Burton and H.St.J.Philby, both became nerve-racked and difficult men in relations with their own people.

My friend the Shaikh much overworked himself. He did make another short visit to Europe, but the leisurely instructive tours abroad he hoped to plan did not mature. His heart was soon giving him trouble and he died in middle age. I did not hear an exact account of the end of this lively, energetic man, but it came following the threat and challenge for which he and most of his people were unprepared.

'Give us a child until the age of seven,' the Jesuits are alleged to have said. It is true that the very young can seemingly be changed successfully. The older men are too fixed in their ways to be disturbed by the coming of great change, deplore it as some may. It was the young adults and the middle-aged, obliged to meet the

challenge full tilt, who suffered most, whether or not they understood the full nature of it. My friend the Shaikh was one of the few
in the front rank at this unrepeatable moment in Arabian history.

A Weekend in England, 1939

The newspapers told us just how long it was since it had been so hot and they prophesied even greater heat over the coming weekend – which as it turned out, was one of the last before the outbreak of the Second World War.

Napier Alington had invited me to stay for the weekend at Crichel, his house in Dorsetshire. The other guests included Mrs Mollie Long, the Baronne de Forrest, patronne of Rugger in the South of France, Edward Stanley of Alderley, the Marchesa Casati, Geoffrey Nares, a son of the actor Owen Nares, and Diana Brougham, Napier's sister. Napier himself used to speculate on the possibility of his having blood of the Doria family in Italy, descendants of the famous Admiral and 'King of the Sea', Andrea Doria. Napier had the vivacity and vitality of many young Italians and was taller and slimmer than his sister Diana and the younger sister Lois, and he differed physically from his elder brother Gerard, who had died of war wounds.

On the Saturday we were asked to spend the day on Edward Stanley's yacht, then at Weymouth. It meant leaving rather early and of course taking bathing things and dressing in a way suited to such extremely hot weather. The men wore open shirts and cool, linen trousers and the women were in similarly light and quite informal clothes. When we had been marshalled in two, or maybe three, cars by Napier, we set off in gay mood, delighted at the prospect before us. Near the end of the grounds of Crichel House, however, Napier suddenly stopped his car. He looked alarmed. 'We have forgotten the Casati,' he said. Turning a car, we drove back to the house. Geoffrey Nares, I following him, ran upstairs to her bedroom and knocked. There was a long pause before she opened. Napier had said that she would know that we had left without her and it seemed he was right. She looked furious. She was dressed in her ordinary day style; in satin pyjamas with lace edges and a hat like a lampshade with a deep fringe that half concealed her blood-red eyes and inch-long artificial eyelashes. Deep borders of mascara circled her eyes.

'*Enfin, tout est prêt?*' she said to Geoffrey Nares who had gone into the room. '*Prenons un whisky?*' she added, turning to the Victorian marble-topped washstand on which was a bottle that she must have brought with her. She had a glass in her hand. She was disappointed when we refused and persuaded her to leave at once.

We were always, I think, rather apprehensive about the Casati's reaction. Once she had been a great hostess, giving fabulous parties that were still discussed some fifteen years later. She had for a time occupied the Palais Rose in Paris and her parties and hospitality were of the Olympian order. Gradually all her money had gone and she was inclined to be resentful and sometimes very bitter in her judgements of people or their motives. She had been painted more than once by Augustus John and by other notable portrait painters. She had indeed been one of the most paintable women in Europe and still retained her slimness and the fine bone-structure of her face.

All the same, it was a fearsome ensemble. People who called her Louisa to her face, called her, I noticed, 'the Casati' when speaking of her to others. (She was still alive in London in 1956 when I made this note.) Such was the peculiar, awesome feeling she induced, in spite of the decline in her fortunes, and her déclassé mode of life in consequence.

At Weymouth, Stanley told us that the glass was giving indications of coming change and he did not feel disposed to go far. We sat on deck as the boat got slowly under way in the calm. At the end of the quay was a kiosk or two, and I saw that a few onlookers had suddenly started to scurry towards them, all seized at the same moment with one idea, or so it seemed. I followed their movements, wondering vaguely what it might be. While we chatted, I kept my eye on them. Now they had reached the booths and were handing over money. They were given, I saw, field-glasses in exchange and were levelling them at us, handing them to their companions and talking with animation. Some were laughing. For a moment it seemed absurd behaviour, then I remembered that we had with us the Casati. A commanding seat on the stern had been made for her, with plenty of cushions. I suppose the spectators were for the most part good people of some inland town, with their wives and children, come for a holiday in August to Weymouth, and maybe with them a local idler or two, to whom the Casati might well have appeared a freak beyond compare. And even though our own 'south of France' clothes, which were then not common in England, would have passed muster if alone, when seen alongside the Casati must have contributed to the impression that we were a band of clowns or troubadors from some far-off land, and contributed greatly to the worth of their holiday journey to the seaside.

Since it did seem that there was to be a sudden change in the weather, we returned to port earlier than planned and drove back to Crichel, though the weather held up. It was still very warm when we arrived, in time for a late tea or for drinks rather early. I seem to remember that we had both, first tea and then, a little later, the men went into the library where the curtains had been drawn and drinks already prepared, since it was usual to assemble there before going into the white salon to wait for the women as they came down before dinner.

We played several games of backgammon and they turned out to be close in result. We were becoming more amused by the game than we generally were. A crisis was being reached in our play with two taking the table in turn, depending upon who had won, when Stavis, the butler, came in and, going up to Napier, whispered something in his ear. Napier turned to look at him in amazement. He said, 'Two foot at least, milord,' and Napier jumped up and went out with him, saying to us as he went, 'There is water in the cellars – I don't know what has happened, don't be disturbed. I'll come back.'

I went to peer out of the window, drawing a little way the very heavy curtains that hung over the great, high windows of the library. Sheets of rain were falling out of a black sky. The heavy curtains had prevented us hearing anything of the storm.

After a time we went to the front door and looked through the windows at the side of it, to see a foot or more of water swirling up to it. 'Don't attempt to open it,' said Edward Stanley, and later appeared outside with a long garden broom and his trousers rolled up, sweeping the water in an effort to free the covers of the drainage sumps and, by breaking down a flower bed, allow the water to run on into the sunken garden on the other, main side of the house.

Geoffrey Nares had driven Diana Brougham to visit some friends and had not returned. We wondered if they were safe. Then Napier came back and asked us to go down into the underground rooms to help the servants remove food from the lower shelves to higher ones, since the water was still mounting. Seemingly some conduit had broken or failed to allow the water its usual course, after a cloudburst. It had as a result come straight at the house and, by an open outside door, into the cellars.

We rolled up our trousers and went to help. There was much to be carried to safety and a good deal to be done. We worked away hard, the servants in the forefront, knowing as they did what must be done first and where everything was to be found. The clearing of the drains had to be done by them, since they had a good idea where to feel for them in the water.

The younger men were energetic, stripping off their clothes and going down into the water in the lower cellar. Henry, a young third footman, was wearing only a white underslip and his dickey and collar. Working in the water as we all were, it did not seem strange, until there suddenly appeared, at the top of the stairs leading down from an open door, Diana Brougham. 'Henry, Henry,' she said in a quite everyday tone, 'has his lordship dined yet?'

The boy replied with daring but deserved tartness, looking up only for a moment, 'No, and he'll be lucky if he dines at all tonight.' She disappeared, evidently set back and feeling, rightly, superfluous.

Henry said that the water was now sinking. Stavis added that the food was all safe and unharmed, that he could give us a cold supper in about an hour's time, that we might even have hot baths, the boiler-room being unaffected. We filed upstairs, an oddly bedraggled party.

A quarter of an hour later, while in a bath, I heard a noise like a bursting shell. I lay listening. Then there was the sound of running feet and screams. Flinging a very large towel about me, I looked out into the passage. A few doors away, Mollie Long was doing the same thing; at that moment there came racing down the corridor a number of young women I had never seen before. They were dishevelled and in a great state of alarm. Their explanations as they hurried along were incoherent. Afterwards we learnt that the flag-staff and its square brick base on the roof had been struck by lightning. The base and the lower half of the mast had partly come through the roof and into the attics where the between-maids, and some of the other women servants, were going to bed. The top half of the mast and the house flag had gone bounding across the garden and ended up some fifty yards from the house.

After supper, Mollie Long drew me aside and said in her habitually rather commanding way, 'No one must mention the crash of the flagstaff. If Napier dwells on it he'll conclude it has a most ominous meaning. We must all go back to London early tomorrow morning. We can catch the nine-thirty train.'

She was right but, do what we might, Napier insisted upon speaking about the fall of the flag. 'It is the end of the house of Alington. We have been bewitched.' Within two years he was dead in Cairo, the last holder of his title. Geoffrey Nares too was soon dead, horribly, in Cairo. He was taken to a military hospital from my small flat in Cairo, having come for a few days' convalescence after being in hospital in Alexandria. He had been taken ill in the western desert with what turned out in the end to be a tumour on the brain. He was one of the handsomest young men in the army.

Some years after the war I went to the brief funeral service for the Casati in the Brompton Road. Her English son-in-law and a daughter were there, but very few others, about a dozen in all, I think.

Lord Wavell and Princess Marthe Bibesco

Having reached Cairo on the first convoy of the Second World War, leaving Glasgow on the first afternoon at 2 p.m., a cable from Reader Bullard, the Minister in Jedda, told me that Ibn Saud was visiting his tribes and it would be some little time before he saw him again. He had no doubt that I would be welcome but he thought it best to deal with such a matter direct with him, rather than with his staff.

Having time to spare, I told General Wavell that I had an invitation to visit George Rendel, the Minister in Sofia, and asked him if I could be of any use to him in going there and making inquiries for him in the Balkans. He approved the idea at once, obtaining a questionnaire from his Intelligence Staff for me.

My journey took me via Yugoslavia and Bulgaria into Romania for a few days. On my return and submission of a report to him, General Wavell sent me a letter of thanks.

GENERAL HEADQUARTERS
MIDDLE EAST
Cairo
16 November 1939

SECRET

My dear de Gaury,
This is just a note to say that I have read with interest your report on

your trip to the Balkans and to thank you very much for the trouble you took in collecting information and impressions.

It is a good and useful report.

Wishing you all success in your new post,

    Yours sincerely,

      (Signed) R.L. Wavell

Captain G. de Gaury, M.C.,
c/o H.B.M. Minister,
Jedda.

I had first met General Wavell, afterwards Field Marshal the Lord Wavell, seven years earlier, in mid-desert between Damascus and Baghdad, at the Fort of Rutbah. He was head of a War Office Mission, studying the use of armoured vehicles in deserts. The immediate cause of the visit to Baghdad was to ascertain and report upon the possibility of bringing reinforcements, in the shape of an armoured column, across the desert to it from Egypt.

The Mission decided, I believe, that it was impossible to do so, though in fact, during the Second World War, it was found quite practicable. It is true, however, that an asphalt road had been built across the desert with a British subsidy in the interval. At the same time when I met the General at Rutbah, I was General Staff Officer, 2nd Grade, Military Intelligence, with the R.A.F., Command Headquarters in Iraq. He asked me at once about water, either on or just off the main car track to Baghdad. I told him that the only known water was at Wiswasiya ('the Whisperer'), a series of caverns which had water, so it was reported, at their very end. A few bedouin and the *solubba*★ sometimes spent the summer there if unable to reach the river in time for settling down before the great summer heat and dryness. Wavell asked to be taken there, though I told him it was quite a distance from the main track and that we should need lanterns and ropes for exploring the caves. These latter, it was found, the party already had.

My guide was a most exceptionally reliable one, the son of the last of the old camel doctors, Jews, of the caravan cities, who

---

★The smiths of the desert, a people different to the bedouin Arab. The name *solubba* might connote 'people of the Cross' and they may have been Christians, or connected with the Crusaders.

annually went out among the Arab tribes in the winter, doctoring their sick camels with physic balls of a secret recipe. I was astonished when, after a few miles, the General quoted to me some lines of Oscar Wilde on the 'Sands of Bokhara'. This must mean, I felt, that he was an unusual General.

After we had travelled for a couple of hours a dust-cloud began to lower visibility. Wavell wondered whether we should not turn back. I reassured him. With the dust, however, worsening, he became fretful. The guide was nevertheless still confident, and I had confidence in him. Finally, when visibility was only about a hundred yards, the General became decisive. 'Here,' he said, 'we halt and turn back.' I told the driver, who stopped the car and explained to the guide. 'But there,' said the guide, pointing, 'is the castle of Wiswasiya.' The ruins of the castle were immediately above the limestone fault, with precipitous sides except at one point, at the bottom of which began the caverns.

The water turned out to be not enough, or good enough in quality, for his military purposes, but the General seemed, from this time onwards, to have confidence in me. At the beginning of the Second World War, having been in touch with him from Kuwait, he showed me some deciphered telegrams of interest.

The last time I saw Lord Wavell was after his return from the Viceroyalty of India, at a Christmas dinner party in London given by a Member of Parliament. I was placed one away from him at the table. After talking to the guest on my left I turned to find the woman between me and the General giving me an appealing look. I knew at once what she meant. Wavell had the reputation of being difficult as a partner in conversation with women. Leaning forward, making it clear that he was being addressed as well as her, I told briefly a story heard from a traveller recently come from Yugoslavia. Though not mentioning it, I knew Wavell had published a book of verse he had called *Other Men's Flowers*. My tale was only that the communists had persisted in making promotion among shopkeepers according to their diligence as party members: a good party member in, say, a furniture shop could be promoted for that reason to be a director of men's clothing stores, and so on. It worked fairly well, but not when applied to the best flower-shop in Belgrade. Then everything went wrong and the wives whose dinner parties were no longer graced by the flowers they wanted created trouble in the highest communist circles, so an exception was made in the Communist Party on behalf of the flower-shops. The flowers had thus beaten the communists. Wavell's smile was faint and unaccompanied by comment, but the lady between us, encouraged, went ahead with an account of her garden in Chelsea.

Glancing back later to see how she was progressing, I saw the General was listening attentively to her story about an isolated garden in the countryside where a centuries' long residing yeoman family had preserved its Elizabethan nature; the poetic old country names of the flowers she was giving him. Satisfied that all was well, I turned once more to my left.

My report to General Wavell in 1939 was primarily on matters of military interest, so I did not write about Princess Marthe Bibesco's dramatic plea for Balkan unity.

She made it to me during a dinner party at the Bibesco Palace in the country beyond Bucharest. There were about twenty covers and she had placed me on her right. During dinner she mentioned the Napoleonic descent of her family. I noticed that she was wearing a rather regal dress with a long train to it in deep red velvet. We talked of the dirigible R.101 and Lord Thompson's death in it. She had been an intimate of his and felt that, had he lived, he could have helped her. It was difficult to bring the attention of the British Government to certain political matters in the Balkans at the right moment. To do so might have most important results. Wars began in the Balkans. Once they were settled and unified, peace in the world would be more likely.

After dinner she led her guests through a wide corridor to one of the drawing-rooms. I walked beside her. She paced slowly. At the end of the corridor, facing down it, was an old wooden armchair on a raised step, looking out of place among the tapestries, gold-framed portraits and *objets d'art* on either side. As we reached it and were about to turn to the left into the drawing-room, she paused in her conversation and stood for a moment. I asked, what was the chair. She had doubtless intended me to do so.

'That,' she said, 'is the throne of the Wallachian Princes, my husband's ancestors. It was for a time lost to us, being preserved by a loyal servitor and hidden.'

From there by easy stages we came to discuss the imperative need and the means of establishing the United Balkan Throne in

Constantinople with, clearly, the Bibescos as the ruling sovereigns. Here was Byzantium revived at last. Here was a pro-Allied Balkan bloc. Propaganda and money and acceptance of this plan by the British Government was all that was needed. Everything was ready for it. If only Lord Thompson had lived in order to be able to tell the British Government.

Princess Marthe Bibesco survived the war. She arrived in London very early after it ended, having been given a seat in a British aircraft by an Air Force Attaché who was in serious trouble afterwards for doing so. Her reputation during the war had been rather doubtful.

I dined with her in Paris at the Ritz with Lady Marriott, wife of General Sir John Marriott, a Guards officer, in the summer of 1953. I remember noticing her regal manner: the waiters treated her as if she were reigning royalty. She wore a cloak that seemed like a coronation cope and she carried a black stick that seemed symbolic. She was writing and making an income out of broadcasting and lectures.

I met Marthe Bibesco again, dining and dancing at Chips Channon's house on Christmas Night, 1954. She looked and behaved extremely well for one who was no longer young. Her grandson George was with her; he was staying with her at the Ritz Hotel for Christmas. Instead of being an heir to the throne of Constantinople – or even to that of Wallachian princes – he was then a British subject and an able-seaman in the British Royal Navy. He told me that he hoped to be an officer very soon. She had had him brought out of Romania, she said, during the war.

Persia

Isfahan, 1940

The archimandrite at Julfa, the Armenian suburb of Isfahan, told me that his three immediate predecessors all died 'in suspicious circumstances'. He said it in passing, without emphasis. Educated in England, Germany and America, he had visited the Far East. In the cathedral museum is an early Rembrandt print from the drawing of Abraham. There was also an Italian wooden crucifix about two foot six inches high, which is very good. It was neglected, having fallen over sideways and covered in dust, in a dark corner of the cathedral 'museum' or sacristy.

Massawar, the miniaturist in Isfahan, is said to have a cat which sits tranquilly beside him while he works and patiently lets him pull out a hair of its whiskers for use in making finer strokes. When we visited Massawar he was out. His two apprentices, who were wrestling instead of working on borders, which is their task, said that the cat too was out.

Teheran

A dapper little clerk from the reception desk of the hotel at Ab Ali, by the new ski-field, asked me for a lift down to Teheran. He showed off his school knowledge of European civilization and pretended to a culture excluding everything old and traditional. By the Shah's orders, travellers were forbidden to photograph camels, donkeys, beggars and so on.

Near the village of Jarj Roud he clapped his hands to his mouth and, being bustled out of the car, was at once very sick. We had just passed a long caravan of camels and I thought he said, '*C'est les chameaux.*' Some time afterwards it occurred to me that he had really said, '*C'est les caniveaux.*' It was a winding mountain road with ruts made by carts and camels.

Gulhek, the house of the British Counsellor in the summer legation where he and his wife invited me to dine. The only other guest was the Apostolic Delegate, a Belgian. After dinner we went out to sit on the terrace facing the tall moonlit trees and long narrow *bassins d'eau*. The moon struck glimmers from the cross and ring of the Apostolic Delegate. A radio placed ready was turned on for the news, news we fearfully half expected. It was of the fall of France. We sat in silence, too moved to speak.

The Apostolic Delegate was the first to do so, in a low voice and gently, with the care of a man habitually choosing his words and pronouncing them well. '*La belle France,*' he said, 'I remember well how much as a boy I longed to make a first visit to France. My brother and I lived with our parents near the frontier. We consulted with a schoolfriend about trying to go into France, if only for a few yards and a short time. The three of us decided to save up our pocket money until we had enough with which to hire bicycles for a day. When at last we had enough and a holiday was near, we told our parents of our plan. They objected at first, but when they learnt how we had saved and bespoken the bicycles, they agreed and promised us a picnic luncheon and a letter to the frontier Customs man, so that we could stop by his post. We did not tell them, I think, how much we hoped for a few minutes on French soil.

'The Customs man thought it was impossible to let us pass the frontier without proper papers, but seeing our faces fall and talking to us and eyeing our only luggage, the small picnic basket from our parents, he told us to wait a moment while he rang his French colleague. He would see what could be done. To our great pleasure the Frenchman agreed, his national pride probably touched by our ambition. He agreed, provided we did not go out of his sight and stayed not long. How much pleasure he gave us! To be, for twenty minutes, at last in France. *La belle France. Ces belles années.*' The Delegate sighed.

We were silent for a time, thinking perhaps of our own first visits to France; for I believe many youths in Britain have a special, not easily explained, sentiment about crossing for the very first time into France. But we were thinking, too, this time and mostly, of what France would suffer.

Teheran, A Glimpse of the Forbidden, 1940

In some Eastern countries in the past, European diplomats were hardly ever received in audience by the rulers to whom they were accredited and were unable to meet members of the ruling family. In Ottoman Turkey, the Grand Signior, the Sultan of Turkey, was seldom seen, even by his own subjects. When he rode or drove to prayers on Fridays he was practically hidden by a forest of attendants, officers and soldiers, screened by their great plumed turbans, their shields and glittering arms. Otherwise, he seldom left his straggling, high–walled great palace, the Seraglio.

Riza, Shah of Persia, the first of his line, though seen more often by the public, adopted much the same attitude towards foreign representatives as the Ottoman Sultans had taken in their day, a practice that in his case lasted into the Second World War. His family were forbidden by him to receive foreigners.

Briefly riding in the early mornings up towards the summer legations at Gulhek and back, I would sometimes pass parties of troops exercising and there see a young, mounted officer regarding them with older men grouped respectfully behind him. The groom with me said that the young man was the Crown Prince, recently returned from schooling in Switzerland; I thought it suitable to salute him, a gesture he returned. I did not expect to see him otherwise.

Although the Shah had in one way adopted the old Ottoman practice, he had been modernizing in other ways. One was the Europeanizing of dress of both men and women. It was said that he had lashed out with a whip at some persons wearing the old dress at a race meeting. Teheran and some other towns had been ruthlessly changed by pulling down old houses, bazaars, mosques and baths, their replacements being drearily straight and parallel streets of similar houses and glass-fronted shops. All this rectangular planning made it hard for a foreigner to find his way about – and did not encourage him to do so.

Among the invitations sent to me from legations, the Iranian Foreign Office and from the one or two established Persian families who had received special permission to entertain foreigners, came notice of a *bal costumé* ('or dinner jackets for men') to be given by a club, called, I think, the Anglo-American Club. Asking a British colleague about it, he told me it was very near, in an old house, but that they did not frequent the place. It was unnecessary to go. Nevertheless, being alone and unoccupied, when that evening came, I went.

Inside the walls of the garden were some large and expensive-looking cars; some were English, rather surprisingly, because the diplomat to whom I had spoken had somehow left me with the impression that the members of the club were mostly not very successful traders. Following a sound of music to the first floor without meeting anyone, I saw that there were few dancers. Scarcely more in numbers were some couples watching them. The waltz music, however, was relatively good although, or because, it came from a machine. The costumes were not at all out of the way. Or so I thought until a masked coupled passed near me, the girl slim and young, wearing a long dress of richly embroidered silk. They were followed by another masked couple, dancing gaily and very well. The man, perhaps twenty, was in doublet and tights, not black to represent, say, Hamlet, but in flesh-coloured pink. His equally young partner was in an admirably well-fitting, pale blue, besequined dress. A third couple, masked and no less well-turned-out, were both wearing startlingly good jewellery.

As the music stopped and the last couple passed out of the doorway in which I stood, the girl lost a slipper. She looked up at me with a smile and I was about to help her when her partner stooped to do so. As they went on their way I turned to ask of a man standing nearby, if he knew who they were. 'If you ask me, old boy, it is a party from the Palace, of the Royal Family; the Crown Prince and his sister, I think.'

'And the young man in pink from head to foot?'

'Maybe it is the son of the botany master at his school in Switzerland. He is said to have brought him back with him as a riding companion.'

I returned to the legation and, telling the Minister what I had seen, he decided to walk with me to the club. When we reached it the grand cars had gone. The music had changed in kind. Only three elderly, British-looking pairs were jigging to it. The few others present had gathered at a buffet table. It was as if what I saw had never been, that glimpse of youth with a longing for splendour of other days risking a sortie. It was the more strange, if true, because made by the offspring of the former trooper of Persian cossacks, hot-headed ruler of a neutral country, and when the whole industrialized world was becoming locked in war.

The Return of Order to Iraq

When on 3 April 1941 one Rashid Ali, a pro-German politician, proclaimed himself head of an illegal government in Iraq, and the Regent of Iraq, the Emir Abdililah, obliged to flee Iraq, had reached Palestine by air from Kuwait, an instruction from London came to the British representative in Teheran that he should send me to join the Regent, if it were possible for me to make my way to him through southern Iraq. The latter seemed doubtful, and was to lead to a curious event for me. Having made my way to the British Consulate in southern Iran nearest to the head of the Persian Gulf and Basra, I was given by the Consul the use of his small launch and a black despatch portfolio so that it would be possible, if still permissible by the situation in Basra, for me to meet the daily down-going launch from the Consulate there. I went out in the early morning to wait for the latter, which was expected as usual to bring and accept mail. The heat by about 10 a.m. was already very high on the river. Some hours later, there was still no sign of the Basra boat. It looked as if it would not be coming. The heat was almost intolerable. Then one of the crew called out that a ship was coming upstream. It was a British battleship. Behind it were two more ships and, behind them, frigates. Clearly these were bringing reinforcements from India. As the leading warship came near, my reaction was to approach it and point to my black despatch-case with its brass crest, then towards Basra and to myself, so that the captain would understand I wanted a lift. Naturally he waved us aside; I naturally indicated my wish again, upon which he gave a gesture showing his concurrence and I saw that he was slowing down. The stern was not high. Sailors lowered a rope-ladder and reached for my small suitcase and helped me aboard. It was doubtless the only time that it would fall to me to hail a British battleship for a lift – and successfully. The rebels were in occupation of part of Basra, but not of Maqil, the air- and seaport where we docked.

A Dutch civil aircraft, with Jewish passengers, had one vacant seat, which was available for me. Before leaving I was asked by the wife of a diplomat at Baghdad if I would be ready to sign that she was undertaking secretarial work for me, otherwise she would have to go aboard a steamer leaving the next morning for India. She was so very anxious about it that I did as she asked . . . as she reminded me with many renewed thanks some forty years later.

On reaching Palestine I heard of the Regent at Lydda and joined him, as Chargé d'Affaires in Jerusalem, the Ambassador being locked up in his Baghdad Embassy, without means of communication. The Regent told me about his escape from Baghdad with the help of the physician, Sinderson Pasha, and the American Ambassador, Mr Knabenshuc, and his wife who took him in their car to the Royal Air Force Camp at Habbaniya, he being concealed under a rug on the floor of the car whenever there were posts of rebel soldiers.

The British Army was preparing to move a column across the desert; the Regent was ready to go with it, and I with him. The Emir of Transjordan had come to say goodbye to us near his frontier and he took me aside to ask, would I make a special effort to restore the power in Iraq. I assured him that we were all just as anxious as he was to see this done.

On conclusion of the operations a month later, and the flight of Rashid Ali over the Persian frontier to safety with the Germans, the Emir sent the following telegram to the High Commissioner in Jerusalem:

Please convey to His Britannic Majesty's Government my hearty congratulations at the collapse of the rebellion which was undertaken by Rashid Ali and his followers in Iraq without thereby affecting the spirit of friendship which exists between the Arabs and the British. I highly appreciate the co-operation which has been maintained between His Royal Highness the Regent and his followers, the great personalities of Iraq, and the responsible British personalities who were by his side, and the considerate policy which was followed by the British Commander on land and in the air. I shall be grateful if you will be kind enough to convey my congratulations and pleasure to all those who took part in this operation and if you will personally accept my thanks for your valuable assistance and noble efforts in this regard. I cannot but request you also to convey to my old friend, the British Ambassador in Baghdad, a message of my greetings and appreciation of his noble attitude.

From: A Distant Fluting
Poems and Sonnets by Christopher Tower, 1941, published by Weidenfeld and Nicolson, London, 1977.

(Christopher Tower was one of the Britons kept in the British Embassy in Baghdad in 1941, until the British military column reached the outskirts of the city.)

TO GERALD DE GAURY
On His Negotiating The Surrender of Baghdad

Baghdad had known the reigns of two Rascheeds –
Haroun and Ali. Each a dictator.
The first of shining legend and renown:
The next of dubious reputation.
Similar names but somewhat different breeds:
Pride of the East – incalculable traitor.

Midnight in our camp. Since the sun went down
We've waited. At last your deputation
Moves between the armies. A captain leads
To the enemy negotiator.
You parley skilfully and soon the town

Has submitted to our occupation.

Haroun enjoyed a Thousand Nights of splendour:
Ali just one or two before surrender.

Deir-az-Zor, 1926 and 1941

In 1926 the walled town of Deir-az-Zor was very little visited by foreigners, even by the French. The 'hotel', so called, was unsuitable for Europeans or for Arabs of any standing, and we went to the *caravanserai*, the French officers not having offered us their hospitality. It was clean and we were offered the room of honour, over the main door on the first floor, the other rooms being smaller all the way round the large courtyard. The ground floor was kept for stabling, lock-ups for merchandise and the drivers of animals of the caravans.

The owner came to see that we would have all we needed. We had our own bedding and simple camp equipment. Did we wish to see the cook-shop owner in order to tell him what we wished to eat? We said that we did so wish. The coffee and sherbet would be brought across in a few minutes' time. When did we want the barber to come? And would we want to reserve the *hammam*? We answered 'Yes' to all these questions. It must have been almost the last time a European traveller would thus experience this age-old kind of life hereabouts.

It was certainly much pleasanter and quicker service than we could find in most of the so called 'European'-style hotels coming into being in less remote small towns in Syria and the Levant countries. The dinner was excellent, the kebabs and rice admirably cooked and brought piping hot, in a stand of containers, with flaps of warm unleavened bread. The barber with his trayful of instruments turned out to be equally efficient though he can hardly have been more than fifteen years old. He was, he said a trifle proudly, from Baghdad, was dressed in a thin silk shirt to his ankles and a black-and-white twisted kerchief in the fashion called *cherawi* and habitual to male inhabitants on the west bank at Baghdad.

Fifteen years later I became the Political Officer at Deir-az-Zor. Just as I entered it, a message reached me that General Slim with his division from India would be arriving from Iraq.

General Wilson had told me that, whatever happened elsewhere, he was determined to keep me there, my area extending from the Turkish frontier in the north to Jordan in the south. He wished to retain this desert corridor which was strategically important to him, and must have a British Political Officer there. A short time afterwards, when I had just about completed my tour and was coming to know the outstandingly important men both in the town and near at hand outside it, I received a cable telling me that a Free French officer was arriving to take over. A decision had been taken over Wilson's head, presumably giving in to demands by de Gaulle. Slim's chief staff-officer told me that the General would like to have me as Intelligence Officer; they would be going back to India and on to countries further east. I thanked him but, feeling that I should be less efficient there and not knowing those countries or the languages, I asked to turn down the offer. Meanwhile the new French officer turned up and Slim invited him to lunch. Since he did not speak any English and neither the General nor his staff from India spoke French, I had to translate. Almost the first question by Slim to the Frenchman was 'Do you speak Arabic?'

'No,' he replied, 'but I do speak Berber.' We were not impressed.

I left for Cairo and became a member of the Minister of State's staff, as 'Liaison Officer for duties in the Arab Countries'.

A curious small incident while I was at Deir-az-Zor in 1941 was that a Military Police corporal came to see me to report that in a remote corner of the town he had found half a dozen Senegalese soldiers working in a garage repairing trucks. He had brought their corporal, who spoke a little French, with him. The Senegali said that they were quite happy and still had a few more days' work in hand, but they were getting short of food. Might they have some? I thought it useless to try to explain that they were prisoners of war, as Vichy French. They were given food. I suppose my Free French successor dealt with them later.

Cavalry Twilight, 1941

A correspondence in the *Daily Telegraph*

22 July 1955

To the Editor, the *Daily Telegraph*,

Sir – The charge of the Royal Bucks Hussars in 1917, mentioned by 'Peterborough', must yield place as 'the swan song of the sword' to that of the Canadian Cavalry Brigade at Amiens on 30 March 1918.

Similarly, charges made in Palestine in 1918 preceded many by British and Canadian cavalry in the last phase on the Western Front.

According to Foch himself, the Canadian charge at Amiens saved the situation when the German offensive was within sight of victory. The later charges completed the German overthrow. All these exploits on the Western Front in 1918 formed part of operations involving a cavalry corps. Thus their pre-eminence, from every point of view, is beyond dispute.

Yours faithfully,
Harwood Steele   Rugby

To the Editor, the *Daily Telegraph*,

Sir – I believe British troops were charged by Italian native cavalry at the battle of Agordat. I think it was early in 1941.

The attack was repulsed.

Yours faithfully,
G. C. Pether   Hitchin

To the Editor, the *Daily Telegraph*,

Sir – Field Marshal Wilson ordered the raising of a cavalry force, which reached 1,100 in strength, from the tribesmen of the Jebel Druze in Syria in 1941.

They were in action under my command on the right flank of his advance, each man having brought his own horse and arms. The squadrons under Wilfred Thesiger and Gawain Bell (now Political Agent, Kuwait) operated until the armistice in Syria, though without any full-scale charges sword in hand.

This may have been the last cavalry unit ever to be raised in war.

Yours faithfully,

Gerald de Gaury   London, NW1   1955

England in Wartime

A Royal Visit, 1943

Emir Faisal of Saudi Arabia and his party from America arrived in England on 17 November 1943, and were put up in the Dorchester Hotel.

They went to a number of Army units and saw the latest armour manoeuvring. The Navy showed them over a submarine which had sunk a large number of enemy ships, whose commander had received the Victoria Cross and proudly produced a woollen sweater knitted for him and presented by Mrs Winston Churchill.

The Air Force arranged for them to see and enter bombers about to leave for Berlin, the pilots and crew giving matter-of-fact accounts of their role and how the bombs were to be released in another hour or so on the enemy capital. The princes were asked not to wish the crews good luck or a safe return as it was felt unlucky to do so. They asked the station commander, nevertheless, if they might know whether the aircraft they had entered did in fact return safely and, by the time they returned to their hotel, found an arranged message conveying that it had in fact done so. It was a long time before they reached London owing to increasing fog; it was only the motor-cycles of two escorting military policemen which enabled the driver of their car to find his way slowly onwards by following very close behind them. Somewhere in south London there was a noise of bombs falling not far away and, when one exploded much nearer, the despatch-riders halted and came to say they believed that there was a shelter not far off. Should they guide the car to it, they asked. Both princes in one voice said that they preferred to go on and put their trust in God, above ground. Very late, they reached their hotel safely. The King of Arabia, as Faisal was to become, and Prince Khalid, later to be his Crown Prince, and later still King, have thus experienced a little, enough to understand, what the people of England experienced in the days of bombing.

As they drove about London and the countryside during their three weeks' stay they saw the hideous results of it, the gaps where houses had come down and people had been buried in them as they fell, the life of the people in days and nights of the blackouts and wartime controls, their purposefulness and courage.

The two princes went on to Downing Street to present an Arab sabre with a jewelled hilt and gold-encrusted scabbard to Winston Churchill from their father. In the absence of the Prime Minister from London they were received by Mrs Churchill on his behalf, and it was decided that she would do so in the Cabinet Room, where fateful wartime decisions had been taken and were still being taken.

Before leaving, they went to Buckingham Palace to see the King. The Palace itself was bombed during the war. It was the King's second war for, as he said to Faisal at another visit two years later, 'I was in the navy in the first war, you know, and in the second one I had quite a bit to do,' using the kind of modest phrasing which Faisal himself employed.

A Night in a Bunker, 1944

Tony Gandarillas invited me to dine at his house in Cheyne Walk one night towards the end of the war, while I was employed in the Foreign Office. He was still an adviser to the Chilean Embassy in which he had been many years.

Towards the end of dinner, the rumble of guns and of bombs falling disturbed us. We were alone except for his manservant. When a bomb fell quite near, Tony said that we had better go to the shelter in the garden. 'It is very good. I paid ten pounds for it at Harrods at the beginning of the war,' he told me. It had three beds, two with a small table between them and one beside the steps that led into the shelter. It was covered by, at the most, two feet of earth and the top was of corrugated iron. It would have barely resisted a rifle bullet. The servant ran off to his wife nearby.

We went to fetch Tony's dog (a huge Great Dane), blankets, books and water. 'Oh, I must get my pipe. Please come to help me,' Tony added.

I helped him bring down his opium pipe and its accessories for cooking opium. It was well known that he was an opium smoker and he did not attempt to conceal it, being permitted a ration of it by the Home Office on medical grounds. As a life-long addict, he would have become deranged without it, and during war it was no longer possible to buy it from his former suppliers.

'You should try it. You know how?' I had once tried it – most unsuccessfully – in Persia. I thought it horrid. He lit a pipe of it and handed it to me but, no sooner had I put it to my lips than he said, 'No, Gerald, not like that. You are so stupid. Like this,' taking the pipe from me. 'You can have the next one.' The Great Dane had climbed on the third bed by the door. Sometimes there was the crash of an explosion across the river. Tony repeated the lighting of his pipe and the expression of disappointment at my inability with it, though I had not had time to take more than one puff. I did not mind his taking it away from me, as I suppose he must have known.

We fell asleep, I think. All I knew, suddenly, was that there had been a great crash right upon us. And yet I did not care much. This might be the end. Were we buried without hope of rescue? Gradually I came to understand what had happened. There had been no enemy bomb falling. We were all drugged. The small shelter had become, as it were, the bowl of an opium pipe. The Great Dane had fallen off his bed and the opium had greatly exaggerated the sound, making it many times more distinct. I struggled up after what seemed – and perhaps was – a long period of cogitation, and made my way home on foot along the Embankment to York Buildings where I then lived, in a small flat on the second floor of a seventeenth-century house overlooking the river, since pulled down.

A Visit to King Ibn Saud, 1944

In all my encounters with Ibn Saud he impressed me as the very great man he was, the maker of his kingdom. He had, which is not unusual in great men, a strongly developed sense of the dramatic as regards his own life. I described his knowledge of how to appear to his sometimes wild people in *Faisal, King of Saudi Arabia.* From being at a dangerously high degree of indignation against him, he brought them back, using the right words and his personality, to a mood of tearful remorse and shouts of renewed acclaim.

In Cairo on my way from London to Riyadh, I met Shaikh Yusif Yassin, Ibn Saud's Political Secretary and envoy to the Arab Committee, then in Egypt. I only saw him for a short time but he asked me at once why it was that the British attitude to Saudi Arabia had changed. I could only say that I knew nothing of it and felt there must be a misunderstanding.

Jedda was in the middle of a 'cold wave' – which means that when wearing a cotton shirt and trousers you are merely cool instead of clammy.

Travelling in the same aeroplane were Jordan, the British Minister, Man, a Secretary of the British Legation, and Shaikh Fowwaz al Shaalan, paramount of the Ruwala Anaza Bedouins of Syria, two of whose sisters married Ibn Saud and his son, the Emir

Saud, and whose daughter had married the Emir Mishaal, a younger son of Ibn Saud.

The Minister invited me to stay with him.

Jedda was growing rapidly and improving in appearance. The repairing and reconditioning of old houses by the Saudi-Arabian Mining Syndicate and the Arabian American Oil Company, and their building of new houses, had stimulated the local merchants to do likewise.

Shaikh Abdulla Sulaiman, the Saudi Finance Minister gave a dinner in my honour. The card of invitation to the British Minister invited him to meet me. Abdulla descended to the door to see me off each time I visited him, and generally paid me the most agreeable attention. Subsequently, on the way to Riyadh, the bodyguard and drivers and servants persistently called me Saadat el Wezir ('Excellency the Minister').

Apart from a courtesy call on Abdulla, two 'business' calls, and the dinner at which there was far from any shortage of food, I visited Abdulla privately at his request, in his house at night.

He said that he was leaving for Mecca immediately afterwards. At this call he spoke frankly and vehemently. His theme was the change in our attitude towards them. He gave several instances. One, which made him quite fiery as he described it, was that fourteen months ago, when he was with the King's sons in India, an official came to see them and said that they were not permitted to send coded telegrams. They said they had not done so. 'No,' he replied, 'but you have received one.' Abdulla said to me that he thought it extraordinary not to permit the King's sons to send a cypher telegram to their father if they wished.

Then they had bought a lot of clothes and personal supplies – some of them for the women at home – and paid for them, but were not permitted to take them, and even now had been unable to obtain them. It was not the Indians who had treated them like this. It was the British. The Indians, some of them princes, had come to offer their assistance and, when they were told that the government had refused permission for the goods to leave, they had offered to smuggle them out, which they said they could quite easily do.

He was much upset as he spoke. He repeated that it was not the Indians who had treated them like this. Evidently what happened then rankled still. The Americans, he said, pushed their attentions and their offers upon them. They, the Arabs, liked and knew us, but could not understand this new attitude.

Since 1943, he said, they had had only one consignment of clothes (shirts, headdresses and loin-cloths, mostly cotton). It was a small consignment. I asked how it was that the people of Jedda seemed adequately clothed. This he no doubt had hoped would be my question. He leapt at it. 'Because,' he said, leaning forward and wagging his finger at me, 'tons and tons of clothes, as a result, are and have to be smuggled in from the Yemen and the Sudan.'

The Saudis have always treated me well, and if they were this time exceeding their former politeness it might be to lend emphasis, by contrast, to their complaint that we had changed our attitude and were treating them badly. Rightly or wrongly, they clearly felt seriously aggrieved.

I saw Coneybeare, retiring American head of the wartime branch of the Middle East Supply Center (M.E.S.C.) in Jedda, and liked him.

He had strongly recommended his British second-in-command, Major Douglas Nicholson, to succeed him. He spoke at length in a sympathetic way about Saudi-Arabian problems. He said that they and we must 'upgrade the standard of living' in the country. He thought that there should be an Anglo-American Economic Advisory Council in Jedda, to succeed, without a gap, the M.E.S.C. organization when it came to an end. He thought that example was better than advice in the case of the Arabs. The Americans would show them and the Arabians would copy when they saw successful results, e.g. in cultivation.

Paul Geier was American Chargé d'Affaires when I arrived. He seemed to be much liked. A British official of the M.E.S.C. said that the Americans had been at pains, it was evident, to appoint a well-qualified man. I saw him several times later when he was in the U.S. Embassy in Rome and in London at the time of the coronation of the Queen.

The pilgrims were arriving in numbers. On 14 November some 8,000 arrived – from India, Africa and the Levant. The atmosphere in the government offices was a cross between that of a mobilization day and Christmas Eve.

Two members of the legation came to see me off to Riyadh, on the afternoon of 15 November, accompanying me as far as Umm al Sallam, the first post on the Mecca road.

I was provided with a 1941 Box Car, a 1942 Chevrolet lorry, food

– including a live sheep – bed, bedding, Arab clothes, a cook and Sudanese servant.

The Emir of the party was carrying a Government Royal Mail 'bag', which he clung to for the first three days but forgot when later we left Riyadh for al Kharj, until reminded by me. We had to go back for it. The Sudanese servant, from Dongola, had evidently been influenced by travelling with Americans. I was given grapefruit to begin breakfast and offered tomato juice when we stopped in the evenings. He laid a camp-table in the European style without fault. Up to 1939 we travelled à l'Arabe in every way. Afterwards the arrangements were a mixture of Eastern and Western methods. Now it is entirely in European style that provision is made, although of course Arab dress is still insisted upon for European travellers on the road to Nejd and in the capital. Ibn Saud has recently permitted an aeroplane to land with the British and American ministers at al Bowaib, only one hour by car from Riyadh.

In Cairo an official of the Minister of State's Office told me that too many British and American officials had entered Central Arabia now for there to be any longer some mystery about it. When I had first gone there, he said, fewer than a dozen Europeans had ever been there; now he supposed some four hundred Europeans had been there. Ibn Saud's mystic power had been lost, he thought. 'You will,' he added, 'find a great difference and there is a different attitude in consequence.' An official of the British Legation spoke on similar lines and thought that Cairo had pressed too many visitors on Arabia. There had been a number of M.E.S.C. officials some of whom were quite unsuitable but had been given facility to travel, in some cases into far corners of the kingdom. In the stress of war conditions, Saudi Arabia had been treated much as any other Middle Eastern country in this respect, or perhaps considered less important than the others, so that no particular care had been taken in selecting officials for the special case of Arabia. On the other hand, Ibn Saud had seldom refused a definite request from the British Legation for officials to travel, whatever his private views.

I spent the first night at Sharaya, near Mecca in the Wadi Fatima. There is extensive new irrigation work, undertaken by Shaikh Abdulla Sulaiman's Finance Ministry. An aqueduct 150 yards long carries water to a depression on the right bank of the *wadi* and there is a deep new well and pumping-engine house in the *wadi* bed. At several places on the road to Riyadh there were changes which showed how much the Saudis have done on their own initiative. There were new forts and government offices around which hamlets have grown up. Wells have been repaired and cement troughs put in at Ibn Saud's orders. These are not isolated cases; almost every well in general use on the most used tracks for cars and by bedouins has been repaired. On some of the wells the date of the work has been inscribed with the King's name.

We were passed by large parties of pilgrims on their way down to Mecca. Among them were camel-riders, each with a led mare for the use of the Emir Faisal and the other princes during the ceremonies, on the road to Muna and Arafat. There were also flocks of sheep going down to be sacrificed on Mount Arafat after the sermon.

Later a long line of camels with litters containing women from Riyadh came by. There were a few lorries full of pilgrims – not many. The rain, which is not always as early as this time, began to fall – a little each evening, on the journey up to Riyadh – and continued from time to time during my visit. The rains this year having been early and quite heavy and widespread; cattle and sheep will not suffer as in the past few years. It is a good winter.

On 17 November near Muwaih, I met the Emir Mansour, a son of Ibn Saud, going to Mecca. He had just been made Minister of War. He said that he wished to see me after my return from Riyadh.

We topped up the cars at the well at Dafina, and reached Afif wells at sunset. Formerly there was nothing save the well, now there is a government office, a hamlet and refilling station. The *mamour* told me that he was an Hejazi and formerly a telegraphist, but he applied for this post for the sake of his three children because it carried an increase of two riyals a day. The climate was better, too. The cost of living excepted, eight riyals a day for such a young man in Arabia is not bad. He also listed for me the cost of clothes and food.

Heavy rain came at last. Everyone was delighted and kept on repeating, 'God be praised.' It is not only early, but heavy and widely distributed, this year after three years of drought.

Hot sheep's milk in glasses was brought. It was excellent.

18 November

We reached Duwadmi fort at midday. A new *diwan* for the King was being built in the old Nejdi style, on the ground floor so that he will not have to climb the stairs to the first floor.

There was more rain during the night.

19 November

Half way across the Nefud sands we met a car sent out by the Emir Saud to meet me and give me messages of greeting. I heard afterwards that the Emir Mansour had telegraphed to his brother, the Emir Saud, suggesting he send out a better car than the one we had.

We reached Marrat at midday. There is a fort here, new since my last visit.

The back-axle ball-bearing case on the relief car sent out by Saud broke soon after reaching Awainid near the Jebel Ruwaiq gorge.

The life of a car in such country as this is (or should not be expected to outlast) two years, and engines should be overhauled after every 8,000 miles. They are having to last far longer now and do without such overhauls.

When the axle broke everyone laughed, and the drivers good-humouredly began their work at once. . . A Baghdad driver would have referred to the more intimate parts of the axle's mother.

We reached Riyadh at two o'clock in the night, Arabic.

The guest-house chamberlain – in the Murabba Palace – and the Officer of the Guard said that the Crown Prince had hardly been off the telephone, to find out if we had arrived, for the last two hours. Shaikh Shalhoub, chamberlain to Saud, came, camel-stick in hand, to make courteous inquiries about my journey. As it was late, it was arranged that I should see the Emir in the morning.

20 November

I went to see the Emir Saud at two o'clock, Arabic (i.e. two hours after dawn) a courtesy call; but he said that he wished to talk to me about some personal matters another time.

I left for al Kharj, to see Ibn Saud, at four o'clock and reached it at 6.40. In three years, immense blocks have taken the place of the former small fort. There is quite a large village at the foot of the Palace. The singular feature of the Palace is the carway which runs round it, going up to the various floors and connecting on arches with the *diwan* palace, some hundred yards away, and even up to the roof. There is a garage on the first floor. It all looks as if it had been designed by Jules Verne or H.G. Wells.

Rushdi, the little Palestinian librarian, archivist and secretary to Ibn Saud who also deals with the organization of the radio news reception for the King, came to welcome me in the absence of

Shaikh Yusif Yassin. I handed over two large bottles of essence of scent from India as a present to Ibn Saud.

I went to the King in the evening – a formal first call – but we talked about Lord Moyne's murder, and so about Jews.

Five days before leaving London for Cairo, I was asked to lunch by Mrs Daisy Fellowes, at the house she was occupying in Chapel Street, London, to meet Lord Moyne. He himself was leaving in a few hours. He invited me to ring him as soon as I reached Cairo, wanting to hear more about Arabia. Arriving at midday in Cairo, I put off ringing the Minister's house until later. It was at that very moment he was killed, on arrival at his house from his office with his A.D.C. I heard it first when the impish Cairo newsboys came into the Continental Hotel dining-room with a half-sheet special edition, singing out in Arabic, 'Death of the High Agent.'

Ibn Saud repeated his well-known views about the Arab *Committee*. He corrected me when I referred to a 'conference' having been held. It was a mistake to embarrass us during the war by bringing up the Palestine question, and any Arab meeting which did not bring it up would be neglecting the main Arab problem. He asked me to describe the V.1 and V.2 flying missiles. I heard later that my description had been repeated by him in his general assembly.

(About this time, like very many of the residents of London, one had experience of the flying-bombs. In return for a small contribution to its outgoings, I was given the use of a mews house, No. 5 Three Kings Yard, conveniently situated near the side door of Claridges Hotel. It had been lent to her son, David Herbert, by Lady Pembroke; David was in the Royal Navy, based in the West Country and only able to come up on leave at rare intervals. One night a friend, Hugh Cruddas, a regular officer in the Royal Artillery, had asked me for a bed for a night; we were kept awake by the start of V–bomb raid, some falling quite near. Then the engine of one coming towards us cut out, meaning – as we knew – that it would fall very near indeed. It did, in Oxford Street, some forty yards away, blowing a taxicab to smithereens, as we learnt later. Hugh Cruddas survived for almost forty more years, dying in the English countryside while tranquilly eating his breakfast!)

King Ibn Saud touched upon Syria and said that he did not quite understand what was going on there. He had given the Syrians good advice and they said that they were following it, yet they did not seem to be doing so. He seemed to imply that he thought we might have changed our policy without his knowing it, but I may be wrong.

He spoke of Philby and the £20 million bribe offered to him by the Jews through Philby. He explained that he had not mentioned it earlier because Philby was, before his detention, considered to be a British agent at his, Ibn Saud's, court, and if he had revealed the story it would have seemed to be a British proposition. He therefore did not tell anyone until he spoke to the American, Colonel Hoskins, about it. I did *not* tell him what Weizman had told me about the arrangements made by him.

He told me that he had made his son Mansour Minister for War and touched upon his supply and transport shortage. It was because of shortage of transport that he had not gone to the pilgrimage this year. I thought that he looked well. He seemed as alert as ever.

21 November

Ibn Saud sent a car for me at three o'clock (Arabic) and I stayed until the midday prayers – at six o'clock, Arabic time. He covered a great deal of ground, including education, the Yemen and 'propaganda' and his neighbouring governments. The Imam of the Yemen, Yahya, was failing and so was his adviser, Qadhi Raghib. Yahya had rheumatism in his legs and sugar in his bowels, but his sickness came and went. Sometimes he pretended to be ill when he was well and sometimes he pretended to be well when he was ill.

Hassan was the best of the sons but he had 'internal whispers' (what we could call 'nerves' and complexes). He had told Yahya that he would lament it if he went to war with him and he had lamented it, but now they worked together. His letters came frequently and he had showed them to the British Legation.

Abdulla el Wazir was a man. He had ambitions; what had upset the country was the Imam's departure from tradition in naming Ahmad crown-prince. Succession had hitherto been by election. Yahya had adopted the system of royalty. It was a complete change. Yahya must (a) have a treaty of bon *voisinage* with the British and a representative from them, (b) quieten his people over the succession and (c) discipline his sons. He had written to him about this, a potent letter. It was a fine country and should be happy.

We were sitting on an open balcony on the second floor of the Palace. Every now and then he looked out over his fields and gardens, and towards the line of trees in the distance which marked the ancient capital of Arabia, al Yamama. He stroked his beard and put his finger to his lips sometimes. He would lean forward to emphasize a point or lean back and smile to denote satisfaction when he had made it. The other subjects were mostly current problems, in the hands of the Legation.

Rushdi came to invite me to dine with the King later in the week and to invite himself to dine with me, together with Hamza Ghauth of Medina and Bashir al Sadawi, of Misurata in Tripolitania. When they left me, Bashir said that if the King gave him permission he would like to speak to me privately about Tripolitania, his home country.

22 November

Ibn Saud sent for me at four o'clock (Arabic) and talked until six o'clock. I left then, it being midday prayer time – making that my excuse.

He spoke about: North Africa; the Americans in the Middle East; the Russians; lack of transport in Saudi Arabia; the high cost of living in Arabia; the extraordinary behaviour of the Government of India on the goods purchased by his sons; the lack of clothing consignments so that Saudi Arabia was forced to purchase smuggled goods; the importance of India as Arabia's mart; and the forms of government in the Middle East. He told me that he was expecting Mr Hamilton of the Oil Company today. On leaving him after this long talk, he said smilingly, 'Gradually – gradually – I want to see you several times more and in Riyadh.'

He asked me what our plan was for North Africa after the war. I told him of the pronouncements so far made. When I told him of that relating to Cyrenaica, he said, 'That's right – that is what we want.' He said that if after the war there were an Anglo-American base in the Mediterranean they, the Arabs, would feel reassured. He said that at their first coming the Americans were more popular than now. He had just had to tell them that they were not to build roads everywhere in Arabia. They could build a road from Dhahran (in the east) to Jedda (in the west), but not at present elsewhere. They had wanted to begin everywhere at once. As to the wireless direct to America, he had passed the matter to the British, saying that if the Americans could arrange it with the British he would agree.

The Americans were impetuous. I asked for enlightenment on

this but he only repeated his remarks in different words. On the other hand, he frequently says that the Oil Company has saved his country. Speaking of its beginnings, he said that the Turks before the last war had introduced secretly German 'engineers' to see the Hasa coast and examine it for oil – seeing my astonishment, he said that there was no doubt about it. The Turks had kept it very secret but he knew about it. At one moment he said that it was well known that the Americans were the richest country in the world with the greatest resources, but the British had . . . he hesitated for a moment . . . better-made armaments – and their policy was better.

He thought the Russians made a new danger to the Middle East and that they were taking much more interest in it. There had been communist demonstrations in Iran lately. Russia would be strong in Eastern Europe.

The effect of the lack of transport in the kingdom was vividly described by the King. He seemed to know where all his transport was. He gave the cost of one tyre-cover as 4,000 riyals. Unless they had more transport soon, he could not say what would happen. After the preceding bad years they had suffered a big decrease in the number of camels in the country. He had stopped export in the north.

The cost of living was unbelievably high. He gave me examples at length. He had all the figures in his head. He fingered his red headkerchief – the chequer-board-patterned one, as used by the bedouins – which he always wears and said that before the war it would have cost half a riyal; it now cost fifteen. I have heard that the cost has been as high as twenty-two riyals. Worse still, the women had difficulty in going properly clothed. One could hardly bear to look at the bedouins now – they were such a distressing sight because of their lack of proper clothes. The only clothes coming now were those smuggled from outside. Some merchants of neighbouring countries were making a fine thing out of it. It was the only way they could get clothes in Arabia. The clothes came from India but via other merchants, the Yemen or the Sudan. Yet when his sons had tried to bring one consignment for their people in Riyadh direct from India, they had been stopped. Taking Ibn Saud and his Finance Minister's descriptions, one has the impression that they feel something like a blockade has been imposed – except that a surplus has been sent to surrounding countries – from India – whence they can be smuggled; thus the only Arabian market of clothes is a black market.

Speaking of Egypt and constitutions in the Middle East, Ibn Saud said that party government was unsuited to Middle East countries. Even in Europe, when there was a crisis a coalition was formed: Mr Chamberlain had formed one. The East was always in a state of crisis and should always have a coalition.

In the evening I went to look at the great pools of al Kharj and found a number of Arabs bathing. They said, 'We learn to swim at the bottom of our wells and many of us go to the pearling banks for a season or two.'

On arrival at dusk, the Oil Company party went straight to the quarters of their engineers outside al Kharj near one of the pools. Ibn Saud thought that they were lost and had sent out a lorry, food, bedding, tents and a cook and breakdown repair party. The next morning, Rushdi came to borrow my cook, the relief party not having returned. He told me what had happened and how their guests had gone straight to the engineers' quarters. Rushdi and Bashir had been moved out of their quarters in the Palace area to make more room for the Americans. Rushdi said that the Americans had no experience abroad. They only had the Philippines. Here in Arabia life was very different. There was more individual independence in America where everyone did what they liked, going their own way. In Arabia, family life was the basis and everyone always deferred to the head of a family.

The weather after rain was unsurpassable – brilliant sunshine, and the clearest air imaginable.

The Americans have said that they hope not to lunch here, intending to leave at noon for Dhahran. They only arrived after dark last night!

Abdulla Bilkhair, who accompanied the Emirs Faisal and Khalid to America and England, came to visit me and left copies of American and European papers and magazines for me.

My car, borrowed by Rushdi, was towed with a broken axle – the third axle, or part of one, to break on cars allotted to me in the last few days.

23 November

Ibn Saud sent for me at 3.30, night-time Arabic. He seemed dispirited. He sat pensively stroking his beard. The conversation was desultory.

When, making conversation, I told him I had been to see the

136

nursery gardens and had admired that of the Bokhari, a Russian Muslim, he said with emphasis: 'Yes. We don't care what people are as long as their personality is all right.'

Without much relevance to anything preceding it, he said, 'We don't want banks in which to lock up money. We want it in circulation.' This was a reference to the American proposition for a Reserve Bank.

Then he began, as if deliberately in order to distract himself, to speak of Arab things. He talked about the Arab traditions, of the strength and beauty of the bedouins, of the trackers – who have knowledge of their own which surpasses the belief of those who have not seen the results of their tracking. He did not touch upon politics, except that he asked about the new Minister of State. Could I describe him? When I said that he was a financial and economic expert, everyone perked up. I left him late in the night.

24 November

I left al Kharj for Riyadh while everyone else was at the midday prayers. Women and children were waiting on the side of the track for Ibn Saud to pass and for his largesse.

The *wadis* had been running – towards the Sahaba plain, 2,000 acres of which are to be irrigated by the new canal, to be finished in December. Seven hundred and fifty acres are irrigated at Baih and about the same number at Khafa Digori. The total acreage will be about 3,500, i.e. under pump irrigation in the al Kharj district, apart from the old oasis in the area – such as al Yamama, Salaimiya, Dilam al Muhammadi, Najan al Hayathim and so on.

We arrived at Riyadh at eight o'clock. Ibn Saud came in just afterwards. There was a double row of soldiers and a band outside the Palace. The soldiers presented arms quite smartly, the band played and a roll of drums was beaten. The men gave two shouts as his car passed between them. Rushdi came in after dinner to ask me about my journey from al Kharj. His car had broken down again and he had come in on a lorry. 'Better than being late,' he said.

25 November

I was woken early and taken to see the King walking back from prayers in the Great Mosque to the Old Palace, Qaar of al Imam Faisal, his grandfather's. It was the first day of the holiday. There was a great crowd. I was put in an upper room of the Palace with a good view over the square and up the main lane from the Mosque. Orphans were given a place of honour at the Palace gate.

Ibn Saud sent for me at nine fifteen. He talked mostly in general – about war news, the news from the Emir Faisal about the pilgrimage and so on.

Bashir came to dine and stayed to talk about Tripoli. He wants to help in the country's reconstruction, provided that it receives its 'rights' *(Haquq),* for which he fought the Italians there. He hails from Misurata. He does not want to go there until the military phase is ended or ending. He had written to the Saudi Minister in London to ask him to tell anyone influential in London about his desire to help when the time comes.

26 November

I spent part of the morning with Nafisi, one of the King's radio listeners – who deals with the Arabic broadcasts. He gave me the fullest details about their views on the various stations, its programmes and broadcasts. He said that London was easily the best Arabic broadcasting station.

He described someone laughingly turning on London and saying, 'Let us discover if Yusif Yassin has lunched yet or the Shaikh of Bahrain gone to sleep.' They thought some of the local news was too trivial for interest lately. Perhaps they are growing out of the 'parish magazine' stage simply because the B.B.C. has given them wider interests and the war has enlarged their vision.

Ibn Saud has three times in his talks mentioned Iskhaishbir, Captain Shakespear, a political officer who was with him at the beginning of the last war and before it and who was killed with his forces at the battle of Jarrab (1915) when Ibn Saud was fighting the Turkish-subsidized Beni Rashid princedom of north Arabia. When he mentioned his name he paused for a moment as if in recollection of him and what they had done together.

In spite of his 'piece' about disliking all foreigners, I believe that in his heart the truth is more nearly what he said in reference to the Bokhari – 'What counts with us is the individual, not the race.'

Last night we spoke of the dark days of the Second World War – when Singapore fell – when I was here and when the Germans came to al Alamain.

Bashir said to him, 'You remember how upset and worried you were,' and recalled what I said to them. 'We shall win in the end – time is on our side.' We all kept murmuring 'God be praised' at the recollection of what had been passed through.

27 November

I lunched with Emir Saud, the Emir Mishaal, a recently married younger son of the King, Faisal bin Saad his nephew, and Bashir al Hamzaghauth. The Emir said that last year his own son married his brother Faisal's daughter, no doubt an important match politically.

After luncheon all the other guests vanished. A grandson aged about three had come in and was introduced to me and then carried out by a soldier.

Saud said that he had something important to say to me. I was to repeat it to the highest minister or official I could see in London. It was this: he was certain that the interests of the kingdom lay with Great Britain, as certain as his father had always been. His father was now nearing definite old age but there would be no change in foreign policy here. He gave three instances of how he, the Emir Saud, had acted in the past which went to show that he was following that policy. He intended in the future to extend his close relations with Great Britain and make them even closer than they were now. He wished to emphasize that this was his policy and wanted to make absolutely sure of its being known in London. I was to make his views clearly known to the highest-placed person I could see in London and tell no one else.

Security in the country was excellent. Foreign affairs, because of their relations with England, were on a firm basis. Financial affairs caused anxiety. They had asked for an adviser. They urgently needed one. It was this side, the financial one, which worried him. He hoped that senior officials of the British Government would come to rely upon him. He wanted his character and way of thought and policy to be known to them and not obscured.

Just before luncheon, Bashir had called to stay a few minutes and walk with me to the Emir's Palace next door.

In the evening while I was out at the Emir Saud's swimming pool in the Wadi Fatima orchards, seven kilometres from Riyadh, I was sent for by Ibn Saud. When I joined him he said that he had had a busy day writing the letters which customarily go with returning distinguished pilgrims to the various princes of the Muslim world, to the Sultan of Morocco, to Tunis and so on.

Almost at once he dismissed everyone. Even the bodyguards, who were out of earshot in any case, were sent away. 'About the matter you have asked me about, have no fear,' he said, 'I am your agent here in the matter and all is agreed to. I have studied the matter. But,' he continued at once, 'I have a matter of great importance I wish to speak about with you upon whom I count as a friend. I should not broach it and it would be incorrect for you to raise it with me. But you are going to London, you are my friend and I cannot miss the opportunity. It is this matter of the change in the attitude of the British towards me. For the first time in my life they are different to me. Not only here but elsewhere. I hear it on all sides. Yusif tells me that it was so and that he had had it from a senior British official. They say, "The British regard for Ibn Saud is now different." Abdulla of Transjordan has taken courage at these stories and has been talking to his tribesmen about it. In Iraq they have the same tale. They even speak of soon being able to move their army into Arabia. It all started about six months or so ago. What is this? I must know. By God it is like a thrust here' – he clutched at himself as if in pain – 'I am very very disturbed. It is all because of the supplies? I spoke to the "Qaid" [General Paget] about it. They sent numbers of officials here to see what they could see, and some of them don't understand about the Arab peninsula and its life, and my word is not taken.

'Jordan the Minister comes to me and says this much is the amount ordered by my Government and I don't know if it is indeed the order of the Government. I know him. I knew him from twenty years ago and they sent him again.

'What am I to do? What can I do? You, as a friend, tell me.'

I said that I could only assure him that in London his reputation was high and that the part he had played both in the past and during the war was unforgettable there.

He seemed to be relieved at the simple statement. He said, 'I know where all this trouble comes from, then. It is Jedda. You are my friend and you are going to London. It is London that counts. See those there who love the truth, my friend. Forget not what I tell you and say it there.' He asked me to dine the following night, and I took the opportunity to ask leave to start for Jedda on the morning following that.

He was genuinely most strongly moved as he spoke. I have recorded his words as briefly as possible.

I felt very sorry for him, enmeshed in a net he had never dreamed existed and pulled down in his pride, as the end of his life came near.

His dinner to me was attended by the Emir Saud and some forty members of his family, and Bashir and Hamza.

140

Little Nowwaf, the pet son of Ibn Saud and of the Palace, aged about nine, was about and met me as I arrived and clung to me as I left, saying pertly, 'Shall I come to England with you?'

The King's last words to me were, 'Then I shall see you again?'

As I went down the road to Jedda the rain fell heavily behind us. The *wadis* were all in spate. We had passed only just in time.

Once when the cars were stopped for repairs near some tents, the bedouins came over to offer us warmed camel milk and sheep's milk. 'This is better than injections,' said Abdulla, the Emir of the party.

One of them, a youth of seventeen, ran back to his tent and came again with two riyals; holding them up, he said to the men, 'A headdress. I beg you sell me, even if old.' It was four times the peacetime price and eight times less than the present price. The men said that they had one to spare for him, as a gift. He was touchingly grateful.

A quite big boy – he might have been thirteen – was stark naked. The men were ragged. Their manners, dignity and hospitality were the same as when they were well dressed in peacetime.

This looks like being an unusually cold winter in Arabia and there will very likely be deaths due to insufficient clothing or, rather, owing to the price of clothing being too high for them to contemplate buying. On the other hand, owing to the price of their foodstuff requirements having risen less steeply then the price of camels, they will in the end be better off and the number of their herds (once the reduction owing to the deaths due to three bad winters is dissipated) will be greater in consequence of their having to sell fewer camels to obtain their requirements.

A day or two after my return to Jedda, the Emir Mansour, Minister for War and Inspector-General of the Army, telephoned from Mecca and asked me to meet him at Bahra, half way to Mecca. The British Minister asked me to tell him that he would like to see him – to discuss flying with him to Khartoum and seeing where men of the Army might be sent for training as mechanics.

We met as arranged, a car being sent from Mecca to fetch me. Mansour came to Bahra driving himself. He put me in his car and drove off behind a ridge – out of view of passing pilgrims and others on the road. A rug was spread. I told him the Minister's message.

He gave me a very polite reply – for him – but said that I was to make it quite clear that such communications had to be through the

Minister of Foreign Affairs. He could not see Jordan about it. He then said, 'I want to speak to you entirely privately. Tell no one about this. Do not tell Jordan or anyone here at all. I want to go to England as soon as it may be convenient. I want to see military things as much as may be possible. You arrange this, please, if possible from your end. My father and I are as one, you know. He would not have suggested this unless he knew it would, if suggested from London, be approved by Ibn Saud. He is Ibn Saud's favourite son, by a Caucasian woman, his favourite wife.' (When Ibn Saud told me he had made him Minister for War he smiled, as if he particularly liked doing so and he said that I should no doubt see him.) He said that the British Military Mission was much admired. They were energetic. They had brought much fine equipment. They got up at dawn, like the Arabs. The effect of such fine men showing such enthusiasm for their work had been excellent. On the whole, only poor men had gone into the Saudi Army in the past. In the last week alone he, Mansour, had received two hundred letters of application to join the Army. There had been brisk recruiting. He was going up to Taif to see things for himself this week. He was anxious to improve the Army, not to enlarge it much. It was the quality they wished to improve. I was not to forget that his message to me was quite secret. I was not to tell anyone in Jedda. He was very polite and pleasant.

During my stay in Jedda, Van der Meulen, the Dutch Minister, and Madame Van der Meulen gave a dinner which the American Minister, as he pushed me into the room before him, said was in my honour. The British Iraqi and Egyptian Ministers, Jordan and Mrs Eddy were present. As we left, Van der Meulen asked me if he could see me alone. I went next morning and he kept me for an hour and a half. Fairly soon after I arrived he began to talk about Ibn Saud's maintenance of his pro-British attitude. He said that he put it down to the officials we had had in the past, that once Ibn Saud had said this to him. He has said, whenever there is a crisis they send me a good man. He, Ibn Saud, had ticked them off on his fingers – mentioning such names as Cox, Colonel Grey at Kuwait, Shakespear and so on. Bullard was a good man. 'Now,' said Van der Meulen brightly – only a very slight questioning in his voice, 'it is you who do this work for England, is it not so?'

I said, 'Of course not. Nowadays it is always a matter for the British Minister for the time being.'

He said, 'Oh, no, it is not like that now.'

I changed the subject, but he came back to it to say how important he felt it to be.

Their Dutch interests, owing to the circumstances of war, were now largely in abeyance, but they would return. They, the Dutch, were a Muslim power and felt the importance of it very much. He asked me if I were returning to London, knowing that I did so plan!

Geier of the American Legation invited me for a picnic and dinner and was extremely nice. I had the impression that he was going out of his way to create a good impression, so that I should not think that they were 'difficult'.

Colonel Eddy gave me messages for some mutual friends in London and said that his party was for me; he apologized for it not being better. These were more than superficial politenesses. They went out of their way to ensure I carried away a good impression of them, and of course they succeeded. The Saudi Royal Family did the same. They, the British, the Arabs and the Dutch Minister, seemed to regard me as a messenger from the outer world who understood their particular difficulties, and they all in turn took me aside in confidence. I believe they felt better for thus relieving their minds. There was less talk of resignation or application for transfer. The British Minister himself seemed to me calmer, and this was noticed and mentioned by his staff.

A Visit to Republican Turkey, 1945

H.M.S. *Ajax* (Captain J.W. Cuthbert, R.N.) left Naples precisely at 6 p.m. on 12 September 1945.

During his tour through Europe, His Royal Highness the Regent of Iraq frequently expressed his delight and said how lucky he felt himself to be in having been able to travel that way. He and his party fully appreciated the difficulties involved and that, without the facilities offered him, such a tour would have been impossible.

He drove his own car every yard of the way from London to Naples and showed a lively interest in everything he saw. The kindness he everywhere received from British officers and men made a deep impression upon him, and he was unlikely to forget the three weeks he spent in Europe and in a British cruiser, just after the final Allied victory.

It was the first visit of an Arab ruler to Turkey since the break-up of the Ottoman Empire, and the first visit of a British warship to Istanbul since the beginning of the Second World War. The captain and officers of H.M.S. *Ajax* were in consequence particularly on their mettle, and the Arabs were unusually stirred. The Regent and the Pashas came on deck when they heard that Istanbul was in sight. They all knew it but had not been there for many years. Nuri Pasha had been at school there before the First World War, in the Harbiya (military) college. Daud al Haidari had also been educated there. The Regent's grandmother still lived there and his family for centuries had had some of its members living there in voluntary, or enforced, exile from Mecca. All the Arabs, like the Regent of middle age, spoke Turkish with complete ease, though without the latest turns of phrase introduced by the Mustafa Kemal modernists since the change of regime. Theirs was the more courtly speech of the Ottoman period.

They usually talked Arabic, only using Turkish as a court language for the conveying of secrets when servants were present. Now, however, Nuri broke into Turkish. He ran from one side of the ship to the other to see again the places he remembered from his boyhood. He pointed out this spot and that to Daud Pasha, recalling this and that memory from long ago, mentioning companions of his youth, several of them killed in wars. While the ship passed the old city and the guns began to fire a royal salute, he stood gripping the rail of the deck and I saw tears in his eyes.

When the A.D.C. to the President came abroad, he brought with him for approval the programme of the visit which included a dinner on the presidential yacht and a naval ball for the first night. 'Istanbul not sleep tonight,' said the A.D.C.

We were conducted to our quarters, the Regent to the Old Imperial Palace of Dolme Bagché and myself and Sinderson Pasha, the royal physician, to the Park Hotel. The Regent showed me round the palatial rooms and into his pink marble bathroom, once used by the Sultan Abdul Aziz. The banquet on the yacht was 'private', only for the party and those attached to it for the visit. The chairs for us were on one side of the table and at its ends, none against the other side of the table though there were empty seats ranged against the opposite wall of the salon. It was only at the end of the meal that it became clear what this portended. A number of musicians and singers filed into their places in front of us. The instruments were the old–fashioned, Arab and Turkish kind. It was a compliment and a pleasant surprise, intended in particular for Nuri Pasha who was known to be a lover of the old Arabic way of playing. We bore it for what seemed like many hours, nibbling sweetmeats and drinking *araq* in the intervals between songs. At long last the Pashas were more or less satisfied and the players more or less exhausted. 'Now,' the A.D.C. said brightly, 'we change into "smokings" for the naval ball.' It was already past midnight.

The visit to Istanbul was short and more or less informal, for the President was in the capital. The Regent took me with him to see his grandmother at Emirgaun. It was an enchanting, rather tumble-down house on the Bosphorus, north of the city. Fine Persian carpets, giant Bohemian-glass chandeliers and elaborate Italian fountains in alabaster gave the motif in the sitting-rooms. We were received in an upstairs room looking over the water through latticed windows. The old lady asked me if I smoked. I said that I did, expecting her to offer me a cigarette or to pray me to smoke my own. She replied, however, 'So do I – like a chimney,' called for her hubble-bubble and began at once. The Regent translated for me since she spoke Turkish of the old kind and had little or no Arabic. She was handsome, even in old age, and had a pleasing expression. It was not known exactly where or in which community she had been born, but she was from the Caucasus. I thought her a good example of her kind, one of the last of the harem-living women of old Turkey. She spoke intelligently of many things and places, and even now in her old age had a brightness in her look and a vivacity of mind that would outdo that of many of her contemporaries of equal standing in the surrounding Christian countries.

The Regent spoke to me of the matters he would mention to the President. He intended to ask for the surrender of one of the four generals who had taken a leading part in the 1941 revolt in Iraq against the regime of the Hashimite monarchy and the Allies. He spoke with rancour of the rebels and was quite determined to obtain the man for execution, his trial having already taken place *in absentia*. The President, I foresaw, might find it awkward to hand over a man who was living in exile in Turkey as if he were subject to an extradition agreement. Changing his mood, the Regent asked me if I thought that he could ask the President, when presents were mentioned, for an Angora cat. 'It would be embarrassing?' I asked why it would be so, surely the request was an easy one? Doubtless that is what the Regent intended me to ask him. 'You see, the President is deaf and has a discoloured eye too, like the cats.' I learnt from him for the first time that Angora cats are deaf and have one eye blue and one green.

In the end the Regent obtained both the cat and the man. The latter, however, caused him concern. The President felt unable to hand over the man officially, but he arranged that he was to be sent to the Syrian frontier 'where your friends the British can arrange to collect and it will be no business of ours what happens once he is beyond the frontier'.

The British security officers did arrange to board the train as it entered Syria, and the general was duly arrested. That evening, however, he asked his escort, a British sergeant of the security intelligence force unit, if he might go to the station lavatory. Once there he climbed very easily through its window. He had a ten-minute start, of which he made good use. The Regent was furious when he heard of it, and sent for me to the Palace in Baghdad to talk about it. 'How could they be so inefficient?' He took it very badly. The Embassy sent a forthright message on the urgent need to recapture the man. After forty-eight hours he was found hiding in a village some twenty miles off. This time he was more closely guarded and despatched to Baghdad, where he was quickly hanged. During the night before the dawn on which he was to be hanged he was taken to see the Regent, who told me afterwards how he had spoken to him. He let the man think he would be reprieved if he revealed all he knew about the events of 1941 and who exactly had taken the leading parts. 'It was most interesting,' said the Regent. 'I learnt a lot that we did not know before.' He spoke with vivacity about this long midnight interview with a man who would die at dawn by his own order. The hanging was in public at the gate of the Ministry of Defence, where the body swung for several days. General Renton, the Chief of the British Military Mission to Iraq, refused to go to this office until it had been taken down.

Some time later, the last of the four guilty generals was hanged. This time the Regent was a little more delicate in the matter. He told me how he had seen the man the evening before his execution. 'I sent my A.D.C. into the cell with a questionnaire and I listened behind the door to his replies,' he said with a chuckle. 'I could see through the hinged side of the door but he could not see me.'

The official receptions in Ankara went smoothly and were boring, as such affairs are. To some of them Sinderson Pasha and I were not bidden and we enjoyed the freedom. We had been in attendance and at official receptions and meals almost continuously since leaving London nearly a month earlier.

The last time I had been in Ankara was in the autumn of 1940 when I went in haste from Teheran to Turkey by car through Tabriz and past Mount Ararat and Erzeroum. The rains had just begun falling and it was with difficulty that I succeeded. Because of the need for passing as quickly as possible before the gullies became too full, and because the only stopping-places were little hovels overfull already with passengers and drivers halted by the rain, I had pressed on without stopping for meals or to sleep between Tabriz and Erzeroum. The two journeys were in strong contrast.

The Victory Parade in London, 1946

Baghdad 30 May 1946

The Prince returned to Baghdad from Egypt in the forenoon.

Shanaishil made a scene in the Palace this evening. I was sitting alone with the Prince Abdililah on the lawn at dusk when he came up, in his uniform of the bodyguard, very neat and clean, and interrupted us. He is black, with huge lips, six foot tall, and lusty looking.

The Prince asked him why he had come without taking leave to do so. The expression in his eyes was that of a faithful fawning spaniel.

'But just one word,' he said, holding up two fingers towards his lips, the back of his hand turned to the front, the gesture of affection and supplication. He had kissed the Prince's hand and tried to kiss mine when he came up to us. I withdrew mine hastily, as is considered becomingly modest, so that he was reduced to kissing his own fingers, as a sign that he would kiss mine if he could.

The Prince with propriety permitted his hand to be kissed. 'Take care to take leave before you come to me,' repeated the Prince to him.

'But, but,' he said, with his dog-like look and pleading air.

'Take leave, I say; go now.' The Prince's voice was rising.

He went. 'His name,' I said, 'was Gayeed Razooki, once upon a time. He used to be in my company many years ago, and he danced well when there was dancing at a holiday. He was the same then as now. I had never succeeded in disciplining him like the others; but his loyalty was unquestioned.'

He repeated my words as if savouring their exact significance: 'undisciplined, but loyal' – or 'disciplined but disloyal'. He gave a little shiver of disgust and called across the lawn for a servant to fetch the officer of the guard and told him to have Gayeed's request examined. The Prince praised my memory. He told me that he had sent for Arshad al Umari to form a Cabinet. We spoke of the Prince's journey to England – to be by air through Cairo and Naples.

31 May 1946
In the evening the Prince showed me his new Miles Messenger aeroplane. We all in turn flew in it. Its ability to land in some forty yards or less is admired.

We sat in the garden at the Qasr Rihab until it was quite dark, at about eight o'clock.

1 June 1946
I telephoned to the Prince to confirm that the Embassy and the Airways Corporation had been able to arrange for an aircraft to fetch him from Baghdad tomorrow. His own aeroplane is damaged (the propeller was hit by the luggage door) at Amman. He had intended to fly in his own aeroplane to Cairo, and continue the journey to London in a chartered Lodestar from the Airways Corporation. The Lodestar will, instead, take him the whole way.

2 June 1946
H.R.H. left in the Lodestar at 2.20 p.m. for Cairo – landing at Lydda for refuelling. He stayed in the Iraqi Legation. He was met by a representative from the Palace, the Egyptian Minister in Iraq, the Secretary-General of the Arab League, Abdur Rahman al Azzam, and many others.

Hugh Cruddas and I stayed with Peter Carter of the British Embassy in his flat, No. 13 Sharia Ibrahim al Nageb, opposite the Embassy. Patrick Kinross came to see me. Peter was as usual very hospitable. He told us that the Egyptian negotiations had broken down owing to the Egyptians refusing our minimum requirements: Lord Stansgate had therefore returned to London.

3 June 1946

We left Cairo (Heliopolis) for al Adem, Malta (where the acting Governor, Sir David Campbell and Sir Harold MacMichael came to receive the Regent), and Naples.

David Lloyd-Owen (Lieutenant-Colonel and Military Assistant to the Supreme Allied Commander) met us and conducted H.R.H. to the General's villa in Naples. He told us that, the elections having been held that day, we should go by a longer route than usual, to avoid the more thickly populated parts of Naples – in case there were any communists rioting.

The Lodestar is cruising at 175 miles, ground speed, per hour.

Party travelling with H.R.H.: Nuri Pasha al Said; Lieutenant-Colonel G. de Gaury; Jasam, Rais Awal of the Iraq R.A.F.; Halim, Rais and Abdul Qadir, Rais, A.D.C.s; and Captain Hugh Cruddas, M.C. (British Military Mission to the Iraqi Army).

4 June 1946

Left Naples at 10 a.m. for Marseilles and London, lunching at Marseilles. We were met, rather to our astonishment, by Shakir al Wadi, the Iraqi Chargé d'Affaires, who had come to Marseilles to meet the King. The yacht had come in earlier than expected and was in the harbour from yesterday.

The party will land this evening. Shakir lunched with us and told us about the arrangements made for the family. The house taken is Grove Lodge, Windsor. They will stay for five days at Claridges. H.R.H. has already told me that the Queen will be unable to lunch at the Palace on the day of the victory march if publicity is given to her presence. He asked me to remind him that she will also be unable to be with the Queen of England during the march-past, as publicity would certainly be made of her presence with the Queen of England, of whom there will of course be photographs taken.

Shakir seems to have been very lucky over the house. It was only at almost the last moment that he heard of this house from an agent in Windsor.

The Prince was met on arrival at Northolt Aerodrome by the Earl of Clarendon, Lord Chamberlain, by Marcus Cheke, Vice Marshal of the Diplomatic Corps, representing the Secretary of State for Foreign Affairs, and Sir Eric Crankshaw, Government Hospitality Fund. He inspected an R.A.F. guard of honour. There was a rather thick drizzle, typical of London weather, but not expected in June.

It has been unusually wet in the last few days in England.

We went to Claridges Hotel. Robert Heber Percy happened to be on the doorstep, and Hughie Cruddas and I slipped away and drank some champagne with him as soon as we had seen the luggage safely sorted out. The same New Scotland Yard detective, Mr Howarth, who was with the Regent last year, reported for duty with him.

5 June 1946

Hughie and I had occupied the suite reserved for the Queen (Ali). I moved to the Travellers Club, although the Regent had hospitably invited me to stay on at Claridges. The party spent the day quietly, walking a little in the neighbourhood of the hotel.

6 June 1946

The ladies shopped, going to the Queen's dressmaker, Hartnell, in the afternoon.

The King went to Selfridges.

7 June 1946

I went with the Prince to see Grove Lodge, the house taken for the summer. The boy King came with us. He had a 'streaming' cold, which stopped suddenly while we were at the house.

Hugh and I went to join the Regent after dinner at Claridges.

8 June 1946

The Regent and the King went to the saluting-base where they were present in the royal stand with the King of England and the Royal family of England for the victory march-past. The Queen, the Iraqi Queen Mother and the princesses were in the seats opposite the stand. The young King conversed with the Princess Alexandra, and counted stretcher cases with glee.

The Regent, the King and the Iraqi Queen Mother lunched at Buckingham Palace, the King interpreting for his mother. He was considerably elated on his return. (The ladies were wearing hats for the first time in their lives.)

In the evening, Hughie and I dined at Claridges with the ladies in the main dining-room – the first time they had ever dined with men not of their own family (except for Dr Sinderson, their physician, and Julian Pitt Rivers, the King's tutor, who had dined on the yacht coming to England with them). It was certainly the first time they had ever dined *in public* with men not of their family. They speak excellent English.

After dinner, the Regent and Hughie and I, with the detective, walked to the Horse Guards Parade and back via the front of Buckingham Palace, through the crowds, to see the illuminations and fireworks. On the way we met Patrick Telfer Smollett in Piccadilly. The crowds down the middle of the Mall were of course very great and we had linked arms, Hughie and I and the Regent, to avoid being separated. Others were doing the same; soldiers, sailors, airmen and civilians. Everyone, naturally, was in great good humour. It was in the middle of this scene of democratic elation and opposite a long crescent of sailors, halted by her stopping in front of them, that we suddenly came face to face with Charlotte Bonham-Carter, curtseying to the ground before the Regent.

The English physician attending the King and the Regent of Iraq told me that he had been asked to visit Grove Lodge because the boy King's asthma was worse and troubling him more than usual. It was a summer day and the front door was open into the long hall at the end of which he could see the garden. There was no one in sight. He rang the bell and there was no answer. He waited and rang again. Then he saw a figure, a female by the dress, but it was bent double, bottom towards him, head invisible near the ground. He gave a little warning cough. He knew that Arab women of the more conservative kind hide their faces from men, yet this way of doing so, and in England, appeared exaggeratedly thorough. Then the figure turned and straightened up. It was Miss Borland, the former nurse of the King temporarily brought out of retirement to help as a member of the household while in England. Without smiling she said, 'I am looking for His Majesty's caterpillar which he has somehow mislaid.'

A Spanish Feather, 1950

Among the books I took to Spain was *Italy, Spain and Portugal, with an excursion to the monasteries – by the author of Vathek*, who was William Beckford. That the writer of that well-known eighteenth-century fantasy saw the world with a romantic eye was certain, but I assumed that in a travel book the bones of fact would be there. It was when I came to the Escurial monastery-palace that I began to doubt if even they were there.

Like Beckford, I was to be shown round by the Reverend Prior of the Royal Monastery and Library in person, and I was glad to wait in his cool anteroom, for it was midday in early July and blazingly hot outside. It was pleasant to be able to relax somewhat, to the drone of voices discussing monastery accounts in the room next door. Through the window far away across a great square, the palace courtyard, the figures of pilgrims, guardians and tourists with their guides were dwarfed by the gigantic, mud-grey walls to the tiny size of people in Italian architectural pictures, reduced in scale by the artists to make their buildings look larger and more imposing. Here the relative size was real and truth seemed put at fault.

Nearby, at the side of the door into the court, a heap of twisted grey objects, piled one upon another and loathsome in their arrested writhing: lead from the roof then under repair, it was said; but in the drowsing afternoon heat taking on some other and disturbing significance like the pictures by King Philip's painter hanging on the Palace walls, where men turn into animals or large sea-shells, and realistic painting by a nightmare imagination is woven into a biblical setting.

Without warning there stood at my side a thin figure in black, skirted and belted, the bespectacled headman, hair cropped almost to the skull and tonsured to the skin, the nose unusually long and straight, the eyes kindly and shrewd, his only decoration a cross on a thin chain. It was the Prior, and a good deal younger than we had anticipated, being, as he told me later, only forty-one years old. He listened attentively to my requests and at once waved us to follow him. I wanted to see first the crucifix by Benvenuto Cellini which, it seems, is not usually shown to visitors; this meant climbing high up above the monastery church, beyond the west end of the gallery, where it hangs behind closed shutters that are opened to reveal it to the congregation sixty feet below, often the regiments of the royal guards or troops leaving on active service. The visitor who may see it therefore does so at very close quarters from, as it were, inside its case.

It is of unsurpassable beauty. I judge it to be a trifle larger than life size for, standing below it with one's head just below the level of the feet, it appears to be only just life size. The head is seemingly of a slightly whiter marble of different texture from that of the body. The arms have at some time been broken near the shoulders – it is said now by Napoleon's soldiers – but the cracks would not be visible from a short distance away. Round the thigh was hung a thin silk veil with a gold-embroidered edge, an ill-conceived substitute for the coarse, twisted linen loin-cloth that Cellini must have intended should be there, if anything at all, for he made the Christ entirely naked. I left with regret the contemplation of this splendid work which Beckford leaves one to suppose is located and facing the choir and which he says is of ivory.★

And now the Prior began to lead us through innumerable galleries and stone corridors and up and down flights of steps, every now and then pausing to unlock a great iron grille, heavy to open and more difficult to close, until at last we came to about where

★See *Naseita e Vicende del 'Mio bel Cristo'* by Piero Calamandrel (La Nuova Italia, Florence, 1950), which has illustrations showing the Christ as made by Benvenuto Cellini in 1562.

(although he is particularly vague at this point in his narrative) Beckford saw what I also wanted to see: a feather from the wing of the Archangel Gabriel.

And when I asked the Prior about it he stopped and, looking directly at me and placing his hand for a moment to his cross, said, 'Many strange tales have been written and invented about this monastery'; going forward again with a quick step, he spoke no more of it. This is what Beckford recorded:

The Prior, who is not easily pleased, seemed to have suspicions that the seriousness of my demeanour was not entirely orthodox; I even heard him say – 'Shall I show him the Angel's feather? You know that we do not display this most-valued, incomparable relic to everybody, nor unless upon special occasions.' 'The occasion is sufficiently special,' answered my partial friend, 'the letters I brought to you are your warrant, and I beseech your reverence to let us look at this gift of Heaven, which I am extremely anxious myself to adore and venerate.'

Forth stalked the Prior and drawing out from a remarkably large cabinet an equally capacious sliding shelf – the source, I conjectured, of the potent odour I complained of – displayed, lying stretched out upon a quilted silken mattress, the most glorious specimen of plumage ever beheld in terrestrial regions – a feather from the wing of the Archangel Gabriel, full three feet long, and of a blushing hue more soft and delicate than that of the loveliest rose. I longed to ask at what precise moment this treasure beyond price had been dropped – whether from the air on open ground, or within the walls of the humble tenement at Nazareth; but I repressed all questions of an indiscreet tendency – the why and wherefore, when and how –. We all knelt in silence, and when we rose up, after the holy feather had again been deposited in its perfumed lurking place, I fancied the Prior looked doubly suspicious, and uttered a sort of humph very doggedly; nor did his ill-humour evaporate upon my desiring to be shown the library.

Beckford's Prior excused himself from conducting him to the library, but our Prior took us there, passing on the way through the main rooms of the Palace where he displayed a particular knowledge of the pictures and tapestries, and showed us the more remarkable of the twelve thousand manuscripts in his keeping.

But that feather was still in my mind. As I looked up from one superb illumination or another, from this or that codex, written before the tenth century, I thought of it again. The Prior had not denied its existence. Was it possible that because of its unusual sanctity, or perhaps a doubt about its authenticity which indeed there must be, it was not now shown to any except the brothers of the monastery? Later I learnt that Boccaccio tells the tale of the Archangel's feather being left behind after the Annunciation, but had I known of it then I should have hesitated to mention such an authority to the Reverend Prior.

I left that man of learning and of charm, the Prior, undisturbed by further questioning on the point, grateful to him for showing me the treasures of that palace-monastery; coming out into the evening sunlight, I was met by one of the guardians, an old soldier with a leg missing who came forward on his crutch at a lurching run, cap in hand, to escort me to the outer gate. He surely must know all the gossip of the place, its old tales, true and untrue. But he only shook his head and answered in the lisping Castilian tongue that the monks were often mighty close and prone to resent inquiry about certain ceremonies to which none but they are admitted.

Rosita Forbes and a Ball Long Ago

The British Ambassador to Turkey explained that it was a private dinner. The only other guest was the traveller and author, Rosita Forbes.

I was sitting with the Ambassador in his huge, softly lit drawing-room before dinner when its door was opened at the far end to admit a young woman in a light-coloured long dress swathed in tulle. Although told to expect her, it took a few moments to understand that this was indeed Rosita Forbes, the already hardened traveller, and not some young unknown girl. Her youthfulness and appealing simplicity were remarkable.

She did, however, mention later her next travel project and spoke enthusiastically of the island she and her husband had bought in the West Indies. We, too, should buy land thereabouts. It was a wonderful opportunity.

Admiring the great room in which we sat again after dinner, the Ambassador told us that it was in it that the guests had danced at the Victory Ball given by Lord Stratford de Redcliffe, in the presence of the Sultan himself, at the end of the Crimean War. It was an historic night. It had been mentioned here and there, in letters or diaries, in the press of the time. He suggested that I might see what I could find and write an account. Rosita supposed that the dances must have mostly been waltzes and polkas. In the low-lit room it was not hard to conjure up the ghosts of those whirling figures, of young officers recently escaped from death in the campaign, of the girls in their arms, of the old Ambassador, Lord Stratford, and the Sultan watching them. If it were not for rugs and tables in the way, I would have invited Rosita to take a step or two so that we could remember we had danced where they had done a century ago.

The ball was held, I found, on Thursday 31 January 1856. Letters said that even on the afternoon before the ball there was a stir of an unusual kind in Pera, the centre of European Constantinople and seat of the Christian embassies. It was noticed that the people were more inclined to loiter and were more curious than usual. The Greek inhabitants were conversing in groups; numbers of troops were moving about, trays of bouquets were being rapidly carried hither and thither; and sedan chairs were evidently in great demand, no doubt for the paying of frantic last-minute visits to late milliners or to dawdling dressmakers. Mounted Turkish Pashas, looking graver and more important than ever, forced their way along with their trains of *kavasses* and pipe-bearers, only just betraying the slightest possible touch of the flurry with which the whole city was already affected. Lord Stratford de Redcliffe, the British Ambassador, alone seemed undisturbed by the preparations going on about him, writing that afternoon four despatches to the Foreign Secretary in London, one of them a lengthy letter on the state of his Turkish Reform Bill negotiations.

As the ladies invited to the ball were finishing their dressing, sending down their sables to the sedans, and their gentlemen were pulling on their jack boots for the ride to the Embassy and the splash through the mud near its gates, the lighting of signal fires and the firing of cannon at Galata Serai announced the Sultan's departure from his Palace of Chiragan, and that the imperial caique was already on its way over the hurrying waters of the Bosphorus.

The long and ill-managed war against Russia was coming to a close. From the moment of the successful assault on the fortress of Sebastopol the previous September (though only the southern face had been taken) the Russians were disheartened. The French, who had provided the largest number of men for most of the early part of the campaign, at once promoted their new general in command to be a Marshal and began to celebrate peace.

In January, plenipotentiaries were summoned to Paris and, by the 18th, Lord Clarendon, the British Foreign Secretary, was writing to Lord Stratford de Redcliffe, 'I suppose that we must now consider ourselves to be on the eve of peace, as Russia has knocked under.' Whatever the misgivings of the British statesmen who were disposed to continue the campaign in order to make sure of lasting peace, it was a matter for great rejoicing. The war with Russia was won.

In Constantinople the Ambassador had a reason of his own for feeling gratified. The Great Elchi, as the leading ambassadors there used to be called, had long had at heart the strengthening of Turkey, till then medieval in its rule, and the Sultan and his ministers had recently agreed to issue a great charter of reform. By January, whatever might hinder the execution of its terms, the Ambassador knew that it would soon be law; and a triumph of the armies on the Crimean peninsula coincided with a personal victory of the Great Elchi.

Sociable relaxation followed the better news from the seat of war and on Christmas Eve there had been a dinner party at the Embassy. It was attended by, among others, Admiral Sir Houston Stewart, second-in-command of the Black Sea Fleet, and by Miss Nightingale; and the midshipmen 'in their old-fashioned coatees and gilt buttons' had come in afterwards. Most of the midshipmen had already commanded men under fire and some of them were scarred by wounds; nevertheless they had at first been a little awed by their surroundings until games had been started by the Admiral. Then the new ballroom had been thrown open for the first time and other Christmas games played, ending with snapdragon. Miss Nightingale, still very weak, had sat on a sofa and laughed until the tears came into her eyes, as the middies, wild with delight, showed a marvellous and unabashed capacity for eating fiery plums.

On New Year's Eve, the Ambassadress had given a dance attended by a splendid gathering of English, French and Sardinian officers, with plenty of stars and orders, and Armenian ladies of the capital literally covered with diamonds, 'who sat and glistened and were remarkable for nothing else', and by the diplomats and their wives, so that it was reported as a brilliant affair, though nothing compared with what was to come.

Lord Clarendon's letter from Paris had arrived in the last week of the month, and it was perhaps the success of his Christmas and New Year parties that inclined the Ambassador to decide upon giving a grand fancy-dress dance. His Excellency had, a day or two earlier, brought to an end a disagreement with Mehemet Ali Pasha, the

Grand Wezir and the Sultan's brother-in-law, and he would ask him and invite the Sultan too. It would be a public proof of the Sultan's wish to modernize the empire if he did accept, for no Turkish sovereign had ever before visited a foreign embassy. Stratford de Redcliffe sought an audience in order to persuade the Sultan to attend and, short though the notice was, His Imperial Majesty agreed to be present at a ball in the Embassy on 31 January.

The British Embassy at Constantinople, built to replace an older one destroyed in one of the numerous fires to which the city of wooden houses had been subject, was still new. It is of white stone, with slated roof, and resembles the Travellers and the Reform Clubs in London designed by Sir Charles Barry, from which it was copied. 'It is wholly fitted up internally,' says an account in 1847, 'with mahogany and papier mâché'; papier mâché then being the mode and only patented for internal and architectural decoration eighteen months earlier. It stands on the crest of the high saddle hill between the narrows of the Bosphorus and the inlet of the Golden Horn, both of which, laden with shipping, are far below, for the hill slopes steeply, almost precipitously, on either side to the very edge of the waters. Opposite, on the Asian shore, is Scutari, where in 1856 lay many wounded and sick men from the Crimea in temporary hospitals. Across the Golden Horn sprawls the great capital itself, ringed with triple walls and defensive moats, dotted with domes of mosques and baths, and by slender minarets, capped at its seaward point by the imperial seraglio, a rambling Ottoman camp in stone, that covers old Byzance. Before office blocks and apartment-houses had half concealed the view, as they do today, the city lay fully open and by the nature of the ground seemed tilted forward, as in old prints of medieval towns, perspective awry, to display itself the better.

On the night of the ball the crowd of carriages and sedan chairs, linkmen and lantern-bearers in the streets leading up to the Embassy and the press of Greeks and *kavasses* at the gates was so great that latecomers could hardly make their way through them. The whole Palace was brilliantly illuminated and on the stairs Mr Doria, one of the attachés who had been entrusted with the outside illuminations, was finishing his inspection of the wreaths of lights and transparencies that, owing to blasts of high wind, were only partially successful. Across the courtyard, hanging as it were on air, the Sultan was to be greeted by the words 'Abdul-Majid' and 'Victoria'.

Two companies of Grenadiers and Highlanders, with the band of the 1st German Legion at their head, formed the guard-of-honour.

The Sultan, with very good taste, left his own guards at the Galata Serai, from where he was escorted by a mounted guard-of-honour of officers of all arms, and a squadron of the 12th Lancers, every other man carrying a torch. The way up from Galata Serai is tortuous, climbing between white- and blue-painted, vine-clad houses, and the Christian populace that seldom saw their Muslim sovereign packed the balconies and narrow streets. The dark route, only illuminated from windows and by lantern-bearers, was lined and secured by pickets of the Turkish army, who shouted with customary raucous enthusiasm, 'Greater than thou is God, Oh Commander of the Faithful,' as the royal procession passed. The dark-blue and gold uniform of the 12th Lancers, with scarlet breast-facings and swan-feather plumes hanging from their caps, looked doubly well in the bobbing light of bitumen torches.

As the Grand Signior's carriage passed through the small Maidan, or ancient tiltyard, near the Embassy and the Lancers clashed up to the gates, the band of the German Legion played the 'Sultan's March' and 'God Save the Queen'. Lord Stratford and his staff, of course, met him at the door, and as he alighted a communication was made 'by galvanic wires' to the ships of the British Fleet, at anchor far below in the Bosphorus, which saluted his arrival with prolonged salvos of cannon.

Dismounted men of the Lancers, specially picked, lined the grand marble staircase, at the head of which he was met by Lady Stratford and her daughters.

His Majesty retired for a time to one of the smaller drawing-rooms to repose a little after his jolting over the uneven streets of his capital and in accordance with the courtly fashion for royalty to have a special apartment and be treated as the owner of the house, rather than as a guest, on such occasions.

Every one of the eight hundred guests agreed that the scene on entering the ballroom was the most splendid and beautiful that it was possible to imagine. The room itself was newly decorated, in white picked out with gold, its chandeliers immense and very fine, a little too large if anything but, with every candle alight, neverthe-less superb; and wreaths of greenery placed here and there relieved the white of the walls. Lady Stratford, standing in the middle of the room, surrounded by and receiving a brilliant throng, was in a dress

162

of the early part of the reign of George III, her tiara of diamonds, her powder and pink roses becoming her very well. Her daughters were somewhat artlessly dressed compared with their mama; Miss Canning sporting the flowing white robes of a druidess, with an oakleaf crown, and Miss Charlotte Canning, not yet twenty, being Mary, Queen of Scots.* Mr Odo Russell, the first attaché, was his ancestor, Lord William Russell: his dress was black velvet, a white plumed hat fastened with brilliants, a point lace collar and below that a splendid necklace-collar of diamonds. Mr Doria was an exquisite of Queen Anne's time in a purple velvet coat lined with figured satin, diamond shoe-buckles, gold snuff-box and 'everything perfect from patch to bow'. The Princess Gregorie Sturdza of Moldavia, one of the most beautiful women in Europe, was in snowy and revealing white muslin, as a lady of the time of the First Consul, with a low crown of regally large diamonds.

The elderly ladies in general wore eighteenth-century costumes, while among the younger ones 'those who had pretty feet' wore the short, picturesque dresses of Spanish, Swiss or Italian shepherdesses, as Colonel Ebor, *The Times* correspondent, rather tartly reported. He himself arrived in the forbidding costume of an Agha or officer of the janissaries, complete with an immense Roman headdress of plumes, and in consequence had to take care to keep out of the Sultan's way, that mutinous corps having been cut to pieces and disbanded only thirty years earlier by the Sultan's father. Beside the English, French and Sardinian officers, the people of the country had appeared in their own national dresses. The Greek Patriarch, the Armenian Archbishop and the Jewish Grand Rabbi were in their robes of state. Persians, Albanians, Kurds, Serbians, Armenians, Greeks, Turks, Austrians, Sardinians, Italians and Spaniards were there in their different dresses and many wore jewelled arms, the Greek *yataghans* and pistols being the most remarkable.

Baron von Prokesch Osten, the Austrian Minister, wore the sky-blue uniform of an Austrian general officer. The Prussian Minister wore a white uniform of the same grade with elk-skin breeches and patent-leather riding boots. Monsieur Thouvenel, the French Ambassador, in his gold-laced uniform of blue carried the

*Lord Stratford's son, long an invalid, died without heirs, and the two Miss Cannings died unmarried, Mary in 1905 and Louisa Charlotte in 1908. His brother Charles, an A.D.C. to Wellington, was killed at Waterloo.

Grand Cross of the Saviour of Greece and the Iron Cross of Austria. The Sardinian Minister, who had been due to sail en route for Turin the same morning, was delayed by the wind being strong from the south; and the British Ambassador, with whom his relations were particularly cordial, had been able to persuade him to stay for the ball. Lord Stratford himself was in his Ambassador's uniform, carrying only the star and insignia of the Grand Cross of the Bath.

Among the English officers were Lord George Paget, Lord Dunkellin, and officers of the Grenadiers and Highlanders, of the 12th Lancers and the 13th Light Dragoons; the smarter the regiment the closer fitting the uniforms, the foot wearing stove-pipe trousers wide enough for comfortable marching, their scarlet tunics looser than the coats of the cavalry. Foot guards were noticeably few, most of them having been called home in the previous year for duty during the visit to London of the Emperor and Empress of the French.

There was every kind of fancy costume to be seen: fakirs and pilgrims, knights in real mail, dervishes, Roman emperors, Pan and various Greek gods, a Negro in a leopard skin and feathers, and two devils who later waltzed with their long forked tails twined gracefully over their arms. The flash of diamonds, especially among the Armenians, Jews and Greeks, was quite astounding.

The bewhiskered and macassar-oiled officers from the Crimea, pausing in the doorway, could hardly believe their eyes, so far was all this elegance and beauty and richness from the discomforts of the camps on the peninsula to which they had become used for so long. Not one of them, it was said afterwards, omitted to declare love to someone before the night was over.

There was only time for half the brilliance of the scene to be taken in before it was whispered that the Sultan was coming.

Everyone made way as Abdul-Majid walked up the ballroom with Lord and Lady Stratford, their daughters and a gorgeous array of Pashas in the rear. He paused with evident delight and pleasure at the scene before him then, bowing on both sides, went on. A velvet and gold chair had been placed for him in the middle of one side of the room, but on being conducted to it he seemed too much pleased to sit down and continued standing, looking about him with undisguised pleasure. He was dressed in a plain, dark blue frock-coat, the cuffs and collar crimson velvet, wearing stars of brilliants. The hilt of his sword was entirely covered with very large diamonds and his headdress was a red fez with a long curving aigrette fastened to it by a giant sapphire surrounded by diamonds. In repose he had ordinarily a languid, careworn air but, whenever spoken to on this night, his eyes brightened and his smile was frank and winning. He was thirty-three years old, had been Sultan since he was sixteen and had inherited from his father a desire for modernizing, in which so far he had mainly confined himself to building a baroque palace at fabulous expense and making changes in military uniforms.

The Pashas accompanying him, in spite of their splendour and high rank of many tails, nearly all of them of nine, showed themselves to be singularly *farouche,* forcing themselves violently in a double row on the Sultan's right hand and pushing everyone right and left – 'like policemen when the Queen is dining in the City', as a young officer remarked. Ladies' dresses were caught in Pashas' swords, until disentangled by their escorts, but in spite of this *gaucherie* of the Pashas on the Sultan's right, everyone agreed that the general scene was not equalled, even by the Queen's *bals costumés* in England.

The heads of the diplomatic missions and their ladies were next presented in turn to His Majesty. The Sultan was kind enough to ask the French Ambassador if he were not thinking of giving a ball, and when the Ambassador agreed that he wished to do so he tactfully expressed his wish to be present.

The orchestra of the Italian theatre was stationed in the gallery of the ballroom and, following the presentation of the diplomatic corps, the dance was opened with a quadrille which the Sultan watched with great interest. The quadrille was followed by waltzes which he seemed to enjoy even more. The Pashas, being used to dances by girls in the privacy of a harem or by boys in public, were quite put out of countenance by the Christian custom of both sexes and any age taking the floor. Habituated as they were to dancing of a more erotic kind, the less supple abandon of Europeans, in couples, deeply stirred their sense of humour; that the Europeans were persons high in rank astounded them even more.

His Majesty then walked through the rooms adjoining the ballroom to the refreshment room where he ate an ice with perfect composure. His eating of an ice in semi-public was a diplomatic entry to the credit of Lord Stratford and an astonishing departure for a Sovereign whose every act had hitherto been so jealously guarded from other eyes that nobody except his chief eunuch was allowed to attend his meals. In his despatch to the Foreign Secretary the following day, the Ambassador took care to record that the Sultan had taken light refreshment, although few now turning the pages of that old letter book in which the copies of his despatches are preserved would notice from the laconic lines their portent.

The Sultan retired to his special apartment for a time. He had intended returning to the ballroom, but found the heat too great and instead sent for Lord Stratford to come and converse with him. He took the opportunity of asking him to convey his sentiment of cordial affection to Her Majesty the Queen and said that he wished Lord Stratford to stay as Ambassador to him for as long as possible; then taking him by the hand he walked down with him to the carriage door, not forgetting to pause frequently and mention his particular admiration of the picked men of the Lancers who lined the staircase, one on every step, nor of the Highlanders or the men of the 13th Light Dragoons and the picket of the Royals who presented arms to him in the gateway, nearly all of them, though youthful, wearing the Balaclava clasp.

The Sultan drove away, as he had come, with an escort of cavalry, to the pavilion of his brother-in-law, Ahmed Fethi Pasha, where, not wishing to re-cross the Bosphorus, he spent the remainder of the night.

Mehemet Ali Pasha, Ali Pasha the Grand Wezir and the young Turkish Beys all remained at the ball. Despite their religious laws, the Pashas were soon seen to be drinking champagne and brandy and taking every kind of refreshment without inquiry as to its nature. 'The reform is already working apace,' said one of the younger diplomats.

Following the Sultan's departure, the dancing continued with even greater speed and spirit. The attachés had been anxiously inspecting the programme of dances before the ball and had contrived to introduce their favourite waltzes from Paris and Vienna, of Offenbach, Lanner and Strauss. These, and in particular Lanner's 'Schönbrunner', were now called for and played over again. The musicians in the gallery above the ballroom found the heat, rising from hundreds of candles and from the great number of dancers, almost insupportable; the air was rendered yet more heavy by oriental perfumes so that they were obliged to strip off their coats, waistcoats and cravats and loosen their frilled shirts. Between dances they were seen mopping their heads and taking large draughts of sherbet, but they played with ever greater verve.

Sometimes the dancers waltzed out into the corridors and down the galleries 'which seemed to please the Grenadiers and High-landers stationed there excessively'. 'The groups in the drawing-rooms were most striking; and splendid knots promenaded the galleries,' says the writer of a letter home to England, penned next day. That prim phrase seems to describe that moment which comes at most balls when the ballroom detains only those who really wish to dance, when the elders are leaving or have left, while others, younger, stay to sit out or to move swiftly, in laughing groups, from one room to another.

Shortly after the conduct of the Pashas in the refreshment rooms had been noticed, the presence of a Muslim lady caused another and greater sensation. She was first seen walking through the ballroom on the arm of General Mansfield, Military Adviser to the Embassy, veiled and wrapped in a grey, Turkish cloak, and appeared to be delighted at her novel surroundings. Many thought that some Pasha, or even the Sultan himself, had permitted a fair prisoner of his harem to view for the first time an infidel festival, especially as all her remarks were made in the true Turkish tongue. As the evening wore on, however, the lady's timidity wore off, and at last she began to behave with excessive levity, walking up to English officers and examining their stars and orders, and looking up into their faces in the most bold and impudent manner. Then a spirit of mischief and fun seemed to possess this lovely creature and she had something sarcastic to say to every Pasha who came within her range: 'Ah! you see we are coming out now. No more cages for us. We are going to see the world and judge for ourselves, and love whom we like. What fine tall fellows these English are, how well formed the Highlanders! I dare say they would be very fond of me, not shutting me up with a foolish rag over my face as you do!' There was a great deal of tittering among the officers and soldiers as the Turkish lady's sayings to the Pashas got translated. She followed Mehemet Ali Pasha about, saying the most cutting and witty things until the handsome Lord High Admiral hardly knew what to make of it; nor were the rest of His Turkish Majesty's ministers spared. It was most cleverly done; the walk and every movement and gesture of a Turkish woman, perfect. At last however Fuad Pasha dis-covered in the beautiful girl the Honourable Percy Smythe, one of the Embassy's unpaid attachés who spoke Turkish and had thus been able to beard the Pashas successfully.

Within a few months, this talented young man succeeded his brother, Lord Strangford, who has secured a small place in history as the last man to fight a duel in England. The new peer took a house in London and was promoted to paid attaché, but soon afterwards gave up his house, resigned from the Foreign Service, and returned to live for two years in Constantinople as a dervish. He had taught himself Persian at Harrow and at Oxford learnt Arabic, matriculating from Merton College at seventeen, and after retirement was long accepted as speaking with particular authority on Near Eastern affairs, being at the time of his death President of the Royal Asiatic Society.

Among eight hundred guests it was not until late in the night, when the ballroom was less full, that some individuals were noticed. It was only then that the chief eunuch was more and more in evidence, strolling through the main galleries, examining everything and everyone with close attention. He was a huge black Negro and 'hideous to a degree positively revolting', but the second man in the kingdom, without whom the Sultan hardly dared go anywhere. He walked about, leaning on the arm of a Negro but little less frightful than himself, their long swords clattering as they went. It was whispered among the European ladies that this creature stalked about the seraglio with a leather thong in his hand ready to strike any rebellious girl who might offend him. The more credulous of the young ladies believed the tales of their escorts that he was even now looking for recruits for the imperial harem; the panache and fierce appearance of his Negro suite lent colour to a story that made its tellers seem doubly chivalrous and trustworthy.

About midnight it was rumoured that Monsieur Soyer was coming with a bear. Accordingly, a little after twelve o'clock a door in the upper end of the ballroom opened and Soyer in a most effective oriental costume appeared leading a monstrous brown bear by a chain. Two Greek ladies screamed; but curiosity overcame most of the guests, and Soyer and his bear were soon being squeezed by the splendid mob. The bear's nose, of too bright carmine, gave him away and soon the Persian princess was persuaded that she need no longer stand upon an ottoman and the Circassian girls that they need not tremble any more, the bear being none other than a friend of the distinguished Monsieur Soyer. The two were escorted from the ballroom by a party of the younger men, Negro kings, devils and pagan gods performing about them a diabolic dance and jumpings. Monsieur Soyer, cook of the Reform Club, an exuberant Frenchman, had not long before invited Lord and Lady Stratford to dine with him at a meal entirely made up of army rations, to show what could be done with them when properly prepared and cooked. He had paid his own passage to the Crimea with that of his companion, 'a gentleman of colour', in order to improve the cooking arrangements of the army. His labours and the climate in the Crimea had undermined his health, however, and he died less than two years later in London.

Lord Stratford left the ball at half past midnight, first walking slowly through the galleries and downstairs, talking to many on his way, returning to the saloons through rooms where the soldiers were supping. It had begun to snow and those person remaining outside, link-bearers, *kavasses* and attendants of the guests, were accommodated inside the Embassy by his instructions.

He must have reflected as he went that it was in all probability the last ball in an embassy that he would give. He was sixty-eight and soon would resign from public service. The ball indeed coincided with the zenith of his career, although he lived on in retirement until he was ninety-three. He remembered another ball of long ago, one of the first grand balls he ever attended, that he described in a letter to his mother as the 'most delightful sight I ever saw', the ball given by Sir Charles Stewart in Paris during the occupation by the Allies, at which the Emperor of Russia had been present and where he had seen Wellington meeting his old comrades-in-arms, Blucher, Platov, Wrede and others. There used, too, to be wonderful dances during the Congress of Vienna. Lord Castlereagh had sent for him, to the Congress, and he had talked with all the great figures there, had been present at the tournament or 'carrousel' in the Imperial Riding School and at the grand supper afterwards in the Redouten Saal; had been invited to dine with the great Prince de Ligne on the very night he had died; had worked with Wellington and seen him 'in a tremendous passion occasionally – a failing for which I have the highest respect'; had been sitting with Talleyrand at the very moment during the Hundred Days when he had received an invitation to Paris by Bonaparte restored; had known well Metternich and Capodistrias. Once he had been in love with Miss Milbanke, later Lady Byron; he had been one of the nineteen who, sitting under a linden tree at a picnic with the lovely Countess Waldstein, toast of the Vienna Congress, had agreed to meet again 'this day twenty years on', a rendezvous that only one of them would keep. As a boy he had seen Nelson come by with Lady Hamilton on his arm; recollected George III, restored to health, being stopped by a cheering crowd of Eton boys of whom he was one, and the King lowering the glass of his carriage, thanking them with tears pouring down his podgy cheeks. His early days in the little house of his father in the city of London and his widowed mother's small villa in the fields at Wanstead, the memories of his long diplomatic career, crowded in upon him with all these young people about him, reminding him of his own youth and dances and days of long ago.

As he walked, the dancers nearby stopped for a moment, to bow and curtsey and say goodnight. The yawning soldiers in the corridor came smartly erect with chink of spurs, stubbing their sword scabbards on the floor beside them, and the old Ambassador went into his room, softly closing behind him the door of his memories.

Outside the snowflakes fell fast and heavier. The orchestra was encouraged with wine and cake, and the attachés went from couple to couple to say that they were prisoners of the snow, expected to stay and to breakfast with Lady Stratford at dawn.

Then fast they danced and long. Age was gone and youth was left, war was done and life was theirs; life and love and all that is true . . . so it must have seemed to those young Victorians, entranced by the magic of such a night, waltzing their way through a candle-lit dream on the arms of their military beaux.

Until the candles were guttering and the footman came to let down with a rattle the great iron bars of the shutters and, flinging open the long windows, let in the day, its morning shadows across snow, cypresses and the sea.

As they made their way home through the glittering cold, there echoed over the Golden Horn the dull boom of cannon, and a long roll of kettle-drums that told of the Grand Signior passing as usual to his Friday prayers.

The Quest of the Holy Grail, 1951

The merchants of Genoa are by repute the most devoted to business of all their kind in Italy. Their astuteness has been the subject of anecdotes and their adroitness the matter for many tales down the centuries; and that is why the Genoese choice of a single bowl at the division of the loot taken at the capture of Caesarea on the coast of Palestine in A.D. 1101 particularly astonished their fellow Crusaders. When that great city of the Levant, midway along what is now the coast of Israel, fell to the Crusaders, the other contingents demanded as their share of the booty costly merchandise, arms and armour, or gold from the treasury. All the Genoese asked was perpetual possession of the Holy Grail, a bowl believed then to have been held to Christ's side while on the Cross by Joseph of Arimathea and to have been used at the Last Supper, a vessel of exquisite dimensions, carved from a single emerald.

Once the Grail was otherwise, a vessel to be sought with a magic lance by young heroes, a symbol of virginity and knightly grace; and earlier still, in pagan days, had been part of the gear of the God of the Underworld, sign of inexhaustible plenty and rejuvenation, not of ascetic but of earthly longings. In the later versions the seeker came to the castle where it was kept and at first, failing to ask for it, was reproved by the 'Fisher King' in whose keeping it was. In consequence he has to wander many years and then comes a second and third time to Grail Castle, makes whole a broken lance and slays with it the enemy of the Fisher King, is hailed by the latter as his nephew, and succeeds him in the kingship. In another, Celtic version, Sir Galahad, Perceval and Bors alone of Arthur's knights succeed in beholding the Grail and follow it to the East, where Galahad and Perceval die and Bors survives to bring it to the West.

Possibly the Genoese, in asking for the bowl, were not so foolish as they must have seemed to their fellows, for all Europe was stirred by news of the return of the true Grail to Christendom. Every year for many years came pilgrims, rich and poor, noble and simple, to revere it in the cathedral church of Genoa, San Lorenzo, where it had been ceremoniously installed by the grateful citizens.

As late as 1503 it was still held in high regard, for the great Spanish Viceroy and General, Gonzalo de Cordoba, coming by sea from Naples to a meeting of kings at Savona is recorded as understandably keeping them waiting while he paid reverence to the sacred vessel that all his life he had hoped to see.

Wandering among newly unearthed ruins at Caesarea and being reminded of the story of the Grail – moreover, bound soon for Genoa – I determined to ask for it as soon as I landed. I had been to Genoa before but had never heard of it being there. Was it even still preserved? An old guide-book, the only one I could find before I embarked, said laconically, under San Lorenzo: 'In the sacristy Holy Grail (sacristan: 2 liras)'.

It was a blazing day in late July and, following upon some weeks in the Orient and quiet days at sea, the sudden noise and scurry in the great Italian port stunned by their first impact. Even under the deep arches that skirt the waterfront and walking on the shady side of the narrow straight street that leads uphill to San Lorenzo, it was very warm. So the nave of the church seemed twice removed and doubly cool after the bustle and heat outside.

In the emptiness an old man dozed on the plinth of a transept column. At first he was silent as if he had not heard. 'The treasury is in the corner and closed, quite closed,' he said at last, very low, and closed his eyes once more.

In the corner an old priest who had lost a key was turning round and round in search of it. And when he found its hiding place and time to answer me, replied too, 'E chiuso,' and shuffled away on some church chore.

Peering here and there in the *coulisses* of the cathedral, I came upon another priest, white stubble on his long jaw, his black frock dusty, who said that the sacristy was closed at all times to everyone and, when I persisted, added that in any case the municipality had taken the matter out of his hands.

A cheerful *maresciallo* of police at the municipality explained that he had never heard that the treasury of the cathedral was in any way under the authority of the municipality, but he undertook to ask his colleagues for their opinion – which turned out to be that the matter fell in the care of the committee of the Belli Arti. So, escorted to the entrance gallery by the police sergeant, I went again quickly on my way.

As I walked, there happened to range alongside me an alert-looking priest, carrying a full briefcase, briskly stepping out, neatly dressed and, because he seemed quite another kind of cleric, I explained to him my mission as we went. He had been, he told me, in Afghanistan, had written books on oriental cults, was a member of the Royal Central Asian Society of England and he was clearly determined upon joining me in my quest. Every now and then in the narrow streets of the old part of the city we were delayed. Once we were misdirected. Then hawkers waylaid us and sellers of lottery tickets stood calling us to come back and make sure of a chance of fortunes. Once my new friend stopped to explain the better some point that he was arguing and we were nearly run over by a truck. Then by chance we encountered his housekeeper who warned him that his luncheon would be spoiled if he were late. If I lost him now I feared that I should not succeed. In the canyons of the mundane world of Genoa he had somehow become for me the symbol of the true companion of the Grail and every petty hazard was significant.

The Director of the Belli Arti was practical and quick. On the official paper of his office he scribbled the name of the sacristan, Don Rossi. 'He has it in his own charge and can show you the bowl,' he said decisively.

So a second time I came back to San Lorenzo and there found Don Rossi, sitting where I had left him, in a shaft of sunlight, unmoving. A second time he replied that the treasury was closed. Then I showed him our trump, our piece of paper from the Belli Arti office and he said that it was mighty difficult, but that he would see what could be done and, taking out key, went to the treasury, three yards away, and came out again and beckoned us in.

The light was not strong. Around us, faintly gleaming, were

silver boxes and reliquaries, carved chests and folded vestments, candelabra giant and small, plates of gilt and a cup of gold, pictures of the Virgin and many crucifixes, all higgledy-piggledy and in their midst the Holy Grail, a great smooth and shallow bowl of glass, dark as cypresses in the evening, a thread of gold binding its rim. 'The gold rim was added,' said the sacristan, 'when it was chipped, a small piece of glass broke away, on being returned from Paris, where Napoleon ordered its removal.' So its fame had endured until the early nineteenth century. By the second half of the century there is only a casual mention in guide-books of the day, and in the twentieth century Goering and the Germans did not find it of sufficient value to remove – perhaps did not even know of it.

Outside in the streets the busy people of Genoa pass and re-pass, unmindful of the treasured object brought to them long ago from Palestine. The industrial age has little use for a bowl of no great intrinsic value. Its only worth was as a symbol, the essence of idealism and romance, and now it is forgotten there, in the closed sacristy of San Lorenzo.

An Evening in Vicenza, 1951

Freya Stark, the author and traveller, known to me since we first met in the East a decade before the Second World War, had several times invited me to her home at Asolo, but she had not, I think, quite appreciated for what kind of surprise we were bound at Vicenza on the night of 3 October 1951, for which two large envelopes arrived containing programmes that would admit us to the palladian Teatro Olimpico at 9.30 p.m.

We were not very sure about the pieces to be played, *La Serva Padrona* (1773), its music by Giovan-Battista Pergolesi, and *Colui Che Dice di Si* (1930) with music by Kurt Weill. The director of the orchestra and of a choir was given as Antonio Pellizari.

A warm evening followed what turned out to be the last day of summer. Arriving rather early in Vicenza, we went off to an empty pavement café in the piazza near the Venetian Columns and the Campanile and were brought coffee and *strega* by a chair-dusting waiter, happy to be interrupted by members of the assembling audience. Freya was wearing a light-grey moiré silk dress, worn, she told me, at Buckingham Palace, and lots of diamonds and paste. It was not until we reached the gates of the courtyard to the theatre that it was clear that this was a special occasion. A small crowd was viewing the arrivals, among it local shopkeepers, country folk in town for the market next morning, 'elderly parties', and boys in shorts holding their bicycles. Police in black were receiving the elegant guests, the women in long evening dresses that glistened as they passed between lamplight and shadow.

Inside the sixteenth-century painted foyer, now only faintly showing its ochre and red figures on panels, two young exquisites in eighteenth-century black dress with chains of office gave us numbered cards that told us it was 'by invitation only' and impressed us anew with our good fortune. Here were all the provincial notables, pleasantly welcoming. Six-foot-four giants with long rods of office, wearing cocked hats, yellow and scarlet frogged coats and white breeches and stockings, stood silently by the inner doors regarding the pigmy gossiping world about them. I began to recapture the delicious sense of anticipation known as a child when going into a theatre. How well the Italians of every kind do these things, and with what easy good taste. These chamberlains wore their eighteenth-century dresses to the manner born, as do the Sienese during the week of the Palio, in even earlier dress.

Someone was saying, 'This is the first time for many years that an opera has been given here.' 'Pellizari, you know, is the industrialist, owner of the factories that make compressors and precision tools. The choir are all his employees. The orchestra to a man work in his factories.' How good many Italians are at doing quite different things. They try to have, Leonardo-like, widely varying interests and abilities.

The crush was parting. Here comes Marina Lulling in a chair fastened to long poles carried by friends, a foot being recently damaged by scaffolding when showing a guest, Bernard Berenson, the repairs undertaken to the work by Veronese at her villa, el Maser. We pass down a sloping entranceway that is a *trompe-l'oeil* street giving on to the stage and into the candlelit theatre, already half full. Designed by Palladio in 1580, it is famous and much visited, but it is one thing to look at it empty in daylight and quite another seeing it by candlelight and ready for an opera. The beauty was such that one hardly wanted the play to begin and quite forgot that we were seated on stone with only small tight cushions between us and it. Beside me was a shy and beautiful young girl, nineteen, daughter of the Italian Minister in Mexico City, in a great black shot-silk dress that billowed and made her seem doubly delicate. 'And what are you doing this autumn?' I ask her, making conversation, with one eye on the ravishing scene, the elegance and beauty of the sixteenth century, and one on the twentieth.

It was the twentieth that responded. 'I shall be going back to Geneva for my interpretership examination, in French, English, Spanish and German.'

'Will you then, if you pass, join the United Nations Organization Staff?' I inquire.

'It is very hard. There are few vacancies. You have to have influence,' she adds wistfully.

A dark and handsome young man passing along the tier below looks back appraisingly at this seeming dewdrop of a girl.

The glow of concealed lighting decreases. The attendants in black come pacing together on to the stage, now lit only by candlelight in order to place 'props', a chest, a table and chairs. They do so unhurriedly and with dignity. The orchestra stand to receive their capitalist conductor. While music begins, a clownish valet hops across the stage, across the 'street' that comes into the middle of the stage and – though only a few yards long – is a convincingly magnificent *corso*. The stout and bewigged, green-velveted widower hero appears. The audience gives close attention to this comedy of manners with its three characters, the master, the deaf-and-dumb valet and a beautiful, wilful washerwoman. It is in two Acts, and afterwards we went out and chattered with friends. The second piece was sinister: a German story about a small boy who volunteers to his master to climb a mountain with his class but, failing in strength before he reaches the summit, is sacrificed by the other little boys. 'It is our rule.' Singing this dirge they push him over the precipice (three feet high). His mother had been rather reluctant to let him start and does not afterwards sing, though I saw her sitting in a chair, hardly off stage, while he was being pushed over the mountainside. The factory choir, all young, were ranged on steps and standing to attention at the back of the stage through-out the second half. As they wore well-fitting though rather convict-like dark grey suits they added to the sinister effect of the whole.

On the way home Freya spoke at length about where and what is civilization. Her views and voice were confident, the words coming from the back of the throat, her rather small eyes twinkling, smile wreathing. Doubtfully, I say that it is rather mercury-like, when disturbed, breaking up into smaller or many particles. But, seeing that this will not do, I add that though prosperous small cities preserving traditional skills and having rich patrons are good for its growth, the vast industrialized capitals of today are less so. Freya's line of thought was different and personal, believing, as she said, that the middle class, to which she belonged, was responsible for producing it, but whatever she was saying was interrupted most suddenly by the elements. Without warning the whole sky, across the plain to the mountains, was illuminated by lightning that lasted longer than usual. When it went out the storm began, thunder and lightning, high wind and hard rain. The summer was ending in style. Our driver began to drive more quickly through the winding country lane, shouting against the wind and the noise that the road ahead could soon become dangerous from falling branches and floodwater. The rain was indeed almost as heavy as a cloudburst, which there may have been not far off. In a lone archway, a young sheltering couple were wringing out their clothes. Freya seemed delighted with the tempest, encouraging the driver as the captain of a storm-tossed vessel might encourage his mate at the wheel, until at last we reached her house in Asolo without harm.

Lady Salisbury, 1952

I only met Lady Salisbury twice, but I was much impressed. The first time was in the house of Diana Daly, sister of the Duchess of Buccleugh. She was telling a story, as I came in, to a small tea-party of about eight people; the conversation stopped while I said, 'How do you do.'

When this was done Lady Salisbury continued with her story. 'Yes, the horses kicked the bottom out of the dog-cart but somehow he succeeded in driving these almost unbroken horses successfully, as he had bet he could do. Let me see,' continued Lady Salisbury, 'yes, that was the weekend the Queen was staying.'

'The Queen' was Queen Alexandra and the date, I suppose, about 1903. It was a little surprising to come straight into such a story in London in the year 1952 on my return from the East only a few hours earlier.

(The sporting gentleman in her anecdote was probably Lonsdale or one of the Lowthers.)

It was to Lady Salisbury, as one learned later, that Kitchener had written in 1912 about our relations with the Turks.

THE TIMES, Monday 7 February 1955
OBITUARY
THE DOWAGER LADY SALISBURY
HOSTESS AT HATFIELD

The Dowager Marchioness of Salisbury died at her home at

Montpelier Square, London, on Saturday after a long illness. She was eighty-seven. She was the widow of the fourth Marquess of Salisbury, who died in 1947, and the mother of the fifth Marquess, who is Lord President of the Council and Leader of the House of Lords.

Lady Cecily Alice Gore was born in 1867, the second daughter of the fifth Earl of Arran. She married the fourth Marquess of Salisbury in 1887. She was Lady of the Bedchamber to Queen Alexandra from 1907 to 1910, and an officer of the Order of St John of Jerusalem. Her second son, Lord David Cecil, is the Goldsmiths' Professor of English Literature in the University of Oxford; her elder daughter married the fourth Baron Harlech, and her younger daughter married the tenth Duke of Devonshire. She was a sister of the Earl of Arran, the Dowager Countess of Airlie, and the Dowager Viscountess of Hambleden.

V.M. writes:

By the death of Lady Salisbury we have lost one of the great personalities of our time. It is very difficult in the crepuscular light in which we now live to imagine the colour and tempo of the old life in which her vivid nature had full play, nor can we easily describe the society in which it was developed. She had immense influence, not only from the gifts and stature of the family into which she married but from her own transcendent charm and the supreme social gift with which she exercised it.

To see Lady Salisbury manoeuvring statesmen and bishops and such unhandy elements into light-hearted enjoyment of their own nonsense was a spectacle of pure joy. The after-dinner games at Hatfield became a frolic of wit under her guidance. One such evening is remembered by those who were there. Mr Baldwin and Archbishop Lang had been induced to play. They elected to take on the characters of Charles I and Charles II and to talk to each other until the company guessed who they were. 'Your Majesty,' said the Archbishop, 'led a very lax life.' 'At least, your Majesty,' said Mr Baldwin, 'I never lost my head.' Lady Salisbury's enjoyment of this joke made the evening. She had a laugh that was as exhilarating as champagne. One Australian Prime Minister said: 'I would come over any time from Australia to hear Lady Salisbury laugh.' This famous laugh has not been heard for several years, not since her husband died.

And she had so much more than mirth to give: wisdom, kindness and complete understanding of all difficulties. And love, too. I say nothing of her work for charity and politics; others have described that. This is only written out of a full heart by one who remembers how her kindness and goodness irradiated a constant intercourse that lasted sixty years.

Reflection from a Christening
in St Tropez, 1953

It was early for the christening to which we had been invited in the tall Renaissance church in the centre of old St Tropez. Two elderly limping women dressed in black came out into the small sunlit *place*, too small to be called a square, in front of it. Inside, it was dark, although midday, except for a faraway lantern. Near it passed and re-passed a figure in white *soutane*, like a daytime ghost.

Suddenly from behind a column there flitted three young girls in clean, pretty, summer dresses. The first laughingly flicked water from the holy-water stoup at the girl following her; she in turn did the same to the last of them. Giggling and exclaiming loudly, they ran on and out of the church. Such natural behaviour is hardly ever to be seen or heard in northern, Protestant churches.

The only time something akin to it was seen was at a most ancient service in a most ancient church, not long earlier. There was then alive something of the ancient spirit. Even outside the Abbey proper before the coronation service began, in the great tent where persons on duty were assembling and eating breakfast, some of the officers with full-dress tunics unbuttoned or laid aside and the Earl Marshal in a military greatcoat above or instead of his full-dress coat, all had an air of unusual animation, of a tenseness and pleasure beyond that habitual in the precincts of a great Protestant church. Inside the Abbey, when the procession of peers, peeresses and others began to move up the aisle some of them gave little waves of a hand or smiles at friends on either side. Two of them singling me out for salutation were, it is true, persons of foreign blood; but others too were greeting one another merrily. It was perhaps partly owed to elation at having arrived successfully, without hitch, for so great an occasion that exhilarated them out of customary 'churchiness'. But was there something more than a sense of the greatness of occasion? The youth of the Queen? There had been Elizabeth I and the very young Queen Victoria. So even that was not singular, appealing as it was. And when at the arranged halt in the service persons on duty could circulate and speak to guests and friends from abroad, the extraordinary air of animation was the same. If few dwelt upon it, was it because of an understood feeling that nothing of its kind could in the nature of things ever be quite the same again? No coronation could ever be quite so brilliant and beautiful. The dresses, the jewels, the quantity of full uniforms could not be again as they were at the coronation of the daughter of the last British King-Emperor. Many present that day in the Abbey had been born and christened during the lifetime, and as subjects, of her great-great-grandmother, the first Empress of the greatest empire known.

And if after the ceremony the question was put to you: 'What was the greatest moment that day?' how could an easy answer be found when everything was wondrous and the whole unique? If some reply were insisted upon, perhaps one of the early moments would be chosen, the Recognition, that is, the Acclamation? As was said in the Order of the Service:

> The Archbishop, together with the Lord Chancellor, Lord Great Chamberlain, Lord High Constable, and Earl Marshal (Garter King of Arms preceding them), shall then go to the East side of the Theatre, and after shall go to the other three sides in the order, South, West, and North, and at every of the four sides the Archbishop shall with a loud voice speak to the People: and the Queen in the meanwhile, standing up by King Edward's Chair, shall turn and show herself unto the People at every of the four sides of the Theatre as the Archbishop is at every of them, the Archibishop saying:
>
> Sirs, I here present unto you Queen Elizabeth, your un-doubted Queen: Wherefore all of you who are come this day to do your homage and service, are you willing to do the same?

> The People signify their willingness and joy, by loud and
> repeated acclamations, all with one voice crying out,
>> GOD SAVE QUEEN ELIZABETH
> Then the trumpets shall sound . . .

'All with one voice crying out', peers and people, old, middle-aged
and very young, the Pages, and all, as loudly and feelingly as they
could. 'And the trumpets shall sound . . .' And no one there present
shall ever forget that moment of the Acclamation.

At what period would you prefer to live if not in your own time?
The elderly and respected French philosopher Gustave Le Bon
reminded his readers at the end of *La Psychologie des Foules*, published in 1909, that 'that was when under 60,000 Englishmen were
controlling 250 million Indians, owing' he says 'not to any other
attributes but their character, built up over several generations, due
not to intelligence or to philosophical or bookish learning, nor to
training or aesthetic ability, it was from something irreplaceable at
the time, that was lingering on from the spirit of their forefathers
and the past.'

A Weekend in Paris, 1955

Saturday, 25 June

I lunched in London. Left for Paris on the last B.E.A. aircraft. Sat next to a young Frenchman who told me that he had come over in the morning only to have suits fitted. He knew no English people at all and merely came to England for English suits, which are cheaper than in Paris. His address is 4 rue Fabert and I am going to 28 rue Fabert, a strange coincidence. He works for Givenchy, he said, and was met by him at Le Bourget in order to go somewhere near Versailles for the weekend.

Dined with Geoffrey Gilmour at 101 rue du Bac, the long windows between his perfectly furnished rooms and the formal garden wide open. His cook is famous and his wines carefully chosen. The evening being fine and warm, we drove in his car along the river and came to the Velodrome d'hiver where the French forces give their annual military tournament, and drank coffee in a café where *légionnaires* and those off duty were meeting their friends. The trumpeters and a detachment of the scarlet-cloaked Senegalese guard sat their white horses with hennaed tails in a dark lane, the horses' feet stamping on the cobbles, the lamplight glinting on uniforms, black faces and accoutrements. Their French officer was in white cloak and high boots. Towards the end of the show we went into one of the stage exits and stood for the finale and the 'Marseillaise' was played by the massed bands and trumpeters.

At the end, the athletes rushed down towards us, all of them stripped to a pair of shorts only, having left their trousers just where we were standing. It was too late and impossible to move away while the naked young men streamed past us on both sides. The smell of clean but sweating men was astonishingly strong. I did not realize how strong their scent could be.

Geoffrey dropped me at 28 rue Fabert, where I have a ground-floor room. It is on the esplanade des Invalides.

Sunday, 26 June

The weather quite perfect. Glittering sunshine. Visited Stewart Cheney, an American playwright at the Crillon for a few minutes and met at the Ritz and lunched with Christopher Warren. Sat next to and talked to Michael Arlen, the American author of Armenian origin: some of his family, they relate, living still in Baghdad, though he denies it.

I went to the Pré Catalan in the Bois for Ali Khan's dinner and dance. Before dinner, I talked to Granard and Astor and their wives, to Mrs Houston, an American beauty married to an Irishman, the Duchess of Devonshire and Madame Stein, who had already invited me to her house in London on the 7th and now asked me to her Paris home at 7 rue Newton, and spoke to several others.

At dinner I was seated between Louise de Vilmorin, the writer, and Madame de Waldner, whose husband's horse won the Derby in 1947. Beyond and next to Louise de Vilmorin was M. Le President, René Mayer, and next to him the Begum Aga Khan. Opposite her was Madame Volterra who had won the Derby in England this year and won the Grand Prix this afternoon with Fildyke. Opposite me was Beatrice Rovasendo and beyond her the Prince d'Alembert and Princess Alexandra of Yugoslavia. Beyond the latter was Arthur Granard and Princess Marthe Bibesco.

There were about three hundred guests. The British Ambassador was in the middle of the next table to ours with his back to us. There were about eight very long tables, four on either side of the dance floor. The Aga himself was there. After dinner we drank a health to Madame Volterra. Ali was a noticeably attentive and good host. Astor, who was staying in the house, helped him.

The table decorations, opposite each third place, were superb, being made like the subject of Dutch seventeenth-century flower pictures, with butterflies, bees and small birds among the flowers;

the food excellent, the champagne pink and also excellent. I danced until 1.30 a.m., every dance.

The women's dresses were splendid, all of them wide and sweeping; the Begum Aga Khan wore white, with a pink wrap; the Princess Marthe Bibesco also in white with a white cloak; Madame de Vilmorin in a black skirt with a white body to it; the Duchess of Devonshire was in very pale blue with a pink rose in her bosom and magnificent diamonds. Nearly all the jewellery was superb, particularly the Begum Aga Khan's diamonds and Princess Marthe Bibesco's emeralds and diamonds. Her emeralds seem to be each about two inches by one inch wide, and there were many of them.

The next morning I was woken at 9 a.m. by military sounds and music. Throwing open the windows, I found that the Cuirassiers de la Garde and the African guard were parading immediately outside my window. Some of the horses' haunches were only a yard from it. Bill Taylor and Fred Haight lunched with me. Before luncheon I had a brief but most useful business talk with Graham Mattison at the Ritz and then met his family who are on their way to Gstaad. I left for England by the last aircraft, on which I found Bobby George, former Air Attaché in Paris and now a Governor in Australia. (He died, killed in the Tottenham Court Road, or nearby.)

This Grand Prix weekend had for me a particular savour in contrast with my days, three weeks back, on the Indian Ocean shore of Arabia. They had in common the beauty of the rare to me: each the best of their own kind and both far from the grey, everyday life of the Western world. Beautiful women splendidly dressed, men in colourful uniforms or oriental dress, well-bred horses were all there, either in Arabia or Paris or both, for my appreciation; the oriental, the Sultanate of Oman, has hardly changed in the last fifteen hundred years, it is said.

Shooting *The Leopard*, 1962

In the summer of 1962 Archie Colquhoon invited me to stay with him in a house not far from Palermo in Sicily. He had translated *The Leopard* by Lampedusa into English and was Director of Dialogue during its filming by Titanus Films. With him I met members of the cast.

Towards the end of my stay we went into the interior of the island to see the filming of a picnic; there Rinaldo Ricci, chief assistant to the director of the film, Luchino Visconti, came across to me and asked if indeed I had to leave; they would like me to stay. It was difficult for me to change plans but was pressed to be photographed there and then.

In Rome three days later, I received a telephone call from Palermo and was told that Burt Lancaster, the leading actor in the film and, indeed, one of the leading actors of America, had himself, in spite of a damaged ligament, been to see the production department to ask for me. I think perhaps he wanted an Englishman or two in the film to whom he could talk. Hitherto there had been only one English actor, a professional whose stay, owing to the nature of his part, was short.

My host in Rome thought it an opportunity not to be missed; returning to Palermo, a month was spent seeing and taking a small part in the 'shooting' of the ball scenes of *The Leopard*. It was scenically rewarding and an instructive experience.

As soon as the shooting of the ball was at last over and the Gangi Palace, its courtyard and a school opposite used as dressing-rooms, were empty, except for debris from filming, the staff of the production or administration had time and the inclination to be more friendly. A red-haired, close-cropped man of about thirty with a skin so pale that by comparison with his red hair it looked almost green came to me and asked if I were going to England and if so could I send him a pair of English handcuffs of the strongest kind. I had never spoken to him and only knew him vaguely by sight, believing him to be some kind of film engineer. He said that the cuffs he had, Italian ones, were useless 'except perhaps for hitting over the head or back' and, suiting words to action, he pulled out a double chain with a small padlock attached and swung it sharply at imaginary shoulders. There were among the employees of the production department some tough-looking men who passed on the 'calls' for extras nicknamed, for want of a better word, 'bullies' which indeed is a word known in the Roman tongue. I thought he must be one of them, and I was wondering why he wanted handcuffs of any kind when he explained that he was a plain-clothes policeman appointed for duty during the filming. Most of his colleagues in the police had acquired English handcuffs through friends in Soho. He had no friend in England.

I had to explain my inability to send him handcuffs by parcel post as he pressed me to do. I was going to France, not England. There was a shop I remembered in the Strand some years ago that used to have such things in the window and I told him that I would look to see if it still existed, next time I was in London; hoping to soften the refusal I had given, I went on to say that there were also ankle-irons, like handcuffs but with a longer connecting chain, in the same shop window. Maybe he had a use for them too?

His eyes immediately changed their light. I cannot say that they brightened; they glowed rather. 'They would be very useful,' he said, 'when making a prisoner walk to the prison.' His enthusiasm radiated. Somehow one felt for the moment an obligation to help in fulfilling such an ardent desire, just as one might feel impelled to help an artist isolated in a far-off corner of the world to obtain painting materials he lacked. His expression haunted me for some days, and I feel sure that I shall not forget him.

In the last days, when most of the dancers had left, the make-up men in the *trucco* room were more at ease. Only a few days earlier they had been continuously distraught. There were numerous arguments over precedence, who had come first for being powdered and prepared, for whiskering, bearding or curling. It had been the longest ball ever known, nightly from early August to mid-September, and the heat in Sicily even at night is almost tropical. Tightly laced crinolines and wigs for girls, dark and thick evening clothes, high collars and kid gloves for the men, made the dancers of the polka, the waltz, the mazurka and the quadrille perspire heavily and feel like dropping. 'Even one of the horses fainted,' said a Sicilian of a carriage horse that slipped in the stone-flagged courtyard when delivering guests. While waiting on benches in the courtyard for their part in the ball, for which they were called by loudspeaker from a gallery above the double stair-way leading up from the court, the officers took off their tunics and remained stripped naked to the waist, dressed only in tight-fitting uniform trousers strapped to their wellington boots. They sat beside girls in crinolines, holding their hands or, stretching out on the benches, rested their heads on the girls' laps. Most of the Roman young men were picked for their beauty and the girls too so that, when a hundred and fifty of them arrived together at Rome Airport where the staff is used to unusual arrivals, there was a sensation. All work stopped until they went aboard, I was told.

Every now and then there was a cry of '*Acqua!*' to the water-carriers who moved constantly among these waiting extras in the Gangi Palace. It was the imperative cry for water which one hears in the hot Muslim countries where water is held to be a gift of God which any man can therefore demand without deference to his host. Sometimes there would be fights, Roman youths versus Sicilians, or an Italian against a German over a game of cards; the latter, arrogant and handsome, looked much put out because obliged to have a plaster on his nose, and left next day. Even the women argued shrilly, say over a chair someone had taken, and each dispute led to arguments for some time afterwards about what had happened and who was right. Once 'Phaebo', one of the two Englishmen in the film, and only there for a few days, was asked to adjudicate – but judicially refused to do so. An Italian explained that '*cortile*', a courtyard, means also in Sicilian 'vulgar'. In one of the crowded dressing-rooms where young officers lounged half-dressed awaiting the call to the Gangi Palace, playing cards, smoking or listening to a gramophone, I saw two diminutive coffee-boys whose small aprons reached only slightly below their short shorts, all they wore, put down their trays and dance the twist with experienced abandon.

Every night, it was said, at least seven girls and women fainted when their corsets were removed at the end of the night. It seems that the blood returning to where it had been restricted caused them to do so. They pulled in their waists as much as they could stand and the dressers tightened them even more at the last moment, before the dances began. The narcissism of the young men far exceeded that of the girls. In the make-up room of the seniors there were bigger mirrors than in their own make-up room and they came in on their way to the Palace courtyard for last moment self-admiration and touches, patting their hair and cheeks, preening themselves, putting drops in their eyes and opening them to see the effect, then going out, returned a moment or two later to go through the whole performance again. One of them habitually returned at least three times. They all had gold necklaces and long hair. Before they were fully dressed, they would walk about in the passage flexing their muscles, shadow-boxing incessantly, engaging in childish pranks such as drawing the attention of another young man in one direction, then, taking him by the arm and crossing a leg behind him, kick him as if from his other side.

Favourites indulged themselves by arriving late and disregarding the shouts of the bullies, 'Andiamo', 'al Palazzo Gangi', 'Tutti al Palazzo'. The favourites in the Visconti court were known to others as the 'ragazze di primo piano' – being, it was said by the elderly professional actors, too often placed in the front rank, nearest the cameras. A newspaper Lo Specchio (The Mirror) mentioned them. There was 'on the set' a constant competition to be near the cameras. Some of the professional actors were said to be competent ones taking a small salary as extras in order to have on their records that they had 'worked with Visconti in the Leopard film'. Others, older, cared for nothing except to be present in order to draw their pay.

The other courts, as it were, were those of Lancaster and Alain Delon. Lancaster, as a world-renowned man, was the most important and also the most impressive. Physically, he is the handsomest and strongest – and probably the richest – of the three, certainly the most talkative and forthright. During the filming of The Leopard he hired a villa, the Villa Scalea, near Mondello, a seventeenth- or eighteenth-century house, well furnished and in good order, where he entertained as much as his work permitted.

Visconti took an old building on the sea between Mondello and Palermo, said to have been used by Nelson's staff ashore. He redecorated it inside and there put up a number of the cast. Delon took a castle on the sea, east of Palermo, belonging to the Gangi family, just beyond the new hotel at Zagarella. He too entertained (but in a quieter way) his personal friends and family, used a speed-boat and a fast car, and behaved as young men behave, without arousing criticism. It is the contrast between his blue eyes and very thick, dark-brown hair that is most striking.

Visconti was feared by the young women, two of whom I saw come off the set in floods of tears, supported by friends in one case and by a 'bully' in the other. They had been spoken to more than sharply for some trifling error or imagined mistake in their behaviour while acting. One or two of the professional actors and junior directing staff fawned on Visconti in a revolting way. Others, if they did not fawn, rushed about carrying out his instructions over-zealously. As a result, an absurd uniformity was to be seen. In a buffet scene, for example, he might say, 'Plates in the hands,' and the junior *régisseurs* would run like athletes through the crowd, shouting, 'Everyone to hold plates,' and everyone obediently took up plates, like children. Or he would say, 'Gloves,' and every man drew on his gloves, screamed at by the young *régisseurs*; or, 'Hats,' and every man would take a *cylindre*. Visconti, it is said, was inclined very much to the Left when he was young and perhaps never attended balls, or else he wished to ridicule and caricature the behaviour of wealthier persons in the last century.

The constant repetition and 'shouting' of rehearsal, sometimes as many as twenty times, gave a kind of unreal, almost nightmare quality to the scenes in the ballroom. It was like some toy, or a scene in a box on a pier which works when pennies are put in a slot; only sometimes, almost before they had started, the performers were brought to a sudden halt with the cry of 'Stop!' and turned back to start again ready for the cry, '*In posta.*' When actual shooting began, though it might be half of the whole to be done, for the 'shooting' too would be repeated much, there was a sigh of relief. '*Lucé!*' with the brilliant lighting that followed and the lighting of candles, marked the change between rehearsal and 'shooting'. Next came '*Motor,*' then '*Azione!*' followed by a shout, sometimes in nearly hysterical tone, of '*Via*', with the inevitable 'Stop!' When 'Stop!' instead became '*Stampa!*', and when '*Stampa!*' was at long last followed by '*Provina!*', the cast would wilt suddenly and stay where they were, like the arrested figures on a run-down musical box.

It was disconcerting to see how, when '*Azione!*' was shouted, the performers, tired as they might be, could become 'animated', smile, laugh and make conversation. If anything, they rather over-did it. It made one appreciate how false 'drawing-room manners' can be and how very easily they can be assumed and aped. Even so, it was not always animated enough for Visconti. '*Allegri!*' would be bellowed through the loudspeaker.

The colour, as seen in 'rushes', is splendid and some of the scenes exceedingly pretty and well composed. Visually at least, it must be a successful film. Lancaster has taken tremendous care to under-stand his part and in America will be a 'draw' for the box office, since he is a topmost film-star. Whether, however hard he tries, he is quite able to assume the part of an old and philosophic Sicilian prince in 1860 is doubtful. But Lancaster, who won the best acting prize in Venice during the filming, is forty-eight, handsome, tall, leonine when made up for the part, with the figure of an athlete who has kept himself fit and has no paunch. The Sicilians – and certainly the Sicilian nobility – are mixed in blood. Carthage, Rome, the Arabs, Normans, Angevins, Spaniards, even the British, were ruling the island at one time or garrisoning it heavily. In the part of Fabrizio, a Sicilian noble, he can therefore be excused for not being dark. Some Sicilians are so, some are not. It is an almost indescribable quality which such an American actor lacks. He is not a European, and no amount of hard application to his acting and studying of the period can make him so, I fear. That will, however, make no difference to box-office takings in America where they do not know the difference. He has a taking personal character and a most unusual one. His emphatic conversation is accompanied by strong gestures with his hands, particularly with both hands raised, the backs outwards and fingers open, approaching you more closely, looking straight at you with his large blue eyes, he says, 'Der yer see what I mean?' He takes pills to brace himself; his output of energy is tremendous, and they make him even more emphatic and energetic than usual, apt to talk without accepting contradiction or argument. At other times, when interested, because of his part for example, he listens attentively. He told me that he began in Marshall Field in Chicago in the linen department at ten dollars a week and commission, and then left to become an acrobat in a circus, to the chagrin of the manager who had noticed sales rising, thanks, no doubt, to the handsome Lancaster who at twenty must have quite knocked out rich and elderly ladies buying sheets. His wife, Norma, is handsome, lively and devoted. They met in Italy at the end of the war when he was in the army and she was engaged in an Entertainment Unit for the welfare of the troops. Norma is an excellent hostess and takes much trouble over their children, now in their teens. They are hospitable and thoughtful towards their guests and their children. It would be impossible not to like them both.

Alain Delon, too, may be not quite perfectly suited in the role of a sophisticated and complicated young Sicilian of the same period and rank. This is one of the difficulties which film magnates create for themselves by promoting superstars, whom they then have to use. In this way they sometimes rule out long-lasting success in favour of a quick financial return. Film being an ephemeral medium, they no doubt hold that it is of no consequence. How permanent is the 'celluloid'? Should not something more permanent that could be revived be attempted? In this case, the script would have to be better too. In any case, the film industry seems to be reaching a climax portending change.

At one of Lancaster's evening parties at the Villa Scalea I met Alberto Moravia, the Italian writer who had criticized *The Leopard*. He was wrong according to published opinion in Europe and America – even the Arabs are translating it, for an official in Jordan is doing it into Arabic; and the Russians, the Spaniards and others are translating it. Archie Colquhoun (who translated *The Leopard* into English) told me that Mario Soldati, a well-known Italian literary man, was noble enough to say, 'Let us face it. He [Lampedusa] has brought it off and we have not.' The book was the only world success in Italian literature for very many years.

Moravia was lugubrious or anyway in lugubrious mood. We discussed 'alienation', its genesis in its present meaning in Italian and English, which he dated back to the end of the last century. In French its meaning is different, medical not 'philosophical', and that is perhaps where it should only be. 'Odd' or 'eccentric' seems good enough and near enough to describe what it is said now to mean, according to such persons as Moravia, if I understand him correctly.

The very young, I think, all much enjoyed being in the film.

Some of them had not taken part in one before, and all was novel and exciting and to be handsome, as most of them were, and surrounded by other handsome young persons and made up nightly to look even more handsome and well paid for it, by their youthful standards was all most pleasing. One of the young dancers brought from Rome for the ball scenes was a Miss McDonald from Blackpool, the only British girl. At the end of one of the most tiring long nights, while breakfasting in an all-night restaurant in the Piazza Bellini with David Lynch, an American teaching Stuppa and Claudia Cardinale English, a very young man called Moroni, from (I think) Milan, was looking unsuccessfully for a table and we called him up to sit with us. Was he decided, as a result of his experiences in *The Leopard,* to go on or to give up the film as a career, I asked. 'Oh, go on,' he said with enthusiasm. He had been recommended by Romolo Valli, the actor taking the part of Father Pirroni, and was a cut above most of the Roman youths in manners, tall and exceptionally good-looking, even in such a collection.

The student who took the part of the dead soldier in the first part of the film, Mario Michele of Palermo who cannot have been more than seventeen, gave much the same reply. He had received 400,000 lire for the dead soldier part, for lying still, and later was one of the yellow-liveried footman, for rather less pay.

There were also black-liveried footmen and butlers. They fought each other now and then, black versus yellow, but spent most of the waiting-time playing a Sicilian card game. One of the black foot-men was a waiter in the Castel Nuova restaurant who had waited on me. Perhaps I had tipped him well . . . at all events, he never ceased, whenever we passed, to give me a little bow. Once he gave me real champagne, when everyone else was getting an imitation, old lukewarm weak tea, during a buffet scene of the film.

The middle-aged actors and the Sicilian nobility and gentry were not too pleased with their work. The Sicilian nobility and gentry, led by the Duchess of Palermo, mostly left early, after about a fortnight, though some, like the Comtessa di Lampedusa, stayed. It was said, I believe correctly, that the descendants of the original of Angelica boycotted the film and did their best to dissuade others from taking part in it, thus only drawing attention to their *mésalliance* within the family cupboard. The semi-professional and professional actors from Rome of middle age and ambition mostly grumbled at the way they had to wait many hours in the courtyard to be called and at the indecision about extra pay when their contracts came to an end. 'They treat us like animals,' one of them said. The elderly and very old, mostly poor, dozed on or sat very patiently with dignity, seemingly quite happy to be left where they were while earning money. 'Another thirty thousand,' they would say when woken up to leave near dawn.

Of waiting, Delon said, 'I have naturally no patience at all. But when working I have all the patience in the world.'

Usually when the 'bullies' shouted, 'All finished – all home,' there would be a rush for the doors and a crush on the steps of the dressing-rooms. The smell of scent and perspiration was strong. But once or twice towards the end, when most of the dancers had been dismissed and the cast was small and had worked until near the dawn, I noticed that they were so tired that the welcome call met with no rush at all. Slowly picking up their crinolines in front, the ladies made their way out and the men too, idly collecting their swords or top hats and cloaks, moved with tired steps, very different from their movements when six or seven hours earlier they had been called upon to perform.

Names were read out through a megaphone: Liguria, la Comtessa di Lampedusa, McDonald, Null, Massimo – a strange mixture. Sometimes many at a time, sometimes few or only one, an old actor, a young boy, three girls, in any order, like meeting death in its uncertain certainty, they went with alacrity from the dark of the courtyard, up the double stone steps, half veiled by palm and banana leaves, towards the brightly lighted grille and landing where drawing-rooms began and Visconti waited and the cameras were poised to 'shoot' them – for immortality, as they hoped.

Some of the actors would disappear quickly after work. Others went to the Bellini restaurant or would stay to eat ices at a small shop open all night.

Then, the dawn coming, they would drive home over the stone-flagged streets, lined with ancient palaces and shops all shuttered up, in fast new motor-cars or in almost as fast ancient victorias, their horses galloping, the wheels and hooves making a tremendous clatter that would have woken the city had it not been, like an oriental city hive, early rising for work before the coming heat. Women peering out as they opened the shutters of windows, and youths already abroad in the street, waved and shouted to them in welcoming recognition as they passed, 'Il gattopardo,' or 'Leopard'.

Murders

It is saddening and depressing to have known quite well a number of men who have been murdered. Two were Pashas, Iraqis – though holding their Pashaliks from Jordan; three were kings, one of Saudi Arabia, one of Iraq and one of Jordan; and one a prince who had long been the Regent of Iraq and who, like the King of Jordan, was a descendant of the Hashimite rulers of Mecca and son of the last of them, King Ali (though he had been left in fact with no more than Jedda to rule for a year).

King Faisal was shot in his Palace in Riyadh by an unstable relative.

King Abdulla of Jordan, great-uncle of King Faisal II of Iraq, was shot in the doorway of the Great Mosque in Jerusalem in 1951, his grandson Hussain, a foot or so behind him, only escaping harm by great good fortune.

An official well-known and liked in Saudi Arabia, Cyril Ousman was shot in his house in Jedda by a member of the Royal Family in a temper.

Jaafar Pasha al Askari, Minister of Defence in Iraq and at one time my landlord there, was shot by rebellious soldiery marching on Baghdad whom he had courageously gone out to try and stop.

Rustam Haidar, like Jaafar a minister at the time, was shot in his office in Baghdad.

Prince Abdililah of Iraq, with his nephew the young King Faisal II of Iraq, his sister and mother and their followers, were all machine-gunned by military rebels on leaving the Palace on promised safe-conduct. Nuri Pasha al Said, Prime Minister, was shot a few hours later. His body, like that of the Prince, was stripped and horribly treated in public. Nuri's son was also killed, as were a number of others, including a British Consul, mistakenly it would seem. Nuri and Jaafar had been brothers-in-law and, when taken prisoners in the First World War as Ottoman officers and sent to India, were then released in order to join the Arab Revolt.

I have named only those Arabs quite well-known to me. An experienced British police officer working as a C.I.D. expert in Baghdad in the 1930s told me that he believed that the rate of murders in that city must be one of the highest in the world.

It fell to me to compose and speak the Address at the memorial service held in the Chapel Royal of the Savoy on Wednesday 30 July 1958, in the presence of the Duke and Duchess of Gloucester, for King Faisal II, for Prince Abdililah, Crown Prince of Iraq and General Nuri Said, Honorary Knights Grand Cross of the Royal Victorian Order, and also for the other members of the Arab Union Government who were killed in Iraq:

> The men – and women and children – we are come to honour and remember were of foreign race, but we in this country throw open our gates to all the world, and the young King, nursed, taught and tutored by British, had been to an English school.
>
> Where he and his uncle stayed often, in their house near London, the people speak of them with affection for their kindly ways. They tell of their modesty and praise their thought for others and their generosity.
>
> They were men unembittered, though their lot from child-hood had been chequered with calamity. The Prince Abdililah was obliged to leave the Hijaz as a child, with his mother, Queen Nafisa, now killed. He never returned to the land of his birth, homeland of the Hashimite family, guardians of Mecca.
>
> When his cousin, King Ghazi of Iraq, was killed, he became regent for his three-year-old nephew, Faisal. He devoted himself to his regency and to training the child for his coming role as a sovereign – in no perfunctory way, but with all his heart.
>
> Experience as a ruler brought ever-increasing wisdom, and knowledge of the West was used to the advantage of his country.

His task as Regent was sharply interrupted by his enemies and ours in mid-war. The boy King was taken prisoner and so remained until order and freedom were restored.

They were our allies in the last war, and they were the off-spring of our allies in the First World War.

In peace and war they were supported by great Arabs; one of the most outstanding of all – Nuri al Said, hero of the Arab uprising – was cut down in the same days. History will give him his place as one of the great leaders of men. Other Arab patriots fallen in Baghdad were members of the Arab Union Government.

If there be any who doubt the devotion to their people or the verity of these princes and leaders, let them consider whether in their place they could have done better. Consider, too, that these men knew how very little their lives were worth and that they might, had they wished, have retired from the contest, without honour though with wealth.

The old leaders, the experienced Prince, the young King, a gentle boy, fallen after so brief a flowering – we who knew them recall their worthiness. None can uproot what is deeply planted in our minds, and so will be remembered always.

God Rest Them All.

Eunuchs

The servants of the shrine in Mecca used to be eunuchs, and maybe there are still some left. It was their duty to clean and sweep, light and guard the Holy Place. Presumably the custom of having eunuchs engaged on the work inside the great mosque arose because women frequent the precincts. From time to time, the mosque has been left many great properties under the wills of faithful Muslims, some of them being abroad; they are administered by the Religious Bequests, or *Waqf*, of Mecca and its servants, the Eunuchs of Mecca. There was a large property of date-palm gardens at Basra in Iraq belonging to the shrine where two of them were always in residence. It was evidently not an onerous post, and was enjoyable because of the revenue. We used to see them nearly every afternoon, being driven slowly in a large car along the waterfront of Basra and out towards the date-palm gardens. They sat in a dignified manner in the back of the open car, dressed in their jaunty Meccan turbans of white lawn, with an end sticking out over one ear and the gold-embroidered skull-cap just showing in the centre, and long striped robes. However, their figures, like those of nearly all eunuchs, were not good: their hands would be crossed over their paunchiness; their cheeks were flabby, and they had the unmistakable, unhealthy look of their kind. Somehow they reminded one of elderly ladies going for an afternoon spin at a watering place in Europe.

These must have been some of the last of the eunuchs of Mecca, and I doubt if there are more than a dozen of them remaining now in Saudi Arabia.

Richard Halliburton, adventurous American journalist, was in Jedda to visit Mecca from there in the mid-1930s, but failed to obtain permission. He had crossed the Alps on an elephant, like Hannibal, and was to be lost at sea travelling in a Chinese junk to one of the great fairs in the United States. He told me he had heard of a club for eunuchs in Cairo and tried to find it. He had nearly given up when he learnt that it was not really a club, but that some of them did customarily meet in an alcove at the back of a certain coffee-shop in old Cairo. He went there and found half a dozen of them, all old and out of work. They spoke of the great harems at which they had been in attendance long ago, of the noble households of the past and of the more liberal days when they were young; like all old men who were once in the same profession, they spoke of their common memories and 'the good old days' with regret for the times that had gone.

(Similarly wistful memories were recalled when, during the Second World War, Donald Mallet asked the famous old Druze warrior, Sultan bin Atrash, what was the population of the Jebel Druze. He gave it as 'twelve thousand matchlocks, no more alas nowadays'.)

A Sub-War in Arabia, the Yemen, 1964

War of a kind has been going on in the Yemen since September 1962, when there was a republican coup in the capital, Saana, and the Egyptian army arrived in the same week. Two years after the arrival of Nasser's army, he controlled less than half the country, though he attacked from it Saudi Arabia and Aden. It is a confused situation and a horrid one for the Yemeni people. Not much has been recorded about the scene in the interior, within the royalist lines, under war conditions.

Yemen is a small country, about the same size as the United Kingdom, but mountains in the centre make for slow travelling. To reach the headquarters of the royalist Prime Minister (only sixty miles or so in a direct line from its northern frontier) takes four days, two of them by car and the best part of two on foot. At first the landscape is open desert dotted with low trees and with areas of sand-dunes. The only immediately noticeable difference is in the dress of the rare passers-by who are without cloaks, wear turbans and carry the large south Arabian dagger. Within an hour or so from the last Saudi Arabian town, still showing signs of bombing by the Egyptians' Russian aircraft, you come upon the camps of the International Red Cross and U.N.O. It was dusk on reaching them, not a convenient moment to pause for long.

An attempt to follow the car track on a new, large-scale map was unsuccessful. You can travel for a week in the Yemen without finding the places you pass marked. Since everyone uses Arabic time, counting twelve hours from dawn and from sunset, you give up glancing at a watch and rely upon the height of the sun or moon instead.

Accepting this vagueness in time and place, the tension habitual in the West leaves you; but in case anyone is attracted by the idea it must be said at once that in the more prosperous villages and valleys you can nearly always tell the hour once a day by the regularity of the Egyptian bombing from the air. At about two o'clock Arabic time, say 8 a.m., the women and children leave their homes for the nearest ravine or caves. The men incline to dawdle until the Ilyushins or Migs are seen glistening in the sun above the horizon. Sometimes they do not come at all or, by some inexplicable exception, are late . . . and you become irritated. One likes to have one's bombing over and done with early and get on with the morning's tasks, or start on the day's march if one is a traveller as I was. My host-to-be was al Hassan bin Yahya, uncle of the Imam, Prime Minister and at the same time Commander-in-Chief of the eastern front on which there had been more fighting than elsewhere.

At the first night's stop, a royalist bivouac among rocks where everyone was awake in spite of the late hour, we were told that we would have to wait to go on until the following night. Apart from the mid-morning bombing-hour pause, all trucks were in use taking up reinforcements to some battle in progress at the Prime Minister's headquarters. It was hard to discover exactly what sort of battle it was. All that the reinforcements knew was that there was a chance of hitting at the Egyptians and republicans. Everyone seemed elated. They fired shots in the air and sang in a repetitive way, though more harmoniously than is usual further north in the Arab world. I had the words written down for me . . . they were unpublishable in Egypt. Yemeni truck drivers paint their bodywork in bright colours and fix decorative ironwork to the rear. Some have a police-type banshee howler and a revolving light on the hood of the cab, both of which they set off to announce their arrival at a post. The scene at night in this rocky valley, lit and shadowed from a moon in its full first quarter and by the lanterns and flashing torches of the embarking soldiery, was lively and romantic, vaguely reminiscent of a setting for opera.

In daylight next morning it was no less unusual, though most of the chorus of warriors had disappeared. The sides of the narrow valley were of cyclopean boulders, as big as small houses, tumbled out by some long-extinct volcano. Between them was cover for hundreds of men. In this maze of grey stone it was not easy to find the way; a captured Egyptian armoured car, painted white and abandoned for lack of spares, made a useful landmark in the gully bottom. Some Egyptian deserters, of whom there were about forty, were working here. I spoke to one who told me that he came from Zagazig in the Delta, and gave as his reason for deserting his dislike of fighting fellow Muslims. He would visit Mecca and stay in Arabia after the war. He looked cheerful and straightforward. Some of the Egyptian soldiers had been told that they would be fighting Israelis. They knew better afterwards. Far from delivering Arabs from Israelis they were asked to fight Muslims. Apart from their pay, their hearts were not in the campaign.

When some trucks returned and our journey was resumed, it was along greener valleys and through straggling oases of fields bordered by stone walls and clusters of palms in which are castellated towers, their upper parts of dried mud and straw, the lower floors of stone.

These settlements of fortified farms, four or five storeys high, are so like one another that you have a feeling when you stop in them that you are making no progress. You are reminded of the Red Queen and Alice's journey: 'A slow sort of country . . . If you want to get somewhere else you must run at least twice as fast as that.' The hospitality, too, is always the same. Brews of tea in small glasses are brought at once and followed by little handleless cups of coffee made from husks, not the bean. Strong coffee is thought less refreshing and, as an intoxicant, is forbidden by the Koran. No one, however, objects to the chewing of the leaves of the plant *qat*, a tranquillizer much favoured. When a supply is in, about one man in three seems to have an abscess in a tooth, owing to the ball of *qat* leaves he is chewing, though happily.

The conversation in these days is often the same, based on hatred of the Egyptians and news of the fighting. Reports of the action at Burqa, the Prime Minister's headquarters, had by now become rumours of a fight at the village of Gharir, a few miles from Burqa. It was clearly a diminishing battle and it was not until the true story was told by al Hassan himself that its nature became apparent, its unusualness accounting for various and shrinking versions.

The end of the car-worthy track is in a village at the foot of high, bare mountains. Its women and children spend the mornings in ravines, sheltering from aircraft. It was a market day but, since markets are bombed, a meeting for barter is held at night on another day of the week. An Ilyushin came over punctually, but sheered off without dropping bombs when heavy Czech machine-guns, captured from the Egyptians, opened fire on it from posts on the surrounding summits. The guard tent provided for my use was much holed by machine-gunning from the air, so that circles of light patterned the bedspreads.

A young fellow-traveller brought news from loyalists further south. He was dressed as a Yemeni fighting man, but turned out to be a technical adviser to one of the youngest of the fighting princes. He is Belgian aged twenty-one, and matriculated as a mercenary in the Congo at seventeen. He told me that his friend and senior, a Frenchman, had been hit by a bomb a hundred yards from him and died in his arms. Two Yemenis were killed at the same time. He spoke with admiration of his eighteen-year-old prince, of the leadership of the other ten princes in the field, and of the extreme toughness of the mountaineers they command. They move mostly at night, living hidden by day, scramble over the rocky heights barefoot, or at most in sandals, for hours at a time carrying a heavy load of arms and ammunition, yet ready for an attack at the end. Hasty retreat is sometimes forced on them, but not before they have made themselves felt and feared. Their operations are always gruelling and it is hard to imagine men physically fitter on so little in the way of food supplies. Their total numbers are doubtful, and anyway they vary. They are probably less than half the strength of the Egyptians. The republican force trained by the Egyptians is small, about two thousand. Loyal Yemenis put the casualties caused by them to the Egyptians at about six thousand or more, though they themselves have no artillery and not a single aircraft.

When the Belgian turned in, putting his head out of a sleeping bag to say goodnight, he gave a final pat to the sub-machine-gun at his side with which he had slept for the last eight months.

At midday we left on foot to surmount the 7,000-foot pass between us and Burqa. It would mean spending a night at a small post in the mountains beyond the pass. As the track mounted higher and higher, finally almost disappearing among the rocks, the three donkeys provided for small baggage and for an occasional ride on any flat ground became more reluctant. They stopped, uncertain before the almost vertical boulders, heads turned as if to say, 'We can just do it, but only if you insist, you wretches.'

The view from the very summit in the evening light was splendid. The air is magnificent after the hot valleys, and cool. The escorting soldiers pointed out the direction of Sada, the northern town where Egyptians are pinned down except for a road southwards to the capital, Saana, itself sometimes cut off by royalists. Nearer was a cloche-hat-shaped mountain, Jebel Barrash, which caught the eye constantly from then onwards, a dominant feature in the landscape between Burqa and Sada.

Men and donkeys plunged on down the steep, at times precipitous path, little interested in the distant prospect or in pausing to recover from the climb.

Night overtook us on the mountain but the moon was bright. The Yemeni mountaineers, unlike nomads in the desert, do not know the stars well. They only name those that herald rain and sowing times. Though they did not even know the North Star, they never hesitated for a moment about their direction when the path was invisible.

It was after dark when we reached our stopping place for the night, some tentage under trees where two narrow and deep gullies met. A belated fellow-traveller in the guest tent saw paperback books in my small bag and asked me about them. The percentage of literates in the Yemen seems high. Almost everyone is prepared to write a note at a moment's notice, taking pen and paper from a container behind his dagger hilt. One highland clerk wrote extremely well, as I noticed while looking over his shoulder; when I asked him about his schooling, he replied, 'My father was my school.'* The percentage of genuine literates in the mountainous Yemen is as high as (if not higher than) in most Arabic-speaking countries, leaving aside the Lebanon.

The next day there was bombing in the valley we had left, and a man and his donkey were killed there. The man was seriously wounded, but his life might have been saved with quick medical attention.

That afternoon we arrived at Gharir and saw at once the results of

*At the often isolated mountain and fortified farms in the Yemen, schooling of sons by their fathers may well have become the traditional method. In hamlets, villages and towns, the mosque was the usual centre for learning letters, as elsewhere in Muslim lands.

damage to it in the fighting two days earlier. The commander of the garrison had come up with the relief force and been wounded in the arm. He took us into his tower and was beginning his story when a messenger arrived from the Prime Minister, saying that he wished us to go on at once to the caves where he spends the day. He would be leaving them almost at once for his night headquarters.

It was not very far, but the country changed much as the valley was left behind. Great sandstone rocks were balanced precariously on others horizontally worn away by aeons of weathering. Here and there, like currants in a cake, were dark entrances to caves and natural arcades.

The Prime Minister was seated, surrounded by his armed men, on an earthen platform in front of his own particular cave. The soldiers formed an avenue down which one advanced to him. He is about fifty-eight, wearing a khaki jacket with a skirt and turban of the same light material, his breast pockets bulging with pens and papers. Some silvered buttons and his shoulder-straps gave his rig a semi-military air. He wore socks and canvas shoes, unusual in that barefoot or sandalled world. He is not very tall, has a very fair complexion with a fluffy beard on the point of the chin and jaw, and a small dark moustache. With his turban off, you see that he is rather bald in front. He does not smile very often and at times is inclined to speak, though with confidence, in a low voice. His secretariat understood him perfectly none the less. Ordinarily he wrote sitting cross-legged on the floor of his cave or room holding his paper on one knee, half the time without spectacles which he generally carries pushed back on his forehead. Papers are put into envelopes, leather cases or tin boxes which surround him and his staff. Other papers awaiting attention are left on the floor. Once one of the younger clerks, unable to find a letter, was seen petulantly to tip the entire contents of a case upside down to search for it. Al Hassan works all the morning with an interval for breakfast. His clerks, and any visitor like myself, are invited to join him for it, squatting round in a circle. The food is adequate, no more: flaps of unleavened bread, rice, a thick brown soup to which they add pepper lavishly, and sometimes the luxury of tinned tunny-fish or peaches. This is a wartime diet, for the country is agriculturally rich and meals are better in peacetime. Excellent raisins are now and then offered to one. About every other morning while I was with him, there was bombing by the Egyptians. Once it came while we were eating and was noticeably near. A bodyguard on sentry duty, peeping round the blast wall of stone at the entrance to the caves, turned to say of one explosion, 'Two hundred yards off' – rather, I thought, as if a telephone had rung while a family in Europe breakfasted and some-one had looked round a screen to say, 'Wrong number.'

My own accommodation was in a cave across the narrow valley from the Prime Minister's cave, about twenty-five yards away, with another cave within call for the use of the three men who had become attached to me for the journey.

In the afternoon, al Hassan emerges from his cave for prayers, then the guards form up in groups with an advance and rear party, the advance is sounded, and they move off for the oasis village in which he has billeted himself. The instrument on which the advance is sounded is a battered bugle that has had its tube lengthened and given a curl near the mouthpiece. I could not decide whether to call that musical mule a trumpet or a bugle.

The guest room is on the fourth floor of the tower next to that in which al Hassan lives. It was furnished with some old country rugs, sheepskins and little bolster-like pillows. I never saw a table or chair the whole time I was in the highlands. The windows, as in medieval towers, are small and steps unlighted. There is a pleasant smell from old brushwood smoke. The women of the house stood about to see the new arrival, not bothering to veil their faces with their head-kerchief. They are sophisticated in this way. In the evening, walking over to al Hassan's, one of the soldiers beckoned to me and pointed out a girl standing unveiled and unabashed in the open. She was a great beauty and light-complexioned. He clearly expected me to express an appreciative opinion, which I did. 'She is a Jewess. They are all like that,' he said. I learnt that there are still Jewish villages in the Yemen. The people come to no harm from the Yemeni Muslims though at least one Jewish village has been bombed by Egyptians from the air recently and one such village had Egyptian prisoners in it.

After dining and late prayers, the Prime Minister was at it again with his clerks, holding a council of war with two princes on their way to an operation, interviewing travellers and messengers, seeing prisoners, trying a case until after midnight. He sat on a low dais, meant for a sleeping-place, at the end of the narrow room lit by a kerosene lamp that hissed and threw strong light and shadows over the turbaned assembly.

When there was a case to be heard and numerous persons in attendance, there would soon be quite a pile of sandals by the door where the Court Usher stood, a tall man wearing a large brown-and-black turban, dagger and cartridge-belt of silver and pale blue. In front of him knelt or squatted the accused, witnesses and sponsors, leaning forward, gesturing to emphasize their words, sometimes leaving a slender hand eloquent with appeal out-stretched towards al Hassan. It could have been a Rembrandt drawing come alive.

Prisoners being tried were three men found hiding in Gharir after the action, something new in this war, a kind of commando raid planned by the Egyptians who had offered £100,000 for the capture of the Prime Minister alive and £10,000 for failure. They were about seventy strong, had infiltrated Gharir at midnight, had raided the unguarded caves where they found only some bedding, papers and a coffer for money in which there was no great sum. It was at first thought that a large force must be present or arriving. By the time the place was surrounded, the raiders were slipping away, including their leader, one Ibn Daaji, a man from the neighbour-hood who had been in Saana when the Egyptians arrived. Some were caught and killed and eighteen were taken prisoner, but not before they blew up a magazine of arms and ammunition. As al Hassan said, the raiders were taught a lesson, adding, 'But we learnt a lesson, too.'

The men brought before him had thought up excuses. They had come because they were forced by threats to do so, had deliberately hidden themselves in order not to go back with the raiders. They brought forward sponsors who would guarantee their good behaviour.

'As for your guarantors,' said the Prime Minister, ending the case, 'there is no need for them. We will be your guarantors for your future good behaviour, by retaining you until the end of the war in safe keeping.'

From time to time al Hassan would break off his business to come and talk to me. Once I asked him about the new constitution which I had heard was planned. 'Is it to be expected soon? News of such reforms to replace the thousand-year-old regime of the past will have a good effect in the outside world.'

He was in New York, at the U.N., when the Egyptians invaded the Yemen on the day of the republican coup; he flew back to

Arabia, leaving his family behind. He is thus aware, and kept aware by his Foreign Minister and by an American special adviser and others, of foreign opinions and pressures. His reply made it very clear that he and the princes and the provisional assembly are set upon the necessary reforms and modernization. He spoke about how the tasks before them could best be tackled and how to avoid errors. 'But,' he ended, 'do you really think that the present time, with the country partly occupied by a foreign army, is the right time and practicable to call a conference of the free and representative kind?' The royalists point out that two days after the coup the republicans and Egyptians summarily executed more Yemenis than were condemned according to the Koranic Law in fourteen years of the previous Imam's out-of-date and often unwise reign. 'This is what is called socialist reform by Nasser,' they add. If the exact figures are unverifiable, there is no doubt that it is broadly true. At one moment, according to the Prime Minister, Americans asked him to make no more attacks on the Egyptians, so that the Egyptians could withdraw. All that happened was that the Egyptians used the lull to their own advantage in consolidating their military positions. If they had more arms, the royalists believe they would have little difficulty in getting the Egyptians on the run.

Whatever the result of the war in the Yemen, it is likely to be one of the last in which physical prowess is an advantage and morale counts heavily, a source perhaps for future films, a new kind of Western, an Eastern in fact.

Already camp-fire stories are told about the young leaders who were some of them at universities abroad when the fighting began and returned to play their part. About one it is said that, hearing that the royalists were short of money, he rode up to Saana and made his way into the city in disguise by night, called upon a loyal leading merchant and, with his help and that of other merchants, collected in one night so much money, enough for several months, that all their ingenuity, and that of their women, was needed to get it away undetected. Another tale is that of a tribe which, short of money and arms, pretended to have quarrelled and sent off a section to tell the Egyptians that they were ready to attack the remaining clans, given (of course) the arms and money for subversion of as many as possible prior to the attack. 'And don't forget to fire high when you do pretend to attack us,' were the parting words of the cousins as they left to carry out their plan, which worked admirably.

Yemenis are encouraged by knowing that often before in the past, foreign armies, Roman, Caliphial, Mameluke and Ottoman Turk, have come out of Egypt to south Arabia and failed to stay. The brother of Saladin invaded the Yemen. The King of the Yemen was arrested in Mecca while on a pilgrimage and taken a prisoner to Egypt in 1350. Aden was captured in 1538 and the Yemen occupied from Egypt in 1569. More than one Ottoman Turkish general lost his reputation in the Yemen. If the result is any different this time, it will be because of foreign aid to Egypt.

Even with this aid and an army of 30,000 men or more, with medium and heavy tanks, several squadrons of bombers and fighters, and a landing-ground for jets, the Egyptians have made little progress. They are losing the support of the tribes in the south, on whom they counted and whom they paid. Foreign occupation is tending to bring the people together more than ever before. One southern tribe, having listened at length to the socialist Utopia painted for them by a republican emissary, is said to have thought it all very promising and asked only, 'And who under this scheme will be our Imam?'

People who dislike or distrust their rulers do not fight for them with meagre pay, short of food and arms, for nearly two years. The oil-less Yemen was to be a back door into Arabian oil-bearing countries and to the port of Aden, so the loyalist Yemenis see it. They themselves in the past made claims in the Aden corner, which only makes Egyptian ambitions more distasteful to them. It is the Egyptians whose motives they distrust.

The care of seriously wounded royalist soldiers and civilians wounded by bombing from the air by the Egyptians in villages is a problem. The International Red Cross Hospital, under the aegis of the U.N., whose main task is to see that no arms come in from Saudi Arabia, is well away from the fighting areas, near the Saudi-Arabian frontier, and by its instructions is not permitted to go beyond a line which excludes even the Prime Minister's present headquarters.

A young Red Cross doctor explained that he was exploring with a view to setting up an advanced post just within the permitted area, though the place he mentioned was off the direct route from the fighting. Asked why it was being considered, he said, 'There are Egyptian prisoners there, twenty of them. We have to be neutral, you know.'

The quite large Red Cross hospital in tents far back near the Saudi frontier deals mostly with sick local civilians. When I asked how many wounded fighting men they had dealt with, one of the doctors told me that in the eight months he had been there he estimated it must have been only about thirty.

Yemen in Arabic has a double sense, not only the political and geographical one, but also the meaning of 'southern, happy land', *Arabia Felix*.

At present the picture that remains most vividly in the mind after a visit there at this time is of a frieze of women and children moving along a background of sunlit rock into the shadow of ravines that shelter them from Nasser's Russian bombers.

Old Age and Youth, 1981

Something one is understandably not told when young is how at about three score years of age you will find yourself looking at the obituary notices and lists of deaths because you find your contemporaries and older persons whom you knew or knew about are in them almost every day, or so it seems. Then, about ten years later, there are far fewer whom you knew, for most of them are dead. You hardly bother to look any more.

Today for me is a little different; the press is announcing the sinking of Field Marshal Montgomery – not that I knew him very well. I was a second Staff Captain in the Brigade headquarters in Cork in which he was the Brigade Major. There were two others with us in the Mess, but he kept himself largely apart, working in his room perhaps. He seemed from his few comments every now and then to be rather a martinet. He chided us for smoking, which was not often. In those days we did not smoke 'gaspers', the Virginian cigarette, but Balkan Sobranje, about four daily, after meals. Taken ill with appendicitis and after sick leave sent to Ulster, I hardly saw him again until I was Political Agent in Kuwait and he was head of the Staff College in Quetta. When he was going backwards and forwards to England from there, he used to send me a cable asking me to meet the aircraft of Imperial Airways, which then used to refuel in Kuwait immediately outside the city walls. He would question me about Arabian politics.

One morning recently, when the daily papers were a trifle late in being delivered, I found myself dreamily thinking of this obituary aspect of the papers, when there was a short sharp ring on the front-door bell. I went out to the door and found a child, a boy about nine years old, in a greatcoat, its collar turned up against the cold, and so big for him that I immediately thought he must have received it from a quick-growing elder brother. Against his size the small number of papers he held under his arm seemed big. With the other hand he offered me my paper. I said that it was quite all right for him, another day, to put it through the letter box, that is if he were to be coming in future. 'I don't know,' he replied and after a pause, quietly added, with a look between pride and uncertainty, with a timid smile, 'this is my first day, you see.'

What does one say to such a child on beginning his working life? I could only smile, as I hoped, encouragingly.